The New Organizational Reality

DOWNSIZING, RESTRUCTURING, AND REVITALIZATION

EDITED BY

MARILYN K. GOWING

JOHN D. KRAFT

JAMES CAMPBELL QUICK

AMERICAN PSYCHOLOGICAL ASSOCIATION

WASHINGTON, DC

First printing November 1997
Second printing April 1998

Published by
American Psychological Association
750 First Street, NE
Washington, DC 20002

Copies may be ordered from
APA Order Department
P.O. Box 92984
Washington, DC 20090-2984

In the UK and Europe, copies may be ordered from
American Psychological Association
3 Henrietta Street
Covent Garden, London
WC2E 8LU England

Typeset in Century Schoolbook by EPS Group Inc., Easton, MD

Printer: Data Reproductions Corporation, Auburn Hills, MI
Cover designer: Minker Design, Bethesda, MD
Technical/Production Editor: Edward B. Meidenbauer

Library of Congress Cataloging-in-Publication Data
The new organizational reality : downsizing, restructuring, and
  revitalization / edited by Marilyn K. Gowing, John D. Kraft,
  and James Campbell Quick.
      p.   cm.
    Includes bibliographical references and index.
    ISBN 1-55798-462-X (softcover: acid-free paper)
    1. Organizational changes—United States—Case studies.
  2. Corporate reorganizations—United States—Case studies.
  3. Downsizing of organizations—United States—Case studies.   4. United
  States. Office of Personnel Management—Reorganization.   5. Chapparal
  Steel Co.—Reorganization.   6. American Telephone and Telegraph Company
  —Reorganization.   I. Gowing, Marilyn K.   II. Kraft, John D.   III. Quick,
  James C.
  HD58.8.N49   1997
  658.4'06—dc21   97-37722
                                                                          CIP

British Library Cataloguing-in-Publication Data
A CIP record is available from the British Library

Printed in the United States of America

Contents

Contributors

Major Joyce A. Adkins, PhD, *United States Airforce, Kirkland Airforce Base, NM*

Ronald J. Burke, Professor, *Faculty of Administrative Studies, York University, North York, Ontario, Canada*

Peter C. Cairo, PhD, *Teachers College, Columbia University, New York*

Wayne F. Cascio, PhD, *Professor of Management, Graduate School of Business Administration, University of Colorado, Denver*

Sarah J. Freeman, Professor, *School of Business Administration, University of Wisconsin–Milwaukee*

John Gordon, *Queen's School of Business, Queen's University, Kingston, Ontario, Canada*

Marilyn K. Gowing, *Director of Personnel Resources and Development Center, U.S. Office of Personnel Management, Washington, DC*

Mirian M. Graddick, PhD, *Vice-President, American Telephone and Telegraph Company, Basking Ridge, NJ*

Michael Grant, *Director of Agency Initiatives, U.S. Office of Personnel Management, Washington, DC*

Clarence Hardy, *Director of the Office of Cooperative Environmental Management, U.S. Environmental Protection Agency, Washington, DC*

Michael A. Hitt, *President of the Academy of Management, Texas A&M University, College Station, TX*

Dennis T. Jaffe, PhD, *Changeworks, San Francisco, CA*

Hank Jonas, PhD, *Manager, Compensation and Organizational Performance, Corning, Incorporated, Corning, NY*

John D. Kraft, *Personnel Psychologist, Vienna, VA*

Lennart Levi, MD, PhD, *Sektionen för Stressforskn, Karolinska Institut, Stockholm, Sweden*

Robert E. Martin, PhD, *Department of Economics, Centre College, Danville, KY*

Joseph Mathey, MD, *Medical Director, Corning, Incorporated, Corning, NY*

Jeff Monroy, MS, *President, Jeff Monroy Group, Pine City, NY*

Lawrence Murphy, PhD, *National Institute of Occupational Safety and Health, Cincinnati, OH*

Debra Nelson, PhD, *Professor of Management and CBA Associates Professor of Business Administration, Oklahoma State University College of Business Administration, Stillwater, OK*

David Noer, PhD, *Noer Consulting Group, Greensboro, NC*

James Campbell Quick, PhD, *Professor of Management, The University of Texas, Arlington*

Eduardo S. Rodela, PhD, *Fairfax, VA*
Robert Rosen, PhD, *President of Healthy Companies, Washington, DC*
Cynthia D. Scott, PhD, MPH, *Changeworks, San Francisco, CA*

Foreword

In the 24 industrialized (mostly Western) countries belonging to the Organization for Economic Cooperation and Development (OECD), there were 24.5 million unemployed workers in 1990 (OECD, 1994). According to the World Employment Report 1996/97 (ILO, 1996), this unemployment figure has now risen to at least 34 million, ratcheting up to an ever-increasing level in spite of some economic recovery. The current cyclical rise in unemployment comes on top of already high levels of structural unemployment. In addition, there is a high, increasing, and persistent youth unemployment rate in all OECD countries. In most OECD countries, the actual unemployment rate is disguised by early retirement or by 5–20% of the workforce feeling discouraged and no longer seeking new jobs. A recent survey indicates that at least 25% of the Swedish population aged 18–64 years are out of work in spite of being both able and willing to take jobs (Berg, 1996).

In sharp contrast, the employment situation in the United States continues to improve, with the unemployment rate falling below the 5% level in 1997. Although the unemployment rate is dropping in the United States, it is interesting to note that job cut announcements rose 33% in March of 1997 from previous year levels. These layoff announcements represent the largest monthly cut in jobs since January 1996. Thus, while the nature of the problems in the United States are different from those in other countries of the OECD (high layoffs versus high unemployment), the resulting condition in the United States is an increased level of organizational turbulence leading to a greater stress potential.

This stress affects not only the person being laid off, but also the person's family members and fellow workers still on the job and it has a probable effect on the morbidity rate (Dooley, Fielding, & Levi, 1996). To be threatened by unemployment, to lose one's job, to experience short- and long-term unemployment, to be forced to rethink one's future, to enter new training or a new occupation, to experience an unsuccessful job search, or to under-utilize one's skills through unqualified short-time (temporary) or part-time work, and eventually to suffer long-term unemployment and the accompanying poverty it produces are all experiences that have a high potential for inducing stress and stress-related ill health.

An additional problem concerns those who are still at work but face demands for ever-increasing productivity due to downsizing. A recent study by the Swedish National Board for Occupational Safety and Health (1996) shows that more than half of all male workers and two thirds of all female workers report experiencing an increased pace of work over the last five years. One third of the labor force report that they skip lunch break, work overtime, or bring their work home to continue working after regular hours.

Increasing earning differentials lead to substandard employment, less income security, and a lower level of living for the lowest-paid workers and represent additional stressors. The elite are paid well to have challenging and interesting jobs, with another tier having more mundane work and lower pay, and a third tier being deprived of work and being blamed for their involuntary unemployment. The Luxembourg Income Study released in March 1997 states, "While the United States has a higher real level of income than most countries, it is the high-income and middle-income children . . . who reap the benefits. The average low-income child in the other 17 countries is at least one-third better off than the average low-income American child."

For these combined situations of unemployment for some and over-employment for others, there are obviously no quick and easy solutions. We first need to identify the quantity and quality of today's and tomorrow's over- and unemployment and related phenomena; then analyze their causes and consequences, particularly in vulnerable groups; and lastly, search for new cures.

Some approaches include (a) a more efficient generation of new and good jobs by the social parties on the labor market, as well as by cooperatives and by individuals; (b) a fairer distribution of gainful employment and the economic benefits which this confers; and (c) a more optimal distribution of employment over the life cycle. Furthermore, old notions may need to be rethought (e.g., the notion that 40 hours per week employment is an absolute prerequisite to health and well-being). Society must help people who have lost their jobs to obtain or retain the content that gives life a goal and meaning; to live their days fully, with a normal rhythm and structure; to preserve their individual identities, self-assurance, and access to a social network; and to achieve an acceptable standard of living.

Interdisciplinary research will also be critical as psychologists, other behavioral scientists, bio-scientists, entrepreneurs, and workers are compelled to reap the fullest rewards from every cent of research money. Wise utilization of research funds and feedback of information to all concerned are essential if decision makers are to be expected to consider and apply the field's research and practice findings seriously. Fortunately, this book contains some excellent examples of the interdisciplinary model. Its publication helps to ensure that decision makers are informed of the benefits derived from such programs. The World Health Organization, in conjunction with the International Labour Organization, and the European Union have called for coordinated preventive action on stress in the workplace (European Commission, 1997; ILO, 1986), including stress caused by downsizing, restructuring, and even by revitalization through change. Until the phenomenon of stress in the workplace is more commonly recognized, political leaders will not be compelled to produce legislation to improve health and well-being in the workplace. In trying to incite government to action, the greatest potential ally is the workforce population. People have a fundamental need to improve both work conditions and the availability of work. Publications such as this book can help to produce a grassroots movement for promoting both objectives. Workplace stress is a human-created problem. As such, its solution should be within our grasp, if complementary "bottom-up" and "top-down" approaches are initiated.

This book presents a state-of-the-art view of the changing organizational structure, its inherent problems, and ways in which solutions have been found. It includes theoretical articles, research findings, and case studies. This book will help researchers to look for new avenues of research, and will provide practitioners and executives with new ways to solve their organizational and employee problems resulting from the new organizational reality of downsizing, restructuring, and revitalization.

Lennart Levi, MD, PhD
Sektionen för Stressforskn
Karolinska Institut
Stockholm, Sweden

References

Berg, J. O. (1996). *Förnyare, frustrerade och fria agenter. Rapport fråu ett forskningsprojekt om abetslösheten och den dolda världen* [Innovators, frustrated and free agents. A report on a research project about unemployment and the hidden world]. Stockholm, Sweden: Sweden: City University Press.

Dooley, D., Fielding, J., & Levi, L. (1996). Health and unemployment. *Annual Review of Public Health, 17,* 449–465.

European Commission. (1997). *Report on work-related stress. The Advisory Committee for Safety, Hygiene, and Health Protection at Work.* Luxembourg: Author.

International Labor Organization. (1986). *Psychosocial factors at work: Recognition and control. Report of the Joint ILO/WHO Committee on Occupational Health* (Occupational Safety and Health Series No. 56). Geneva, Switzerland: Author.

International Labor Organization. (1996). *World employment 1996/97.* Geneva, Switzerland: Author.

National Swedish Board of Occupational Safety and Health. (1996). *The working environment 1995.* Stockholm, Sweden: Statistics Sweden SM 960.

Organization for Economic Cooperation and Development. (1994). The OECD jobs study. *OECD Economics Outline, 55,* 1–4.

Foreword

This is an important book about the human impact of the forces for change moving us toward a new competitive landscape in the 21st century. It is also about the strategies in which organizations may engage to help employees respond constructively, positively, and in healthy ways to the new organizational reality. Martin and Freeman's opening chapter sets the stage by addressing the importance of economics as a force for change that is shaping the new competitive landscape. Technology is another important force shaping the new organizational reality. While Martin and Freeman mention technology and other chapters touch on this aspect of the new reality, I emphasize the importance of several technological trends and their direct and indirect effects on people at work. These trends illuminate the primary theme of this volume and complement the important subthemes developed by the diverse chapter contributors.

As an organizational strategy scholar who began his career in human resources management, I have an ongoing concern for how organizational and business strategies affect people at work. From a technological standpoint, there appear to be four sets of forces or trends contributing to the shape of the new organizational reality. Each of these trends also has direct effects on people at work, the central concern of this volume, and on competition and organizational strategies, which, in turn, have effects on people at work.

First, there is an *increasing rate of technological change and diffusion*. This has two important implications for people at work. Not only are employees challenged to continuously learn to maintain currency and competence related to new technology, but they also face employment uncertainty that may be created by technological advances, which either automate work activities previously done by workers or significantly restructure the nature of the work individuals do within the framework of the new technologies. Hence, new technologies may affect restructuring in organizations.

Second, the *information age* has produced an information-rich, computation-rich, and communication-rich organizational environment. While an abundance of information characterizes the new competitive landscape, such information abundance does not necessarily mean clarity nor consistency. People working in information-rich and communication-rich environments are increasingly challenged to organize, integrate, interpret, and evaluate the volumes of information available to them. This presents a new and potentially stressful challenge for people working in the new organizational reality.

Third, there is an *increasing knowledge intensity* resulting from technological change, because the development and use of technology inherently involves knowledge. Increased knowledge is at the core of revitalizing and reeducating people at work. No longer can an employee expect to learn a definable set of skills in trade school, college, or graduate school and expect to sustain his or her career on that knowledge base. Rather, individuals must expect life-long learning, reeducation, and knowledge enhancement as they progress through a series of developmental phases in their careers. The concept of continuous development is a key feature of the new organizational reality that enables individuals and organizations to be competitive on the new technological battlefield.

Fourth, increased knowledge is also the basis for the emergence of the *positive feedback industry*. Conventional economic theory emphasized self-correcting mechanisms and was formed from natural resource-based industries. In knowledge and information-based industries, it appears possible to achieve continuously increasing returns where new knowledge and new information are created on an ongoing basis. Hence, individual expectations about organizations and economics again must be adjusted to the changing reality of the new competitive landscape.

In addition to the direct effects that the four technology trends have on people at work, there are indirect effects mediated through competition and organizational strategy. Graddick and Cairo's chapter 4 on the AT&T experience is an excellent illustration of how technological advances affected AT&T's competitive environment and organizational strategy, thereby affecting tens of thousands of employees throughout the organization. In addition, there are four sets of indirect effects related to how the technological trends affect competition and organizational strategy.

The new competitive landscape is a perilous place for organizations and businesses in the 1990s due to *increasing risk and uncertainty coupled with decreasing ability to forecast important environmental events*. Because technological change is fast, pervasive, and unpredictable, organizations face greater risks of failure and adversity, which place individuals within these organizations at greater risk as well. Organizations cannot easily buffer their employees from competitive pressures and environmental discontinuities. While employees may seek security in employment and in their careers, few organizations can guarantee such security because of the uncertainties in their technological and competitive environments.

In addition, there is an *increasing ambiguity of industry*. The boundaries that once defined industries and helped provide a modicum of environmental buffering for organizations have become permeable. Organizational boundaries are no longer permanent; they are in flux as new suppliers are found and different strategic business alliances are formed. This ambiguity produces uncertainty and stress for organizations, and, in turn, individuals. Thus, people need to maximize their knowledge and skill sets, developing a portfolio of knowledge, skills, and abilities that enhance their general value and marketability as industries shift and change.

Furthermore, the new competitive landscape is moving *managerial mindsets* away from formalized strategic planning, a watchword of the late 1970s and 1980s, toward a managerial mindset of flexibility in strategy and organization. Therefore, rather than developing long-term fixed strategies and stable organizational structures, managers are moving toward fluid business strategies and agile organizational forms. The need for flexibility in response to the firm's environment also requires a flexibility on the part of employees. This response to a turbulent, dynamic environment is counter to the normal human response to resist change because it is threatening. Therefore, people are being asked to behave in ways that are counter to their typical predispositions under threatening conditions.

Finally, the new competitive landscape is also *dramatically changing the imperatives* to which organizations must respond, such as the decreasing transaction costs discussed by Martin and Freeman in chapter 1. Organizations must emphasize increased learning and strategic response capability. The new competitive landscape is a constantly changing battlefield upon which winners are distinguished by (a) their ability to learn from feedback and create new products, designs, and services in response to that feedback, and (b) their capacity to forge and then change quickly their mission and strategic focus. People may experience the new organizational reality as akin to surfing a constantly changing and shifting wave. This somewhat disconcerting atmosphere is the result of the new competitive landscape where the ground rules have dramatically shifted for organizations, and therefore for individuals working within them.

Although this collected volume emphasizes the human side of organizations and focuses on what is happening to people at work, it is important for the reader to be aware of the broad context of organizational behavior such as systemic forces of economics, technology, organizational strategy, and organizational design shaping the new competitive landscape and the new organizational reality. These forces for change may help one understand the downsizing, downscoping (selling off businesses unrelated to the company's core business), and restructuring activities that have such dramatic effects on people at work. Furthermore, it is in the context of the new competitive landscape and the new organizational reality that individuals and organizations must be revitalized and invigorated if they are to survive and succeed.

Michael A. Hitt, Past President
Academy of Management and
Paul M. and Rosalie Robertson Chair
of Business Administration
Texas A&M University

Introduction

A new organizational reality is emerging on the current competitive landscape that is having important, and in some cases adverse, effects on people at work. The purpose of this book is to increase understanding of this new organizational reality and competitive landscape. Organizations and businesses are facing increasingly competitive environments and, as a result, employees are at risk of obsolescence, job loss, and adverse health effects. The new organizational reality calls for organizations to create systems, processes, and structures to support employees in meeting the ever-increasing challenges that both individuals and organizations face in the present economic climate. Psychologists can play an instrumental role in counseling executives, employees, groups, and organizations to respond to this new reality in healthy and constructive ways rather than defensive and dysfunctional ways.

The hallmark of the new organizational reality is change. Work life is changing in the United States and around the world (Lawler, 1996). Individuals, groups, and organizations often experience change as a threat to their well-being or survival (Staw, Sandelands, & Dutton, 1981). As a result of this predisposition to experience change as a threat, individuals, groups, and organizations have a tendency to respond with dominant, well-learned responses that are sometimes not appropriate responses to the changing reality. They tighten up and become rigid and, thus, are not maximally competent, capable, and productive because their energy and resources are committed to defense, not achievement or accomplishment. Hence, "threat–rigidity effects," described by Staw, Sandelands, and Dutton (1981) begin to emerge. Seen as a threat, change carries with it the implications of impending loss and costs for individuals and organizations. Employees become less open to new information and management controls behavior more strictly. Defensiveness and rigidity are counterproductive in the face of the new organizational reality.

Although change carries risk, it also has an upside. Change offers an opportunity to learn, to grow, and to develop new products, new services, new patterns of behavior, and new ways of doing business. Some economists believe that the United States is in a time of crisis, and well it may be. In this critical time, it may be helpful to recall that the Chinese symbol for crisis is composed of two underlying symbols: One represents danger and the other represents opportunity. The concern of this book is to help individuals and organizations see an overview of the new competitive landscape and, by doing so, look for new opportunities and challenges on that landscape so as to facilitate the process of personal and organizational transformation to fit into the new organizational reality.

Our thesis is that organizations around the world are in the midst of a dramatic systemic revolution similar to the agricultural revolution that occurred in America from the late 18th century through the early

20th century. That agricultural revolution saw an enormous increase in the agricultural productivity per farm worker due to great technological and crop management advances. Hence, the proportion of Americans engaged in agriculture shrank from nearly 80% of the population to less than 2% of the population (Scott, 1967). Jobs in farming and agriculture became increasingly scarce, and the emerging jobs in farming and agriculture became transformed with each new year into manufacturing and service occupations. Workers today need to learn new skills for the emerging jobs created by the new organizational reality just as agricultural workers needed to learn manufacturing and industrial skills to be successful during the industrial age.

The Bureau of Labor Statistics of the U. S. Department of Labor released its employment outlook for 1994 to 2005. The report notes that manufacturing will lose 1.3 million jobs, a continuation of a decline. Employment is projected to increase to 144.7 million (out of the United States population of 265 million) from 127 million or only 14%, compared with a growth rate of 24% from 1983 to 1994. Jobs in the service and retail trades are expected to increase by 16.2 million. Business services, health, and education will account for 9.1 million new jobs (U.S. Department of Labor, 1996).

Also, in a wide range of organizations throughout the manufacturing and service sectors of the economy, jobs are disappearing in large numbers never to be replaced, due to technological and information management advances. A study by Henry Farber of Princeton University found that the rate of job displacement from 1991 to 1993 exceeded the rate in the much deeper 1981–1983 recession ("Downsizings' Impact," 1996). The displacement was caused more by companies permanently abolishing positions than by the more traditional reasons of slackening demand for a company's work or plant closings. The Bureau of Labor Statistics included systems analysts, computer engineers, and operations research analysts among those occupations projected to have significant growth in the future, a reflection of the oncoming and ever-expanding information age.

These dramatic shifts in the nature of work are occurring during a period of relative economic prosperity. Growth in the first quarter for the inflation-adjusted gross domestic product was 4%. Compared with the economies of the other members of the Group of Seven industrial countries (which are Japan, Germany, Britain, France, Italy, and Canada), the United States economy looks vigorous—job growth is much stronger, and the economy is expanding more rapidly while the unemployment rate remains low ("Growth," 1996).

In fact, the U. S. Department of Labor reported that the nation's jobless rate dropped to 4.9 percent in 1997, while employers brought on board hundreds of thousands of workers. Interestingly, the National Association of Manufacturers, the Business Roundtable, and the Committee for Economic Development all released studies in 1996 asserting that the economy is creating new jobs of increasingly high quality. Since 1992, 10.7 million payroll jobs have been added ("Soul-Searching," 1996).

Other good economic news includes a decline in the seasonally adjusted Consumer Price Index to 2.9% from nearly 6% five years ago, a decline in the annual federal budget deficit to $23 billion from over $290 billion in 1992 ("Forecasts," 1997). Additionally, the Census Bureau reported in September 1996 that household income rose for the first time in six years and the proportion of Americans living below the poverty line fell during the last year ("Household Income," 1996). Median household income rose 2.7% to $34,076 after being adjusted for inflation. The poverty rate declined from 14.5% to 13.8% and the number of poor fell by 1.6 million, the largest decrease in 27 years. One reason for the increase in average wage rates was the pressure that employers are facing to recruit and retain workers in a relatively tight labor market.

The one disappointing trend in this bright economic recovery is the earnings distribution across the white- and blue-collar jobs. Wages for white-collar workers rose 1% during the first 3 months of 1996 and 3.3% for the past 12 months. Blue-collar workers' wages rose only .2% for the first 3 months and 2.3% for the past 12 months, a rate of increase lower than inflation. In essence, the gap between the rich and poor is rising. Family incomes for the poorest 20% of the population have lagged the gains made by families in the top 5% and top 20% according to the 1992 *Survey of Consumer Finances of the Congressional Budget Office* ("The Gap," 1996).

What this economic picture suggests is that while employees will continue to lose their jobs due to downsizing and restructuring, mergers and acquisitions, and the introduction of advanced technology, those employees will have an easier time locating new work. Nonetheless, the stress associated with job loss, relocation, and adjustment to the new, fast-paced environment will require attention to ways to help individuals, groups, and organizations maintain their health and well-being as they work their way through this period of transition on the way to the future.

This book develops a number of themes through conceptual and theoretical chapters, research-based chapters, and organizational case study chapters from the public and private sectors of the United States economy. Some of the themes developed in this book are competitive economic pressures of the 1990s, the financial impact of downsizing, the challenge of revitalizing workforces, and the importance of the human side of enterprise. The concerns and issues addressed in this book are not uniquely American, although their variants may be uniquely American. Rather, the new organizational reality and emerging competitive landscape are global in nature.

Most books dealing with the new organizational reality have one or the other of two distinguishing features. One category of these books, such as Hoskisson and Hitt's (1994) discussion of downscoping as a way to better manage diversified firms, address specific aspects of the new organizational reality. Another category of these books, such as Lawler's (1996) discussion of the new logic corporation, represent a single author's point of view concerning the new organizational reality. *The New Organizational Reality* is distinguished by its multi-topic, multi-perspective presentations of the new organizational reality.

This book is intended for two audiences. One audience is composed of executives, organizational leaders, managers, and employees who are working to be both productive and healthy in the context of the new organizational reality. These are the people who make the wheels meet the road by manufacturing the products and providing the services that are essential to the functioning of a mature, advanced society. Another audience is composed of the psychologists and other health-care professionals charged with the responsibility to attend to the health and well-being of those working in the new organizational reality. The wealth of a nation and its people rests upon the health and well-being of the productive, working members of its population. Hence, the two core audiences for this book are the people at work and those who care for the people at work.

This book offers these two audiences a collection of 13 chapters organized into three major parts and a concluding chapter that describes a conceptual framework for coping with the new organizational reality. A part introduction precedes each of the three major parts of the book and provides a brief overview of each chapter in the part. Part I addresses the question "What Is Changing at Work?" It is composed of three chapters that address the economic, organizational design, financial, and transformational aspects of the new reality. Part I is intended to help define the new organizational reality while providing a context through which to see and understand the diverse case studies to follow in Part II. Part II consists of case studies from both the private sector and the public sector. The five case chapters in this part of the book come from AT&T, Chaparral Steel Company, the United States Air Force, the United States Office of Personnel Management, and the Environmental Protection Agency. Part III of the book is composed of four chapters that address management issues and are written by external or internal organizational consultants who are working to help organizations and individuals accommodate and adjust to the new organizational reality.

James Campbell Quick
Marilyn K. Gowing
John D. Kraft

References

Downsizings' impact on jobs begins showing up in studies. (1996, March 21). *The Washington Post*, p. B9.

Forecasts on the federal deficits are declining. (1997, October 4) *The New York Times*, p. A11.

The gap widens. (1996, October 14). *The Washington Post*, p. A1.

Growth to crow about, quietly. (1996, April 2). *The Washington Post*, p. E1.

Hoskisson, R. E., & Hitt, M. A. (1994). *Downscoping: How to tame the diversified firm*. New York: Oxford University Press.

Household income climbs. (1996, September 27). *The Washington Post*, p. A1.

Lawler, E. E. (1996). *From the ground up: Six principles for building the new logic corporation*. San Francisco: Jossey-Bass.

Scott, M. (1967). *The bifurcation of work and family life. Seminar on the church and the world of work*. Chicago: Presbyterian Institute of Labor and Industrial Relations at McCormick Seminary.

Soul-Searching time in the corner office. (1996, May 13). *Business Week, 3475*.

Staw, B. M., Sandelands, L. E., & Dutton, J. E. (1981). Threat–rigidity effects in organizational behavior: A multilevel analysis. *Administrative Science Quarterly, 26*, 501–524.

U.S. Department of Labor. (1996, July). *Employment outlook: 1994–2005—Job quality and other aspects of projected employment growth, Bulletin 2476*. Washington, DC: Bureau of Labor Statistics.

Part I

What Is Changing at Work?

Introduction

Understanding the new organizational reality involves appreciating the economic forces that redefine the boundaries of the firm and shape the ways in which organizations are designed. This new organizational reality may be an opportunity or a threat, depending on how an individual or an organization sees, interprets, and responds to the forces shaping this changing reality. Environmental change is most often experienced as a threat, with impending loss or costs. When individuals, groups, or organizations feel threatened, they are less open to information and more controlling in their behavior, which leads to rigidity. Rigidity in response to change is often dysfunctional. An alternative is a healthy, flexible response.

A healthy response to environmental change requires a proactive strategy of adjustment, accommodation, and transformation. To develop such a strategy requires knowledge and information. Knowledge is power; information is empowering. In Part I, the chapter authors present an impartial and realistic, if sobering, picture of the new organizational landscape. The changes portrayed here are both personal and systemic. The changes do impact people, and there may be personal loss and costs with which individuals and organizations must come to grips. Once this painful aspect of the new reality is accepted, then the processes of designing and building new individual and organizational realities can begin.

Trust is an essential ingredient for healthy interpersonal and organizational relationships,[1] yet the new organizational reality is challenging the bonds of trust among employees, employers, and the whole host of participants in business, commerce, and enterprise. Experiencing threat in the absence of trust can be especially stressful for people in organizations, often leading to behavior that is competitive rather than cooperative or collaborative. In trusting relationships competition challenges us to achieve our best, but in nontrusting relationships, competition becomes corporate warfare played out between enemies and allies.[2]

Chapter 1, by Martin and Freeman, addresses the economic origins of firms, examines the revolution in manufacturing, or mentofacturing (i.e., mind-based manufacturing such as computer-assisted design, etc.) and its implications for the service sector of the economy, and discusses the impact of these economic, technological, and informational forces on the design of

---

[1]Hosmer, L. T. (1995). Trust: The connecting link between organizational theory and philosophical ethics. *Academy of Management Review, 20,* 379–403.

[2]Nelson, D. L., Quick, J. C., and Quick, J. D. (1989). Corporate warfare: Preventing combat stress and battle fatigue. *Organizational Dynamics, 18,* 65–79.

work and organizations. The trends Martin and Freeman discuss are at times complimentary and at times conflicting. The chapter raises important and difficult questions, which must be answered within the new organizational reality.

Chapter 2, by Burke and Nelson, presents a North American perspective on three core organizational transformations that are central to the new organizational reality: mergers and acquisitions, downsizing, and privatization. These three forms of organizational change may create individual problems such as underemployment, occupational *locking-in*, career entrenchment, or job insecurity, without ever quite realizing the organizational benefits proposed in restructuring objectives. The authors conclude that organizational decline is all too often the organizational consequence of restructuring efforts. The chapter suggests actions that individuals and organizations may take to cope with the new organizational reality.

Chapter 3, by Cascio, reports on a study that examined the financial performance of 311 firms that downsized their workforces by more than 3% in any year between 1980 and 1990. Downsizing did not appear either to help or hinder systematically the financial or stock performance of these firms. Financial performance did vary as a function of industry variables, suggesting the relevance of the firm's industry context. The chapter offers a model for responsible restructuring as an alternative to downsizing. The model challenges top management to articulate a vision for the firm that is embedded in a supportive corporate culture in which employees are understood as valued assets to be developed rather than costs to be cut.

These three chapters highlight the ways in which the new organizational reality is fundamentally different from the reality 10 years ago, or even in the more recent past. Many things are changing at work: the economics of markets and industries, core competencies and competition, the relationships among employees and organizations, the ways in which firms are defined and organized, and a whole host of related aspects of organizational life. The new organizational reality succeeds only if trust and collaboration remain intact, and fails if trust is lost in the transition from old to new.

1

The Economic Context of the New Organizational Reality

Robert E. Martin and Sarah J. Freeman

The purpose of this chapter is to set the economic stage for the discussions of corporate restructuring that follow. Our intent is to identify the economic forces that are leading firms to focus so intently on their internal organization. The following section considers the economic theories that explain the origin of firms. Understanding why firms evolved in the first place can help us understand why they are changing so rapidly today. The third section reviews lessons learned from the revolution in manufacturing that began in the 1980s. In the fourth section, we consider the social forces that affect internal and external transaction costs and how this changes the size of the representative firm. Special implications for the service industries are discussed in the fifth section, and the general summary and implications are contained in the last section.

It is tempting, although egocentric, to view our own time on earth as a historic turning point, a watershed period, or a golden age. As we approach the year 2000, there is an even greater tendency to view the world and its events through this cataclysmic lens, and a host of books with millennial themes attest to its appeal. Writers have addressed change in all domains, as well as the acceleration of change in general, and how change can lead to feelings of uncertainty and turbulence.

Something important appears to be taking place in the evolution of firms and market economies. Diverse writers from the varying perspectives of theory and practice, from a multitude of academic disciplines, from new and old line manufacturing and high-technology industries, and from East and West agree on how organizations must change and what forces are driving this change (Davidow & Malone, 1992; Drucker, 1988; Hammer, 1990; Harris, 1993; Kanter, 1989; Maruyama, 1992). Organizations must become leaner, less hierarchical, more adaptive, more responsive to customers, and more willing to empower their employees. They must make their internal and external boundaries permeable, and at the same time

We are indebted to the editors and an anonymous referee for their comments and suggestions. All remaining errors are our own. Part of this work was completed when Robert E. Martin was a member of the Economics Department at the University of Texas at Arlington.

they must permeate the boundaries of other organizations and institutions. A fluid network of relationships with suppliers, customers, competitors, collaborators, contractors, and employees will result. These relationships will vary in duration and in the level of commitment they demand. Organizations must identify their core competencies (Prahalad & Hamel, 1990; Wernerfelt, 1984) and jettison or outsource other functions of the firm. It will be very difficult for firms to simultaneously preserve their core competencies and open their "borders" to suppliers, customers, competitors, collaborators, contractors, and employees.

The sources of this change include globalization; integration; new competition based on quality, speed, and customization; and new demands from varied stakeholder groups. Perhaps most of all, change is enabled by new technology and the speed of technological advancement. This is particularly the case with information and communication technology.

Organizations have responded to these forces by downsizing, delayering, restructuring, redesigning work, reengineering processes, and outsourcing noncore and support activities. As organizations seek to rely less on hierarchy and become more flexible and responsive, they also try to establish work processes and relationships that will enable them to both produce goods and services at low cost and be nimble in their decision making and market responses. A primary strategy for firms today is to become a market leader through the creative innovation of state-of-the-art technology. These innovations can lead to much lower costs for goods and services and innovative products that heretofore were unimaginable.

The logical extension of many of these organizational changes is not just a reduction in hierarchy, but its elimination. That is, organizations have the option of placing the work—and the employee—outside the boundaries of the firm. This outsourcing has been a result of some of the layoffs, outplacements, and announced restructurings of late. Outsourcing sometimes means spinning off organizational subunits that formerly operated in-house, so that the original parent firm may become a client of this former subunit, rather than its owner. Similarly, although the business and general press prints much about mergers and acquisitions, lately there have been some prominent examples of breakups (e.g., AT&T, ITT, General Motors' EDS unit, Ford Motor Corporation's recent announcement of its plan to spin off The Associates Corporation of North America in a public offering), disaggregating extremely large firms. Although a majority of the workforce is still employed full-time with a single employer, there is increasing use of temporary employees, contract workers, and suppliers that provide anything from subassemblies for manufacturing to contract CEOs for relatively short-term turnaround efforts. Trends such as telecommuting and increased use of information technology allow many workers to perform their jobs from their homes or other remote locations. In turn, this has made it easier for the "employee" to operate as a private contractor, providing some specified output, service, or project for the client firm.

The revolutionary potential of computer technologies has been recognized for decades, but to date their promise has not been exploited fully. However, as the costs of information technology decrease and its capabilities increase, considerable change is taking place, particularly in manufacturing. A question has arisen regarding whether we are in the midst of a second industrial revolution. Whereas the Industrial Revolution created the factory system and destroyed cottage industries, the second industrial revolution seems poised to destroy the factory system and create new forms of cottage industry.

Today's turbulent situation is redrafting the implicit, or psychological, contract between the individual and the organization. The implications of this changed contract are many. Before addressing the new contract, it is useful to ask why firms exist to begin with? What led to individuals' holding more or less permanent, relatively secure positions, and performing specified or unspecified tasks within a given organization? The economic theory of the origins of the firm can yield useful insights regarding reengineering, downsizing, and outsourcing.

The Economic Origins of the Firm

Conceivably, all economic activity can be conducted through arm's-length market transactions. Under these circumstances, every agent would be an independent contractor, and all tasks would be outsourced. Cottage industries in Europe before the Industrial Revolution represented such a system based on independent contracting (Mathias, 1979; Mokyr, 1985). Although possible, this system in which all economic activity is conducted through markets is rare. Considerable economic activity is carried out within firms, all at less than arm's length. The pure theory of transactions suggests firms are not necessary. But the existence and the survival of firms are important empirical evidence indicating that firms have some economic advantages over systems based on market transactions.

Holmstrom and Milgrom (1994) suggested that the "make-or-buy decision" may be the most studied question in economics. The forces that drive the make-or-buy decision also explain the existence of the conventional firm. At the extreme, a firm can cease to exist by choosing to buy all of its activities. While the traditional firm then disappears, the residual firm is a contract monitor or a broker of independent production activities.

There are at least five traditional explanations for the existence of firms: risk, information asymmetry, transaction costs, inseparable team production, and control of assets. These are not competitive explanations, but rather are complementary in many respects. Furthermore, their influence is not constant or linear.

Risk

Knight (1933) suggested that firms arise because of the distribution of attitudes toward risk. Some individuals are less risk averse than others. Those who are more risk averse choose employment, while those who are less risk averse become entrepreneurs. Market forces determine the profit returned to entrepreneurs in each industry, which varies with the risk in each industry and the distribution of potential entrepreneurs. An equilibrium point exists, then, where the reward for risk bearing matches the distribution of risk-bearing entrepreneurs.[1]

Knight's explanation is not entirely satisfactory. The reward for risk bearing explains why an entrepreneur makes a market with the output of others. It does not explain why they integrate backward or forward to bring the previously independent contractors into a firm. That is, it does not explain why an entrepreneur would take responsibility for these independent contractors by making them employees. The risk averse worker's demand for security can be satisfied by a long-term contract. She or he does not need to become an employee to gain security.

Information Asymmetry

Information asymmetry can also explain the existence of firms. A "complete" market is a market where information is complete and is uniformly distributed among all agents. There are no trade secrets, no proprietary information, and no uncertainty. In actuality, all markets are incomplete. Agents do face uncertainty, and the information that is available is not uniformly distributed. Some agents have more information than others, and agents with more information about profit opportunity are in a position to receive greater returns by coordinating inputs as the manager of the firm.

Transaction Costs

Coase (1937) brought us closer to understanding why firms exist. He asserted that market transactions are not without cost. Buyers must search for sellers, and sellers must search for buyers. This searching is costly. Once located, contracts between both parties must be negotiated and enforced. Negotiation and enforcement are not without cost. Similarly, there are costs associated with each transaction conducted inside the firm, such as monitoring and coordination. Coase speculated that firms evolved as the market's solution to the problem of minimizing transaction costs. If the internal transaction cost is less than the external transaction cost, the activity will become part of the firm. If the internal transaction cost is greater than the market transaction cost, the activity will be accomplished via a market transaction.

Coase's explanation also emphasizes the dynamic nature of the optimal firm structure and suggests that firms should be reengineering themselves continuously. The "border of the firm" is defined by the point where the firm ceases to perform economic activities with employees and begins to contract with independent firms for these services. The locus of the

---

[1]The entrepreneur's expected reward for bearing risk is economic profit, a return on his or her skills that is above his or her second-best employment opportunity.

border, in any direction, reflects where total transaction cost is minimized. Minimization requires the marginal cost of an internal transaction to equal the marginal cost of a market transaction. The firm is analogous to an amoeba with an irregular border. Like the amoeba, the firm's border is constantly changing. Any factor or condition that changes either set of transaction costs will also change the optimal border of the firm. The firm's ideal structure varies with time and across different circumstances. Firms sometimes fail to recognize when organizational changes are needed. When firms do undertake change, their adjustments are discrete while change in the ideal structure is continuous.

Team Production

Although the concept of transaction costs aids our understanding of the firm, it is not precise enough to explain the major historical changes in the representative firm's structure. Alchian and Demsetz (1972) provided the next step in the explanation. They emphasized the inseparable concepts of team production, shirking behavior, and monitoring. Furthermore, they focused on the system of incentives that organize behavior inside the firm. The theories of risk bearing and transaction costs alone do not tell us much about what happens inside the black box called the representative firm.

Alchian and Demsetz considered the critical role played by production technology in the evolution of the firm. Suppose we have two workers (w_1 and w_2) and two different production technologies, one old and one new. The old production technology is strongly separable in labor input, such that output is the sum of each individual worker's labor (i.e., $x = f[w_1] + f[w_2]$). The new technology is inseparable in labor inputs, such that output is a function of the two workers' joint labor (i.e., $x = F[w_1, w_2]$). Adoption of the new technology requires that output of the two workers be greater under the new system, that is, that $F(w_1, w_2) > f(w_1) + f(w_2)$ for all pairs of workers. The new technology must lead to greater production for the same input levels, or there is no economic incentive to adopt it.

Consider, for example, the weaving of cloth before and after the Industrial Revolution. Before the Industrial Revolution, weaving was a cottage industry. Looms were hand driven by individual workers. The output of each worker was independent of the effort of other workers and was easily measured at the end of the day. Therefore, the total output was the sum of all workers' output, $x = f(w_1) + f(w_2)$. With this technology, production could be dispersed to wherever the workers happened to be. The Industrial Revolution brought the factory system. The steam engine used to drive mechanized looms was a centralized power source that never got tired and could work much faster than any human or animal. A factory was created by bringing many workers to this power source.

The most significant incentive problem with this new technology was that the output of one worker now depended on the effort of other workers. The workers' productivity was a team effort. Therefore, total output was no longer a simple sum of individual outputs; it was instead $x = F(w_1, w_2)$. In the market system, productivity determined rewards, but a system of market transactions cannot set wage rates for individual workers who are members of a team. The market can measure the team's output and fix the team's reward. However, the reward distribution among team members must be left to some other mechanism. Distributing the reward equally among team members gives each worker an incentive to free ride or shirk at the expense of other team members. Someone must supervise or monitor the team to measure members' output and allocate rewards.

One problem remains: Who monitors the monitor? What will prevent the monitor from shirking? If the monitor has claim to the residual profit, he or she has the necessary economic incentive. The entrepreneur's role as residual claimant is to measure individual output and allocate rewards within the firm. She or he will attempt to do this efficiently because her or his return is the profit residual. If he or she allocates rewards within the team in a way that does not represent each member's actual contribution to team productivity, he or she will decrease residual profit and his or her own return. That is, team members who are underrewarded will now have a disincentive to perform, whereas those who are overrewarded will have incentive to shirk.

Asset Control

Finally, Hart and Moore (1990) and Grossman and Hart (1986) considered the role of property rights and the corresponding control of assets in the organization of the firm. Like that of Alchian and Demsetz (1972), their analysis focused on the internal structure of the firm. Asset property rights are important because contracts are incomplete. A complete contract specifies actions for both parties for every conceivable event that may arise. In an uncertain environment, there are an infinite number of possible outcomes, and writing a complete contract is impossible. With incomplete contracts, the parties to a transaction must rely on other incentive mechanisms to ensure compliance with the spirit of the contract. A *performance bond* is an example of this type of incentive mechanism. A construction contractor may guarantee his performance by purchasing insurance on the work. Because the insurance is performance rated and the contractor pays for the insurance, the insurance is a bond posted to guarantee the quality of the work.

The location of asset property rights has different incentive effects. Suppose there is an entrepreneur, B, who buys the output sold by a second entrepreneur, S. Entrepreneur S also employs several workers who produce this output. Initially, the asset property rights, that is, the rights to the machinery that is used to produce the output, are held by entrepreneur S. Further, assume that the machines (assets) are specific to the output sold by S and used by B; that is, the machinery is not well suited to produce other products. The workers and the machines are complementary in that the workers' skills are also machine-specific. Thus, the market value of the workers' output depends on having access to the machines. Therefore, the workers' loyalty goes to whoever owns the machines. Entrepreneur B has a make-or-buy decision. If she makes the product, the workers' loyalty will be transferred to her, and she can fire individual team members without having to fire the entire production team (Hart & Moore, 1990). Note that firing the entire production team means terminating her arrangement with Entrepreneur S and thus firing the output-specific machinery as well as the team of workers. Under uncertainty, it can be demonstrated that all agents (regardless of attitude toward risk) prefer flexibility to inflexibility in production (Hey, 1979). It is preferable to adjust team composition rather than to adjust the whole team. Control of assets, either firm or product-specific, engenders flexibility.

Firm-specific assets are not restricted to plant and equipment. For example, the firm may hire engineers in a general market for engineering labor. Once hired, a given engineer builds human capital through experience. This human capital can be a firm-specific asset. Oliver Williamson (1985) called this the fundamental transformation of general labor skills to managerial skills. The more firm-specific human capital a manager holds, the more he or she has to lose if the firm goes bankrupt. Managerial loyalty will be attached to whoever controls the assets. The relationship between the entrepreneur and the manager becomes a bilateral monopoly.

In a sense, we have defined five musicians—risk bearing, information asymmetry, transaction costs, team production, and asset control. Each musician is melodious, yet harmony escapes us. Holmstrom and Milgrom (1994) considered how these influences work together as an incentive system to coordinate behavior within the firm. They identified three major groups of incentive instruments: compensation, asset ownership, and job design. *Compensation structure* is limited only by ingenuity; it varies from fixed hourly wages with virtually guaranteed employment to strict performance-based pay with freelance employment status.

Asset ownership promotes a longer planning horizon among managers. Managers, who may control but do not own the assets, may make short-run maximizing decisions at the expense of longer term profit. This is the principal-agent problem (Holmstrom and Milgrom, 1991). The composition of assets also is relevant. The owner is most vulnerable to principal-agent abuse when the firm has firm-specific assets and the manager has few firm-specific assets in her or his inventory of human capital. The more firm-specific assets owned by the manager, that is, the less portable the manager's skills, the less serious is the principal-agent problem. Here, the manager's firm-specific assets act as a performance bond. The firm is subject to similar problems with suppliers whose assets are not specific to the firm that purchases their output. This is why, for example, the major automobile manufacturers require subcontractors to invest in specific assets.

Job design comprises tasks and procedures included in the job description, work rules, hours, and excluded activities (Holstrom & Milgrom, 1994). Freedom of choice in job design is a powerful incentive.

Holmstrom and Milgrom (1994, p. 972) argued that the three most powerful incentive instruments are performance-based compensation, manager ownership of assets, and freedom to design the job. However, they note that employment and entrepreneurial incentive systems appear to be opposite of each other. Employees generally receive fixed wages, they do not own the firm's assets, and they have little freedom in job design. Entrepreneurs, on the other hand, receive performance-based pay, own the assets, and have complete freedom of job design. Of course, these dimensions are not dichotomous but exist on a continuum. Many firms have experimented with variations in these incentive instruments, often in attempts to make employees behave more like entrepreneurs. However, one does not normally observe a mixture of, say, fixed wages, employee ownership of all assets, and no freedom in job design. This observation suggests a strong complementarity among the three incentive instruments. As Holmstrom and Milgrom (1994) observed:

> So one has to ask what explains the choice between different incentive systems: Why are some workers employees and other workers independent contractors? To address this, we have to introduce exogenous parameters that move the system solution around. Variations in the cost of measuring performance, in asset specificity, and in uncertainty about the future are all good candidates. (p. 973)

This suggests that freedom of job design and fixed wages are competing incentive instruments, in the sense that reducing performance-based pay toward fixed wages also reduces the positive incentive effect of freedom to design the job. Freedom of job design and performance-based pay are complementary in the sense that an increase in either increases the incentive effect of the other.

Holmstrom and Milgrom (1994) explored how risk, transaction cost, inseparable team production, and asset property rights jointly influence these complementary incentive instruments. They found the two most important factors to be monitoring difficulties and multiple work tasks. All else being equal, if individual productivity is easily monitored, the worker is more likely to be an independent contractor. If the job requires the worker to do multiple tasks with diverse members of other teams—that is, if the job is characterized by high variety, complexity, and interdependence—the worker is more likely to be an employee. The entrepreneurial incentive instruments are powerful enough to discourage cooperation and coordination in a multitask environment. Therefore,

> the natural economic hypothesis is that bureaucratic constraints can serve a purpose. To the extent that there is a need for reduced bureaucracy today, it may be because the environment has changed. Our modeling approach identifies some of the environmental changes that could account for the current trend toward greater worker responsibility ("empowerment"), as well as the implications such a change is likely to have for the other components of an incentive system. (Holmstrom & Milgrom, 1994, pp. 989–990)

Thus, according to the economic theory of the firm's origins, individuals sometimes prefer to operate as employees rather than as individual contractors due to varying propensities for risk and uncertainty. Likewise, entrepreneurs bring workers into the firm as employees, rather than contracting with them in the market for the same outputs, because internal transaction costs are sometimes lower than market transaction costs and because some output is best obtained via a team effort that is inseparable into its component units of labor. Control of some asset property rights, both tangible and intangible, confers the manager with job description flexibility, a powerful incentive. At the same time, the manager's firm-specific human capital ties the manager and the firm to one another through nontransferability of assets. This promotes longer planning horizons in most managers, because their long-run well-being is more closely tied to the firm. All of these factors influence the incentive systems meant to encourage productivity and job performance on the part of the worker. Environmental change, particularly advances in technology, can influence the extent to which worker productivity is easily monitored, the degree of interdependence required in the production of a service or product, and the extent to which the individual worker must be expert in many varied tasks.

Lessons From the Revolution in Manufacturing

Recent trends in manufacturing reveal much about the evolution of the modern firm. According to Milgrom and Roberts (1990),

> manufacturing is undergoing a revolution. The mass production model is being replaced by a vision of a flexible multiproduct firm that emphasizes quality and speedy response to market conditions while utilizing technologically advanced equipment and new forms of organization. (p. 511)

Whether this revolution can be applied to the service industries and government, which together account for nearly three quarters of the economy, has not yet been demonstrated. However, there are some interesting parallels.

Several authors have recounted a variety of remarkable changes taking place in manufacturing (Davidow & Malone, 1992; Milgrom & Roberts, 1990). The new production technology allows firms to utilize extremely short production runs, so that products are, in effect, custom-made. Furthermore, technology enables immediate shifts in production from one product to another. Linking computer-aided design (CAD) with computer-aided manufacturing (CAM) results in computer-integrated manufacturing (CIM). This dramatically reduces the cycle time for product development. Products leave the drawing board and reach the market in a fraction of the time formerly possible. These engineering developments, combined with organizational innovations such as synchronous manufacturing and concurrent engineering, are forcing changes in the rest of the firm's structure.

Engineering developments affect marketing strategies directly. Computer sales monitoring completes the return link from design to the market and back to production. With electronic networks, the firm receives sales volume information and order requests in real time. It has immediate information about what products are popular and what products are languishing on the shelves. Production is literally pulled by demand, and therefore, inventories are minimized. In addition, the very products the firm sells are different. It can customize products that were available previously only as mass-produced items. Furthermore, it offers immediate delivery. A firm's marketing strategies and organization clearly must be different for these new products and services. The rigidity of the old production technology protected firms from the market's volatility. The new technology demands that firms be nimble.

The next step in the firm's evolution is the "virtual corporation." (See Davidow & Malone, 1992; Gargan 1994; and Goldman, 1994, for discussion of this new type of corporation and its concomitant trends in product development, manufacturing, marketing, and organization structure.) If the individual firm's internal functions can be integrated by computers, then why not integrate manufacturing across firms? Electronic information networks are the platform for this step. The virtual corporation may be a temporary entity that exists only in the information network. In each production period, manufacturing firms have a certain amount of plant capacity available to produce their own products and, perhaps, some excess capacity. Any excess plant capacity is a wasted resource. However, the new production flexibility has created a market for excess plant capacity. The availability of machine time, with certain technical capabilities, can be posted on the information network. The "virtual entrepreneur" combines these productive services to produce a custom-made product. This virtual corporation can have a very short life in the information network. Information network technology will make it easy for firms to change from one market to another at virtually no cost.

These developments also have important implications for economic theory, particularly for the theory of production. Neoclassical production theory assumes the existence of a "production function," which describes how inputs are converted into outputs. A firm's engineers are expected to choose the most technologically efficient production function. Economists assume that engineering optimization has already occurred. Notice how this compartmentalizes the structure of the firm. First, the engineers select the optimal technology for the plant design. Next, the firm's managers take the technology as given and try to maximize profits. In today's reality, these activities are inseparable. While the neoclassical model predicts that all input choices will be made individually at the margin, Milgrom and Roberts (1990) have noted that production decisions today are made across systems of organizations. The firm simultaneously chooses organizational form, technology, and input levels; it does not take form and technology as givens and then choose inputs.

Thus, in addition to their impact on economic theory, these developments have implications for organizations. On one hand, more activities can be performed outside the boundaries of the firm, and the costs of these external transactions are reduced. Thus, technological change has enabled downsizing and restructuring, and competition has made these adjustments necessary. On the other hand, the workers who do remain within the boundaries of the firm as employees are likely to possess more firm-specific knowledge. Furthermore, the interdependence of their work increases as many activities take place simultaneously rather than sequentially and thus necessitate greater coordination.

Social and Economic Forces That Affect the Border of the Firm

The representative manufacturing firm is becoming smaller and simpler. By focusing on a few core competencies (Prahalad & Hamel, 1990), firms hope to do a smaller number of things better while outsourcing or contracting for the remaining activities. This indicates that the costs of market transactions are falling relative to the costs of internal transactions. Therefore, more transactions are taking place outside the border of the firm, causing it to shrink.

Transaction costs are influenced by technology. The first effect is on what economists call the *minimum efficient scale*. This is the smallest output at which the firm achieves the minimum average cost of production. Long production runs imply a large minimum efficient scale, and short production runs imply a small minimum efficient scale. "Mini" steel mills and "brew pubs" are examples of firms with short production runs and a small minimum efficient scale. A smaller minimum efficient scale increases the deadweight loss of bureaucracy per unit of output. So, as Holmstrom and Milgrom (1994) noted, the environment is moving away from bureaucratic incentive systems. The second technology effect on transaction costs comes from computer information networks. *Information networks lower the cost of market transactions by decreasing the costs of search, coordination, and contracting.*

Demographic and social trends also influence transaction costs. For example, as the population ages and life expectancies increase, the contingent liabilities associated with every employee also increase via three direct effects. First, the incidence of serious illness increases with age, and we can expect greater medical liabilities as the average age of the workforce increases. Second, the date at which the firm acquires the representative employee's pension liability is closer as the average age increases, so that on a present value basis the pension costs to the employer rise. Third, an increase in life expectancy increases the entire pension liability. All of these costs rise if health care costs rise. Of course, there are also benefits associated with older workers, such as reliability of performance and their store of firm-specific knowledge.

Legal trends affect transaction costs as well. The legal position of *em-*

ployment at will has eroded over the last several decades. *Employment at will* is the legal concept that firms have the right to hire and fire employees as economic and other conditions dictate. Congress and the courts are awarding job property rights to workers. Richard Epstein (1995) noted that "worldwide, the regulation of labor markets has created a legal edifice of stunning complexity. Protective laws abound on every conceivable aspect of the subject: health, safety, wages, pensions, unionization, hiring, promotion, dismissal, leave, retirement, discrimination, access, and disability" (p. 151). It now may be much easier to "fire" the entire production team managed by a supplier than to selectively fire members of one's own production team (Hart & Moore, 1990). Therefore, internal transaction costs rise compared with market transaction costs.

Implications for Service Industries

Reengineering projects have been successful in both manufacturing and service applications. There is some indication, however, that success rates for these projects are not the same for manufacturing applications and service applications. There are many "white paper processes" in manufacturing, as well as in services.[2] Expediting inputs and outputs, accounts receivable, and customer service are examples of service activities carried out by manufacturing firms. These activities are different than applying cutting edge technology to the design and manufacture of physical products. We draw a distinction here between actual manufacturing and service activities, wherever they occur.

Several basic differences tend to make reengineering more complex in service applications than in manufacturing. First, unlike manufacturing, well-accepted measures of service output are elusive and problematic (Griliches, 1994). The productivity improvements that follow organization change may be less obvious in service industries. While it can be relatively easy to identify the direct reductions in costs that follow reductions in staff, the quantity and, particularly, quality of service output may fall as staff is reduced, making any improvement in productivity illusory. Units of service with uniform quality cannot be counted with the same dispatch as the number of computer chips from alternative manufacturing processes.

Second, linking machines with computer networks is easier than linking people with computer networks. Adjusting machines for consistent performance is more easily accomplished than adjusting people for consistent performance. Machines do not suffer from fear or the persistence of inappropriate work habits. Furthermore, a firm encounters ethical issues when replacing an older employee with a new one but encounters no such ethical issues when it replaces an older machine with a new machine de-

---

[2]*White paper process* refers to administrative or staff systems. These are clerical procedures for booking orders, billing, shipping, collecting, etc. There are systems for handling these tasks just as there are systems for assembling auto parts components.

signed for new technology. Unless a historical preservation society intervenes, the firm is free to dispose of the old machines with impunity.

Third, service workers make frequent judgments. Their work often is characterized by uncertainty, high information-processing levels, and low routinization. Whereas much manufacturing is characterized by repetitive tasks that are ideally suited to computing, human judgments in the service industries imply numerous conditional subprocesses that one does not find in manufacturing. Therefore, the process flow diagrams are considerably more complex and probabilistic than in manufacturing. Technology can enhance judgment and may accelerate it; for certain relatively well-defined problems, like those in expert systems, technology may replace judgment. However, technology cannot eliminate judgment. This is most obvious in health care. While technology can improve the physician's speed and accuracy, it cannot, at present, replace the physician. For the time being, knowledge workers play an indispensable role in the service industries.

Fourth, consumers may resist service automation. Consumers are indifferent to automation in manufacturing because they are not directly involved. But automation in services frequently requires the consumer to take a direct part in the production of the service. Consider the automation of prescription refills. The patient must call the pharmacy and respond to a series of automated options and inquiries. Following these responses, the computer queues the prescriptions and brings them up for the pharmacist to fill. This can both improve service quality and lower the cost. However, some patients may not have the inclination or aptitude to use such a system. Although there has been widespread acceptance of automated teller machines, fast food ordering, and various kinds of self-service, the customer may participate less willingly or ably in the production of more complex services.

Generally, reengineering comprises two phases, process design and implementation. Simpler processes make for simpler process design. Process design is likely to be more difficult in service applications, due to the complexity and nuances of the service process. In addition, the critical role played by knowledge workers and the direct participation of customers in service production suggest that implementation will be both difficult and critical to the success of service reengineering. For these reasons, empirical efforts to measure reengineering success rates and to identify the strategies that work should control for the inherent differences between manufacturing applications and service applications.

Summary and Implications

Firms exist because of risk, information asymmetry, market transaction costs, inseparable team production technology, and asset control issues. The firm's optimal structure, assuming that it exists and can be known, depends primarily on the interaction among relative transaction costs, technology, and competition. New technology grows exponentially

(Davidow & Malone, 1992), and a considerable share of this is communication technology. The new communication technology accelerates the innovation of all technology. Therefore, the optimal structure of any given firm is constantly changing. Ideally, the firm's organizational structure should evolve continuously as market conditions evolve. Although incremental change is accomplished via continuous improvement, in reality most changes in organization structure occur as discrete steps. There is a lumpiness, if you will, in organization change. Any divergence in the actual firm structure from the optimal firm structure gives rise to an opportunity cost. By definition, an *optimal firm structure* is a profit-maximizing firm structure. Therefore, any firm structure that is not an optimal structure must earn lower profits. The difference between what the firm is earning and what it could earn is an opportunity cost. If unrecognized and unattended, opportunity costs can be fatal to the firm.

The current wave of corporate restructuring is driven by many forces, all of them connected to or facilitated by rapid technological change. Firms must become smaller and more agile and may have shorter life cycles. This suggests greater risk for both the firm and its employees. Flexibility is necessary for survival. Although inflexible organizations may survive for extended periods under conditions of slow to moderate rates of change, globalization of trade, new information technologies, and new science have greatly accelerated the rate of change in markets.

Complex systems exist on a knife's edge, balanced between rigidity and flexibility. Too much of either can result in collapse or chaos. Hence, the natural tendency is for complex systems to degenerate. In a smaller sense, this is the problem for today's firms. They require structure to accomplish tasks consistently, but they require flexibility to accomplish the next set of tasks. A familiar phrase in economics is "all production takes place in the short run, and no production takes place in the long run." The firm's planning horizon extends over the long run, where it is free to choose the optimal combination of inputs, including plant size. But to actually produce a product or service, the firm must have an existing plant; thus, production takes place only in the short run. Existing resources provide the structure, and planning manages change.

The labor service provided by workers can be obtained by employment or by purchasing their services as entrepreneurs. Market transactions are more flexible than employment. Current trends seem to select for fewer employees and more entrepreneurs. In one respect, this shifts risk to workers. Smaller firm size, more flexible organizations, and shorter life cycles suggest that workers will be forced to make adjustments similar to those being made by firms. New computer-based communication technologies can decentralize production, especially that of knowledge workers. Many workers no longer need to function at a common location. Furthermore, this technology permits the product of work to be monitored at remote locations. Therefore, these technological trends lower the cost of market transactions relative to internal transactions.

In this context, organizations, managers, and individual workers must explore new relationships. Changes in the relative cost of external compared with internal transactions, differences in asset control, and other factors that affect the economic boundaries of the firm have led to conditions favoring entrepreneurs over employees, that is, favoring the use of independent contractors and freelancers to accomplish the work of the organization. However, the remaining employees are likely to have more firm-specific knowledge. Processes such as reengineering and concurrent engineering seek to eliminate non-value-added and noncore work, by taking out steps such as travel, hand-offs, approvals, and waiting time. Information technology facilitates these processes by making information available to the individual worker at the point where the work is accomplished. This removes the need for much hierarchy that previously performed functions of information gathering and relaying. It also enables decisions to be made closer to where the work is performed. The individual performing the task can make decisions, provided he or she has both the relevant information and any firm-specific knowledge required to use it.

Today's knowledge workers are choosing alternative and distinct paths. First, there is a growing number of individuals working as independent contractors, carrying their bag of tricks to a variety of organizations. They may contract with a firm or entrepreneur for a specific length of time, a specified output, or a particular service. These individuals, while allowed a great deal of flexibility in their job design and location, also face greater risks and lower job security. They also remain responsible for their own training and skill maintenance, for ensuring that their knowledge and skills are indeed portable, for their own career paths, and for their own retirement planning. Some of these individuals may be working as independent contractors to firms where they had previously worked as employees.

Second, we have the remaining core of organizational employees. These individuals will have both organization-specific and job-specific knowledge and will thus have greater job security as long as their particular skills are required. Due to the pace of technological and environmental change, there is no guarantee that any skills will be required indefinitely, or that it will always be least costly to incorporate them within the firm rather than purchase them in the market. However, employers will also be more dependent on these employees, due to their possession of firm-specific knowledge. As noted previously, this dependence creates a bilateral monopoly of sorts. Therefore, it will behoove the employer to address issues of training, skill maintenance, and so on. Neither finding employees nor contracting for work is cost-free. Thus, employers may be willing to make a greater investment in the employees that remain in the organization.

These changes in the environment and the employment relationship lead to several questions. For example, if individual skills are to be portable and the individual is responsible for his own training and development, then how is the organization to ensure its access to the skills it needs in the market? How do organizations distinguish between core and noncore employees and tasks? What do organizations and managers need to know about managing across boundaries and managing nonemployees?

What level of commitment can be expected, on the part of organizations, employees, and independent contractors alike, in these fluid relationships? What kind of leadership is required for employees and contractors alike in the changed organization? These and other questions remain to be addressed.

References

Alchian, A. A., & Demsetz, H. (1972). Production, information costs, and economic organization. *American Economic Review, 62,* 777–795.

Coase, R. H. (1937). The nature of the firm. *Economica, 4,* 386–405.

Davidow, W. H., & Malone, M. S. (1992). *The virtual corporation.* New York: HarperCollins.

Drucker, P. F. (1988). The coming of the new organization. *Harvard Business Review, 66*(1), 45–53.

Epstein, R. A. (1995). *Simple rules for a complex world.* Cambridge, MA: Harvard University Press.

Gargan, E. A. (1994, July 17). "Virtual" companies leave the manufacturing to others. *New York Times,* Section 3, p. 5.

Goldman, S. (1994). *The era of the virtual enterprise* (Working paper). Bethlehem, PA: Lehigh University, Iacocca Institute, The Agility Forum.

Griliches, Z. (1994). Productivity, R&D, and the data constraint. *American Economic Review, 84,* 1–23.

Grossman, S. J., & Hart, O. D. (1986). The costs and benefits of ownership: A theory of vertical and lateral integration. *Journal of Political Economy, 94,* 691–719.

Hammer, M. (1990). Reengineering work: Don't automate, obliterate. *Harvard Business Review, 68*(4), 104–112.

Harris, T. G. (1993). The post-capitalist executive: An interview with Peter F. Drucker. *Harvard Business Review, 71*(3), 114–122.

Hart, O., & Moore, J. (1990). Property rights and the nature of the firm. *Journal of Political Economy, 98,* 1119–1158.

Hey, J. D. (1979). *Uncertainly in microeconomics.* New York: New York University Press.

Holmstrom, B., & Milgrom, P. (1991). Multitask principal–agent analyses: Incentive contracts, asset ownership, and job design. *Journal of Law, Economics, and Organizations, 7,* 24–52.

Holmstrom, B., & Milgrom, P. (1994). The firm as an incentive system. *American Economic Review, 84,* 972–991.

Kanter, R. M. (1989). *When giants learn to dance.* New York: Simon & Schuster.

Knight, F. H. (1933). *Risk, uncertainty, and profit.* Boston: Houghton Mifflin.

Maruyama, M. (1992). Changing dimensions in international business. *Academy of Management Executive, 6*(3), 88–96.

Mathias, P. (1979). *The transformation of England.* New York: Columbia University Press.

Milgrom, P., & Roberts, J. (1990). The economics of modern manufacturing: Technology, strategy, and organization. *American Economic Review, 80,* 511–528.

Mokyr, J. (Ed.). (1985). *The economics of the industrial revolution.* Totowa, NJ: Rowman & Allanheld.

Prahalad, C. K., & Hamel, G. (1990). The core competence of the corporation. *Harvard Business Review, 68*(3), 79–91.

Wernerfelt, B. (1984). A resource-based view of the firm. *Strategic Management Journal, 5,* 171–180.

Williamson, O. (1985). *The economic institutions of capitalism.* New York: Free Press.

2

Mergers and Acquisitions, Downsizing, and Privatization: A North American Perspective

Ronald J. Burke and Debra Nelson

Hardly a day goes by without a story about job loss appearing in the media. Consider the following headlines:

> "Montreal Job Losses Predicted: '96 Will be 'Horrible' Economic Chief Says," *Globe and Mail*, December 13, 1995.
> "Kimberly-Clark to Cut 6,000 Jobs: Impact on Canadian Plants Under Review as Tissue Company Digests Scott Paper," *Globe and Mail*, December 14, 1995.
> "Toy Maker to Close Guelph Plant: 165 Employees of Ohio-Based Rubbermaid's Canadian Unit Will Lose Jobs to Restructuring," *Globe and Mail*, December 6, 1995.
> "Corporate Killers: Wall Street Loves Layoffs, But the Public Is Scared as Hell," *Newsweek*, February 26, 1996.

Three types of organizational transitions have received increasing attention during the past few years: mergers and acquisitions, downsizing, and privatization. These three newly emerging sources of organizational change share some common features. First, they are interrelated because all represent the effects of the economic recession and attempts by organizations to survive and to increase productivity (Marks, 1994). Second, all are fairly new areas of research in which relatively little empirical work has been completed (Kozlowski, Chao, Smith, & Hedlund, 1993). Third, these changes have vast implications for psychological practice and intervention at both individual and organizational levels (Cameron, Freeman, & Mishra, 1991; Cascio, 1993).

Some of the dramatic changes affecting work and organizations include increased global competition, the impact of information technology,

Preparation of this chapter was supported in part by the Faculty of Administrative Studies at York University, Toronto, Ontario, Canada, and the College of Business Administration at Oklahoma State University. We thank Graeme MacDermid for collecting material for the chapter and Louise Coutu for preparing the manuscript. Esther Greenglass and Rekha Karambayya provided helpful comments on the chapter. The authors names are listed alphabetically; both contributed equally.

the reengineering of business processes, the decreasing size of companies that leads to fewer employees, the shift from making a product to providing a service, and the increasing disappearance of the job as a fixed collection of tasks (Cascio, 1995). These forces have produced wrenching changes to all industrialized economies. These changes have made a most profound impact on the number of job losses.

In addition, companies were not downsizing simply because they were losing money. Fully 81% of companies that downsized in a given year were profitable in that year. Major reasons for downsizing reported in the American Management Association's 1994 survey (see Marks, 1994) were strategic or structural (to improve productivity; to accommodate plant obsolescence; to adjust to mergers and acquisitions, transfer of location, and new technology).

The economic downturns of the 1980s highlighted the stress of not having a job. In the United States, 10.8 million people lost their jobs between 1981 and 1988 (Fraze, 1988). Even in the growth periods from 1985 to 1989, 4.3 million American workers lost their jobs (Herz, 1991). From June 1990 through July 1991, 1.6 million lost their jobs (Greenwald, 1991). In the European countries of France, Germany, Italy, The Netherlands, and the United Kingdom, 2.1 million lost their jobs in 1989. In this same year, 320,000 Japanese and 522,000 Canadians lost jobs (Sorrentino, 1993). And in Central and Eastern Europe, 3.7 million lost jobs (Organization for Economic Cooperation and Development, 1992). Global job loss is predicted to continue throughout the 1990s as organizational downsizing and restructuring continue (Haugen & Meisenheimer, 1991).

Changes such as these over the past 10 years are challenging workers' traditional expectations of career advancement. In the past, workers typically saw their careers develop with one (or a few) organizations. Career advancement was equated with career success. The advent of reorganization, restructuring, and downsizing has constrained career advancement prospects. Company loyalty seems to have suffered in the process, with many firms pursuing initiatives (flexible structures, decentralization) that further undermine employees' personal attachment to the firm. Employees may increasingly be left on a plateau as a result of the constraints in career paths. Some develop or pursue other options (e.g., starting their own business), but many remain entrenched in unsatisfying careers. Some entrenched individuals continue to be productive; others become organizational liabilities.

A major characteristic of the total restructuring of American business in the 1990s is the change of traditionally secure managerial and professional jobs into insecure ones (Heckscher, 1995). *Business Week* reported the loss of over 1 million managerial and professional jobs over a 2-year period as organizations restructured, merged, downsized, and divested ("Downside to the Jobs," 1994). The public sector, too, has also evidenced substantial job loss as governments try to contain costs by privatizing services and reducing budgets.

Other studies have shown that anticipation or concern about job loss may be as damaging as job loss itself (Latack & Dozier, 1986). Job insecurity has been found to be associated with increased medical consultations for psychological distress (Catalano, Dooley, & Rook, 1987) and with increased disability claims for back pain (Volinn, Lai, McKinney, & Loeser, 1988).

Furthermore, laid-off workers who return to the job market often take pay cuts. This downward mobility is common ("Downside to the Jobs," 1994). Of approximately 2,000 workers terminated by RJR Nabisco, 72% eventually found jobs but at wages averaging about half their previous pay ("Jobs in an Age," 1993). These jobs were not lost temporarily because of a recession; they were lost permanently as a result of new technology, improved machinery, and new ways of structuring work.

Organizations are becoming leaner and meaner. More and more companies are focusing on their core competencies and outsourcing all other tasks. Continental Bank Corporation, for example, has contracted its legal, audit, cafeteria, and mailroom operations to outside companies. American Airlines is contracting out customer service jobs at 30 airports. Flattened hierarchies also mean that there will be fewer managers in smaller remaining organizations.

This chapter examines mergers and acquisitions, downsizing, and privatization, highlighting research in the United States and Canada. It begins with a description of the context for these organizational transitions. It next illustrates the degree to which mergers and acquisitions, downsizing, and privatization efforts have taken place. Consideration is then given to the consequences—both personal and organizational—of these widespread changes. An attempt is made to identify process characteristics of effective implementation of these changes. Finally, future research directions are identified. Potential roles that psychologists might play in assisting individuals and organizations during these trying times are proposed.

The Canadian Context

The Canadian economy, like those of many other industrialized countries, is currently not performing very well. The unemployment rate in 1995 averaged 9.6%. Company bankruptcies were also at near record highs. In addition, many Canadian companies are branch plants of international corporations headquartered in the United States or Europe. These Canadian organizations have little influence in corporate decision making. Similar to other industrialized countries, Canada is struggling to reduce deficits. This involves budget cutting and associated job loss. The budget deficits in Canada are higher than those of some of the industrialized countries because Canada has developed a more widespread (and costly) social welfare system. And similar to the United Kingdom during the Thatcher years, various levels of government are reducing expenses by privatizing services. Finally, the trade union movement in Canada, although it lost membership over the past 10 years, is still stronger than the movement in the United States. Strong trade unions add to the potential for increasing social tensions within Canada as it struggles with massive restructuring.

First, consider the Canadian experience with organizational restructuring and downsizing in broad overview. Murray Axmith, a Canadian consulting firm providing career transition services for corporate clients, has conducted periodic surveys of Canadian firms on their dismissal practices. The most recent survey, conducted in 1995, included questions on downsizing and beliefs about the future. Their findings were based on 1,034 organizations across Canada representing every type of business (private, public, and nonprofit). Data were collected in the fall of 1994. The typical participating organization had gross annual revenues of $100 million and employed about 550 employees (300 salaried, 250 paid hourly). About three quarters of organizations surveyed had downsized or restructured within the last 5 years. During the previous 12 months, the typical organization had dismissed 35 employees (2 executives, 8 managers or supervisors, 10 professionals or technicians, and 15 other salaried employees). Position redundancy was indicated by 53% of the survey respondents as the most important reason for dismissal. Because respondents were senior managers, the results may actually portray a more favorable picture than actually existed.

Virtually all organizations in the survey offered reemployment counseling services to dismissed employees. Eighty percent offered these services to help employees become reemployed as soon as possible. These services were also intended to help maintain good employee relations. In addition, about 40% of these organizations had used voluntary early retirement programs to reduce the size of their workforces. Of those organizations offering such programs, just under half of the eligible employees (45%) accepted the early retirement option.

Was there life after downsizing? Considering organizational outcomes, 85% of the surveyed organizations reported lowered costs, 63% reported improved earnings, 58% reported improved productivity, and 36% reported improved customer service. Considering effects on remaining employees, 61% reported decreased morale, 50% reported decreased company loyalty, and 37% reported decreased job satisfaction. Respondents also indicated ways their companies would change their approach in future downsizings and restructurings. Forty-three percent would improve communications, 24% would plan more carefully the jobs to be eliminated and employees to be dismissed, 11% would move events more quickly, and 10% would increase managerial involvement and visibility.

Almost 90% of the organizations surveyed believed that organizations could no longer offer job security to employees. Forty percent of these organizations had implemented programs to help employees adjust to and manage this change. These programs involved career management, skill-based training, change-management seminars, communication of organization's current conditions and future prospects to employees, and educating employees about the new employment contract—employability versus job security.

Having briefly considered the Canadian context, we move now to an overview of mergers and acquisitions in the United States and Canada. Particular attention is paid to the effects of mergers and acquisitions on the individual and the organization.

Mergers and Acquisitions

Marks (1994) coined the phrase "organizational MADness," referring to the impact of mergers, acquisitions, and downsizing that result in a fearful, suspicious, and cynical workforce. Several forces lead to MADness: increasing global competition, government deregulation, technological change, total quality management (TQM) and other reengineering movements, delayering, broader economic conditions, and corporate rationalization.

Marks and Mirvis (1986) indicated that 3,284 U.S. companies were acquired by other companies in 1985, with the dollar value of these acquisitions estimated at $150 billion. They also presented statistics showing that between 50% and 80% of all mergers are financial disappointments.

Mirvis (1985) illustrated some of the heightened work stressors in a case study of negotiations over the combination of a small manufacturing firm into a multi-billion dollar conglomerate following its acquisition. Strategic and tactical conflicts surfaced between the two firms during the first year of negotiations following the sale. Mirvis traced these conflicts to the parties' emotional reactions to the combination. Some heightened work stressors during this period (and preceding the sale) were each party's sense of uncertainty (Gill & Foulder, 1978) and the loss of personal and organizational identities. Feelings of conflict arose that were associated with the ambivalence of loss versus gain, dependence and counterdependence, proactive versus reactive control, and incompatibilities in company managements, business systems, organizational cultures, and goals for the combination itself (Sales & Mirvis, 1984).

Marks and Mirvis (1985b) found the "merger syndrome," a defensive, "fear-the-worst" response, to be a common response to the uncertainty and stress of a merger. Those at the top of the acquired organization report disbelief, uncertainty, fear, and stress. Lower level employees circulate rumors of mass layoffs and forced relocations, pay freezes, loss of benefits, and plant closings. Fear of job loss after a merger or acquisition was the top-ranked worry of 54% of the senior executives in the 1,000 largest U.S. companies in 1991. The second most common worry was burnout, reported by 26% of the executives (Robert Half International, 1991). These concerns are not limited to hostile takeovers. Crisis management should be the order of the day (Marks & Mirvis, 1985a). Instead of managing crises, senior managers too often seal themselves off, become less accessible, and limit their lines of communication, leaving their staff uninformed about the changes in the organization.

Merger syndrome is manifested by increased centralization and decreased communication that leaves employees in the dark about what is happening in the merger. Rumors are fueled by this communication break-down. In addition, employees focus on worst case scenarios and become preoccupied with the merger. The result is that employees are distracted, productivity decreases, and key people leave the company. Marks and Mirvis (1985b) cited a *Wall Street Journal* survey that found that nearly 50% of executives in acquired firms seek other jobs within 1 year and another 25% plan to leave within 3 years.

Mergers are stressful not only for the executives embroiled in the pre- and postmerger discussions and plans but also for the employees involved (Burke, 1987). Executives are under stress for the following reasons: They have more work to do and less time to do it, there is a great deal of uncertainty about the future, and it is a time of insecurity for executives. They worry about losing their own jobs due to task redundancy or simply not fitting into the newly organized structure. Furthermore, they worry about having to demonstrate their value and skills to a new superior (Marks & Mirvis, 1985a, 1985b).

Lower level employees are under stress for some of the same reasons. They have uncertainties about the impact of the merger on specific job factors. The employees may wonder, Will there be layoffs or dismissals? Will I have a new boss? New duties? Do I keep the same title, or will it be different? Is a transfer to a new location pending? Will the present compensation package be affected? Will the benefit plan change?

Mergers and acquisitions in North America represent a powerful source of organizational change. Downsizing represents an even more powerful force for change, as indicated by the following review.

Downsizing

The early 1990s were characterized by economic slowdown, plant closings and layoffs, and budget cutbacks. This mood of austerity has affected private and public sector organizations alike, and is expected to continue through the late 1990s. More organizations are working toward balanced budgets and fiscal responsibility; they are becoming "leaner and meaner" (Hirschhorn, 1983; Levine, 1980).

Leana and Feldman (1992) focused on layoffs. Several institutions play a role in how layoffs are implemented: companies, unions, and provincial and federal regulations. Other people are affected besides those laid off: spouses, children, parents, friends, and coworkers. In the United States between 1980 and 1985, about 2.5 million jobs were lost each year, most of these blue-collar. From 1985 to 1988, a different pattern occurred. Over one third of Fortune 1000 companies reduced their workforces 10% each year. They were reducing their workforces not because the company was losing money, but because they aimed to increase productivity and cut costs. Hourly workers in manufacturing still are the hardest hit, suffering about 50% of the job losses; the rest are spread fairly evenly over the other organizational levels. The experts believe that downsizing, now seen as an organizational initiative to increase profitability, will continue through the

1990s. White-collar workers now are as vulnerable as blue-collar workers. Job loss will continue to be a problem and will quite likely worsen.

Downsizing has affected hundreds of companies and millions of workers since the late 1980s (Cascio, 1995). The list includes all the blue-chip firms. More than 85% of Fortune 1000 firms have downsized their white-collar workforces between 1987 and 1991, affecting more than 5 million jobs. More than 50% of these firms downsized in 1990. Champy (1995) indicated that over the past 5 years, 1.4 million executives, managers, and administrative personnel have lost their jobs, a large increase from the 787,000 who lost their jobs from 1981 to 1986. This phenomenon is so common we now have words for it: *downsizing* and *rightsizing*.

Cascio (1993, p. 102) drew several conclusions from an exhaustive literature review and interviews with managers having downsizing experience. He pointed out that downsizing would continue as overhead costs remain noncompetitive with domestic and international rivals. He also pointed out that there were risks for the employer, for former employees, and for employees who stayed on the job, which needed to be addressed. See chapter 3 for a further discussion of Cascio's work.

The number of jobs lost through downsizing are staggering. Chase Manhattan cut 12,000 and Digital Equipment cut 20,000. CEOs have been highly criticized for their roles as hatchet men—as employees lose jobs, CEO pay persists at incredibly high levels, and some CEOs profit from the increased stock prices that result from the announcements of downsizing.

In view of this evidence, we conclude that downsizing is likely to be followed by more downsizing. The experiences of many companies (e.g., IBM, Xerox, TRW, Digital Equipment, Kodak, Honeywell) bear this out.

- Downsizing is now a major theme in organizations and management. Even organizations that are profitable downsize, in anticipation of an increasingly competitive marketplace.
- Downsizing is too often done indiscriminantly. Downsizing is limited to reductions in head count rather than part of a broader search for waste.
- Some organizational philosophies suggest that firms manage people as they manage other inventories—keep both as low as possible.

"Downsize first, ask questions later" is a dominant theme.

Many companies say they turn to layoffs only as a last resort. The facts indicate otherwise. Right Associates, in surveys of 1,204 and 909 organizations that had downsized, reported that only 6% of employers had tried cutting pay, 9% had shortened work weeks, 9% used vacations without pay, and 14% had developed job sharing plans. Yet 80% of respondents in a *Time*/CNN survey indicated that they would rather see all employees of their firm take a 10% wage cut than lay off 10% of the workers to cut expenses to stay in business.

Why do firms downsize without incorporating other changes in the reorganization of work? Cascio (1993) suggested that firms downsize because of the existence of outdated organization and management concepts (e.g., command from the top, control through supervision, compartmentalizing through rigid job descriptions).

The pursuit of organizational effectiveness through downsizing, rightsizing, and restructuring is predicted to continue. Whatever the term used, employees translate it to mean job loss. Privatization is another force for change that must be considered.

Privatization

Privatization has been broadly defined as a strengthening of the market at the expense of the state. A narrower interpretation refers to the conversion of public corporations into private ones, or at least hybrid ones, in which the state has less than a 50% equity stake. There are two main reasons for privatization: The goals underlying the formation of the public corporations no longer exist, or the goals are still valid but there are more efficient ways to achieve these goals (Kierans & Stanbury, 1985).

The viability of privatization has long been discussed by federal, state, and local governments in the United States. However, there has not been as much need for privatization in the United States since the various governmental units have not owned as many manufacturing and service organizations as are found in Canada and the United Kingdom. Some large government-owned corporations, such as Amtrak and Comsat, have been privatized. However, government-owned private corporations like the Bonneville Power Plant and the Tennessee Valley Authority will probably remain as government-owned corporations because of local political conditions. That is, various levels of government will want to be seen as providing both jobs and particular services. Privatization of traditional government functions such as prison management and trash collection has taken place. Also, many government agencies have hired contractors to provide support services.

Governments in Canada have sold off more than $9 billion worth of taxpayer-owned, (government-owned) companies in the past few years. Thirty crown corporations have been sold by the federal government since the mid-1980s. Another 72 companies have been sold off by provincial governments. The list includes airports, air traffic control systems, federally owned grain cars, and the St. Lawrence Seaway. In Ontario, it includes Ontario Hydro, liquor stores, and TV Ontario, which could total more than $4 billion. Other possibilities in Canada include the Canadian Broadcasting Corporation, schools, health care, and municipal services such as garbage collection and homes for the aged. Kierans and Stanbury (1985) noted that the United Kingdom has proceeded down this route sooner, and in more industries, than has Canada.

Lipsey (1985) noted that over 400 fully owned crown corporations exist in Canada, about half of which are owned by the federal government and half by provincial governments. These corporations include deHavilland,

Canadair, Atomic Energy of Canada Limited, Eldorada Nuclear, Air Canada, Telesat Canada, Teleglobe Canada, and Canadian Arsenals Limited.

Berg (1988) reported on the privatization of Air Canada by the government of Canada. The privatization was announced by the federal government on April 12, 1988. Air Canada (initially known as Trans-Canada Airlines) began operations in 1937, when the federal government concluded that a coast-to-coast national airline would be useful in providing air service to Canadians, particularly because no Canadian private sector organization was interested in providing such services at that time. Air Canada received significant government financial assistance in the early years but no such support since 1970. Studies have indicated, however, that government ownership hindered the cost efficiency of the airline. In 1977, the government of Canada passed legislation requiring Air Canada to act like a private sector firm with a bottom-line focus.

Other factors supported the 1988 privatization, including the development of an integrated airline industry in North America, deregulation of the airline industry, the emergence of Canadian Airlines in 1986, the need for a large capital infusion to support Air Canada's renewal program, and the fact that the airline was not playing a dominant public policy role.

As might have been expected, there was considerable disagreement with the government's decision to privatize Air Canada. Many of the firms' major unions were opposed, along with the two opposition parties. They saw this initiative as unnecessary and potentially damaging to airline service because the less profitable routes would be dropped.

Other examples of privatization include contracting out work to the private sector, selling off public enterprises, transferring previous state functions to the private sector, and allowing private sector firms to enter markets previously supplied only by the public sector. Contracting out refuse collection is one example of privatization that is growing because it is cost-effective.

Galal, Jones, Tandon, and Vogelsang (1994) examined the effects of privatization in four countries: the United Kingdom, Chile, Malaysia, and Mexico. They also provide detailed case studies of three British examples: British Telecom, British Airways, and National Freight. Privatization started in the United Kingdom but is now being pursued in developing countries, industrialized countries, and countries emerging from socialism. Galal et al. drew some general conclusions. In most cases, privatization provided modest economic benefits, and workers did not lose out. There was, however, significant job loss in all United Kingdom examples. The authors do not attempt to explain this discrepancy.

Brown (1991) developed a brief case study of the Canadian firm Novatel Communications Ltd. after its privatization in 1990. Established in 1983 as a subsidiary of Alberta Government Telephones (AGT), Novatel never made a profit as a government-owned company. The provincial government provided the necessary financial support to keep it afloat. The company had laid off over 700 employees as part of a restructuring plan aimed at saving the financially troubled cellular phone maker. The company posted a $200 million loss for 1990 after projecting an $83 million profit for the year. The privatization of AGT in the fall of 1990, which the government hoped would better enable the company to compete, did not improve its situation much. In December the government stepped in to help the struggling firm by buying it back from the Telus Corporation (formerly AGT) for $174 million. Novatel blamed its poor sales on new product launch scheduling problems and price erosion in the U.S. marketplace.

The *Economist* (1992) noted that privatization in Britain continued to lead to job losses and cited British Telephone as an example. The planned selling of the coal and steel industries will contribute still further to job losses. Without a greater commitment to industrial training (and retraining), the jobless will find it harder to find work, and the British economy will find it increasingly hard to provide work for them to do.

A. Nelson, Cooper, and Jackson (1995) conducted a study of a workforce during the process of two major organizational transitions. The organization was a regional water authority about to move from public to private ownership as a result of the government policy to privatize the U.K. water industry. Two significant events took place during the period the research covered (October 1989 to July 1991): (a) privatization, at the end of November 1989, and (b) structural reorganization in March 1991. These changes occurred in the context of previous changes including staff reductions. Between 1983 and 1989 the workforce had been cut 25%, reducing the number of employees from 6,000 to 4,500. This reduction affected many levels of management, and some employees changed jobs. The privatization plans called for a major restructuring and rationalization of the existing system of autonomous geographic regions, each with its own service functions. These service functions (e.g., personnel, finance) were to be centralized at the head office. These changes would have significant effects on large numbers of employees (e.g., new reporting relationships, changes in jobs and responsibilities, relocation to other sites).

The research examined the effects of these changes on employee morale and well-being. From a total workforce of 6,500, every third employee from each of the nine divisions of the organization was selected (N = 1,500). Data were collected from 332 employees (84% of whom were male) at three time periods: preprivatization, November 1989; postprivatization, June 1990; and postreorganization, July 1991. The three dependent variables included were job satisfaction, mental health symptoms, and physical health symptoms. Job satisfaction dropped after privatization and increased after reorganization. Symptoms of poor mental health increased after privatization. There was also a significant increase in symptoms of poor physical health after privatization.

Cunningham and Mitchell (1990) undertook a project to predict the effects of privatization on labor relations in British Columbia. The government of British Columbia undertook a program of privatization in late 1987. By the end of 1988, $840 million worth of Crown corporations and other government-run services had been sold off. The B.C. government had as its goal reductions in the size and cost of government. Some individuals have expressed concerns about efforts to privatize government services. Privatization can involve the transfer or loss of public sector jobs, so it has become of particular interest to the union movement. The union movement in countries with traditionally strong labor movements (e.g., Britain, New Zealand, Canada) has waged campaigns against privatization and its impending job loss.

Cunningham and Mitchell (1990) involved three groups of "experts," union, management, and neutral–arbitrator participants. Each individual possessed considerable expertise in labor relations. These experts reported the following privatization results: an increase in job instability for job holders in the short run, lower wages, greater fragmentation of management's approach to collective bargaining, increased costs for unions, more militancy, and greater difficulties in improving labor relations.

As the preceding review indicates, mergers and acquisitions, downsizing, and privatization are potent forces for change in North American organizations. They portend many changes both for individuals and for organizations. We turn now to the effects of these trends for individuals and for organizations.

Consequences for Individuals

Mergers and acquisitions, downsizing, and privatization have many consequences for individuals (Meyer, 1995). Some of these consequences are the stressors and attendant symptoms of strain. Jick (1985) proposed that individuals in organizations undergoing cutbacks are subject to various sources of stress. These include role confusion, job insecurity, work overload, career plateauing, poor incentives, office politics and conflict, lack of participation in decision making, tense organizational climate, ideological disagreement, and conflicts between job and personal life.

Rosellini (1981) observed that federal budget cuts had a significant role in a recent increase in federal employees' usage of health services. In the light of anticipated staff reductions, almost triple the number of federal employees were treated at the Department of Health and Human Services for stress-related symptoms such as dizziness, stomach upset, and high blood pressure. Blundell (1978) reported that government employees in Denver whose staff had been reduced and reorganized were found to be so fearful and concerned about their futures that productivity suffered.

Schlenker and Gutek (1987) examined the effects of being reassigned (demoted) to nonprofessional jobs on professionals in a large social service agency. In the administration of staff cuts, one group of social workers was abruptly reassigned to nonprofessional jobs while keeping the same salary and benefits. Data were collected about 9 months after the reassignments, sufficient time for workers to adjust to their demotions as much as they were likely to. The sample of 132 included 66 reassigned workers and 66 nonreassigned workers. Individuals who were reassigned (demoted) reported significantly less self-esteem, significantly less job and life satisfaction, and significantly greater intention to leave the agency. No differences were found on measures of professional role involvement, professional role identification (commitment to social work), and work-related depression.

Studies that examine survivors' attitudes in the aftermath of corporate layoffs consistently indicate that their job attitudes such as job satisfaction, job involvement, organizational commitment, and intention to remain with the organization become more negative (Brockner, Grover, Reed, & Dewitt, 1992; Brockner et al., 1994; Hallier & Lyon, 1996). These negative reactions, combined with the fact that survivors must do more with fewer resources, make the aftermath of layoffs difficult to deal with.

Noer (1993 and chapter 10, this volume) offered a vivid description of the state of layoff survivors. Individuals who survive cutbacks must deal with their own feelings as they develop a new relationship with their organization in which they are more empowered and less dependent. Managers must help other survivors through a painful but irrevocable change in the psychological contract between employees and employer. Employees need to develop a more autonomous and less dependent link with the organization, and should not assume job security. Unlike discarding machines, discarding people has an effect on those who remain (Gottlieb & Conkling, 1995).

According to Noer, time did not heal all the wounds. Five years later in the same firm, the same symptoms of stress, fatigue, extra workload, decreased motivation, sadness and depression, insecurity, anxiety and fear, loyalty to job instead of company, self-reliance, one-way loyalty, sense of unfairness, anger over top management pay and severance, resignation and numbness, and lack of management communication to employees were evident.

O'Neill and Lenn (1995) interviewed middle managers from one organization involved in a significant downsizing effort. They found that emotions among middle managers ran high. Common among them were anger, anxiety, cynicism, resentment, resignation, desire for retribution, and hope. Anger seemed to be correlated with tenure and hierarchical level. Anger tended to be directed at two types of organizational activities: use of superficial slogans to rationalize the downsizing and condemnation of the former structure. Anxiety over not fully understanding the downsizing strategy was created in part by a lack of adequate communication. Cynicism was expressed by the victims of downsizing and senior executives who could not trust middle managers or who in turn were not trusted by middle managers. Resentment illustrates the importance of equity in both real and symbolic sacrifices by all employees.

In addition to the increase in stressors, strain symptoms, and the "survivor syndrome" (see chapter 10), three individual effects of restructuring and job loss warrant more extensive consideration: underemployment, occupational locking in/career entrenchment, and job insecurity.

Underemployment

In their study of 2,000 laid-off steelworkers in the United States, Leana and Feldman (1992) reported that only 66% of the reemployed were working full-time, 85% were making 40% less money than in their former jobs, and 70% were receiving fewer fringe benefits than in their previous jobs. Previous research on laid-off workers had defined underemployment in terms of wage differentials between the current job and the job held before the layoff.

Feldman and Turnley (1995) considered underemployment among recent business school graduates. Some estimates cited by them place the number of underemployed among recent university graduates at about 25%. Underemployment has been consistently found to be related to poorer general mental health, lower overall life satisfaction, and lower job satisfaction.

Occupational Locking In/Career Entrenchment

Kay (1975) identified several factors associated with increasing discontent in middle management ranks. One of these was a boxed-in feeling when individuals had almost no opportunity to move from their present jobs or when the only position for which they were qualified was the one they currently held. Quinn (1975) used the term *locking in* to refer to the same phenomenon. Quinn distinguished three components of locking in: (a) low probability of securing another job as good as or better than the present one, (b) little opportunity to modify a presently disliked employment situation by securing a change in job assignments, and (c) low likelihood that a worker who was dissatisfied with his job could take psychological refuge in the performance of other roles not linked to this job. Thurley and Word-Penney (1986) suggested this phenomenon will be present through the 1990s and beyond.

Burke (1982) and Wolpin and Burke (1986) studied the relationship between self-reported locking in of two groups of administrators and their personal and situational demographic characteristics and personality variables, occupational and life demands and satisfactions, lifestyle, and emotional and physical well-being measures. Individuals reporting greater locking in were older, less educated, had more children, had longer organizational tenure, had made fewer previous geographic moves, and were less interested in further promotion. Locking in was also associated with interpersonal passivity, emotional instability, and an external locus of control. Work experiences and satisfactions were generally unrelated to degree of locking in although administrators more locked in reported greater underutilization at work and greater life dissatisfaction. Locking in, however, was associated with negative emotional and physical health consequences in only one of the samples.

Carson, Carson, and Bedeian (1995) outlined the development and construct validation of a 12-item career entrenchment scale. Three dimensions of career entrenchment were examined: *career investments*—investments in one's career success that would be lost or be worthless if one pursued a new career; *emotional costs*—costs associated with pursuing a new career; and *limitedness of career alternatives*—the perceived lack of available options for pursuing a new career. Career entrenchment considers organizational attachment in terms of the extrinsic rewards that an employee would lose by leaving the organization. Data from 476 women and men employed in a variety of occupations were used to validate the career entrenchment measure. Other measures included in the survey were career commitment, job involvement, calculative organizational commitment, affective organizational commitment, and withdrawal cognitions.

Job Insecurity

One of the most dramatic changes in organizations during the 1980s has been the transformation of traditionally secure managerial and professional jobs into insecure ones (Hunt, 1986). Managers and professionals now must come to grips with the same job insecurity long experienced by blue-collar workers. Lifetime employment and a guaranteed standard of living are now no longer realistic. Real income has remained essentially level, or even declined, for large numbers of workers in the industrialized world. Those who were fortunate enough to maintain their jobs often faced a more demanding work setting (e.g., increased performance requirements, fewer rewards).

Although the number of managers and professionals who have actually lost jobs may be relatively small, some writers (e.g., Greenhalgh & Rosenblatt, 1984) postulate a "ripple effect." That is, managers and professionals who are currently employed but see that it is increasingly difficult to get and hold managerial and professional jobs will become insecure about their own jobs. They may become concerned about maintaining their own jobs, see decreased promotional and career development opportunities within their organization, and find diminishing prospects of finding another job similar to the one they have.

Research on the stressful effects of job insecurity is just beginning to emerge (Brockner, 1987; Hartley & Klandermans, 1987; Jick, 1985). The data indicate that the effects of job insecurity appear to be similar to job loss itself. Depolo and Sarchieli (1987) compared the emotional well-being of individuals who had lost their jobs with that of survivors in the same organization. They found no difference in well-being between the two groups. Interestingly, the level of emotional well-being was extremely low in both groups. Cobb and Kasl (1977) conducted a longitudinal study of job loss and reported that workers were in greater distress when anticipating job loss than when they had actually lost their jobs.

Several studies have examined the effects of job insecurity on work commitment and job behavior. These studies (Hallier & Lyon, 1996; Jick, 1985) show that survivors exhibit levels of reduced work commitment and effort. In addition, other research findings show increased resistance to change among survivors (Greenhalgh, 1982; Noer, 1993). Thus job insecurity becomes a critical factor in accelerating organizational decline.

Ashford (1988) found that high levels of individual strain were associated with ambiguity about prospective work roles and job activities within the organization and concerns about whether there would be job losses. In addition, she observed that individuals having a high tolerance for ambiguity and reporting greater control over their job showed significantly smaller deterioration in psychological well-being.

Dekker and Schaufeli (1995) conducted a repeated measures study of the effects of job insecurity in a large Australian public transport organization undergoing significant change and downsizing. At the time of the study (1990–1991), the organization employed about 20,000 people and provided train, streetcar, and bus service to passengers in urban and rural areas. Although the public service in the Australian state in which this study was conducted did not typically terminate employees, recent events had suggested that job insecurity was a real and justified concern. Four departments were identified as being at risk of closure or employee cutbacks. Data were collected using questionnaires distributed twice with a 2-month interval between distributions. Job insecurity was associated with a deterioration of psychological health as well as job and organizational withdrawal. Social support from colleagues, management, or unions had no effect. Dekker and Schaufeli suggested that the job stressor itself (job insecurity/job loss) should be directly addressed instead of trying to render its effects less harmful by providing more social support. Interestingly, Dekker and Schaufeli found that those transport workers who knew they would lose their jobs seemed to suffer fewer symptoms of psychological stress and burnout than those workers who stayed with the organization but felt prolonged job insecurity.

Most research has focused on the effects on employees of actual or imminent job loss as opposed to job loss further in the future or loss of valued aspects of the job (e.g., salary increases, promotions, perks, working conditions). Roskies and Louis-Guerin (1990) examined reactions to perceptions of job insecurity as a chronic ambiguous threat in a sample of 1,291 Canadian managers. Three companies participated in the study, each having multiple divisions, sites, or both. Two high-risk companies participated: One was a large manufacturing company in a traditional declining industry that had undergone major restructuring and repositioning to address survival issues in the preceding 5 years; the second was in a high-technology industry characterized by cyclical employment that was dependent on the needs of projects in progress. The one low-risk company participating was engaged in high-technology research and manufacturing and had rapidly expanded in the 5 years preceding the research.

Employees at the foreman level or higher in these three firms were given anonymous questionnaires. Respondents indicated whether they had previously experienced job dislocation in the form of termination or demotion. Four conditions affecting perceptions of risk were also included: whether individuals worked in a high-risk company; whether they worked in a department or division that had experienced downsizing or reorganization in the previous 2 years; whether they experienced "danger signals" in their immediate environment (e.g., formal announcements or general policy statements indicating threats to job security, rumors of downsizing or reorganization, significant management changes); and whether they were aware of changes in technology or business conditions that could adversely affect their job security.

Let us now consider some of the questionnaire results. First, significantly more managers in the high-risk companies than in the low-risk company saw themselves as insecure. Second, substantial numbers of managers in the high-risk companies felt insecure in their jobs. Third, various facets of insecurity showed different effects. Less than 5% of all respondents reported high likelihood of termination or demotion in the short term; 15% reported high likelihood of deteriorating work conditions, and over 40% reported a high likelihood of job loss in the long term.

Roskies and Louis-Guerin (1990) also found significant relationships between the measures of insecurity and health problems: The higher the levels of perceived insecurity, the greater the number of health symptoms. A similar pattern was found in relationships between levels of job insecurity and work-related outcomes: The higher the level of perceived insecurity, the lower the job commitment and more negative the appraisal of one's career. Interestingly, subjective perceptions of job insecurity had significantly stronger relationships with the physical health measures than did the objective index.

Consequences for Organizations

Modern restructuring processes have several effects on organizations, and research evidence regarding these effects is in its infancy. Long-term studies are needed to provide more thorough investigations of the consequences. Preliminary evidence shows that organizational effects form two categories: organizational benefits and negative or unintended consequences.

Organizational Benefits

Businesses expect downsizing to have economic as well as organizational benefits. The major economic benefit is increased value to shareholders. The rationale is that future costs are more predictable than future revenues; therefore, cutting costs will improve profits. Employees can represent a high percentage of costs. Thus, cutting the workforce seems to be a natural step. Other anticipated results are lower overhead, less bureaucracy, faster decision making, smoother communications, greater entrepreneurship, and increased productivity. Some organizations have seen benefits. In the Canadian study by Axmith (1995), 85% of the downsized organizations cut costs, 63% improved earnings, 58% improved productivity, and 36% reported improvements in customer service. But other evidence suggests that most restructurings fall short of objectives (Cascio, 1995).

Negative/Unintended Consequences for Organizations

Many restructurings fail to reach anticipated financial objectives. To understand why these attempts fail, we must consider the impact of downsizing on organizational functioning. Most firms mismanage the downsizing process (Cascio, 1993, and chapter 3, this volume; Marks, 1994).

A recent survey of 1,142 firms conducted by the American Management Association (Greenberg, 1990) reported that more than half of them were unprepared for the downsizing, with no policies or programs in place to reduce the effects of the cutbacks. Surviving managers found themselves working in new and less friendly environments, where they were stretched thin from managing more people and jobs and from working longer hours. In addition, these companies sometimes replaced staff functions with expensive consultants. Some severed employees were hired back permanently while others returned to work part-time as consultants.

What about productivity? More than half of 1,468 firms surveyed by the Society for Human Resources Management (see Cascio, 1993) reported that productivity either stayed the same or deteriorated after downsizing. Similarly, a study of 30 firms in the automobile industry indicated that in most companies productivity deteriorated relative to pre-downsizing levels (Cameron, Whetten, & Kim, 1987).

Studies consistently show that after a downsizing, survivors become narrow-minded, self-absorbed, and risk averse resulting in a drop in morale and lessened productivity. Survivors distrust management (Brockner, 1988). The long-term implications of survival syndrome—lowered morale and commitment—are likely to be damaging for organizations. How likely are such surviving employees to strive toward goals of high-quality services and products?

Cascio (1993) reviewed the literature on the economic and organizational consequences of downsizing. He concluded that in many firms, expected economic benefits (e.g., higher profits, lower expense ratios, higher stock prices, greater return on investment) were not realized. Similarly, many expected organizational benefits were not achieved (e.g., better communication, greater productivity, lower overhead, greater entrepreneurship). Cascio attributed this failure to continued use of traditional structures and management practices. He advocated that downsizing instead be viewed as a process of continuous improvement that includes restructuring along with other initiatives to reduce waste, inefficiencies, and redundancy.

Cameron et al. (1987) identified 12 dysfunctional organizational consequences of any organization's decline. These include centralization, the absence of long-range planning, the curtailment of innovation, scapegoating, resistance to change, turnover, decreased morale, the emergence of special interest groups in politics, loss of credibility of top management, conflict and infighting, and across-the-board rather than prioritized cuts.

Four of 10 companies that downsized had unintended business consequences (Marks, 1994). These included need for retraining, more use of temporary workers, more overtime, increased retiree health costs, the need for contracting out work, loss of the wrong people, loss of too many people, and severance costs greater than anticipated.

According to Cameron and his colleagues (1987), organizations in the automobile industry sowed the following negative outcomes as a by-product of downsizing in the 1980s:

1. increased centralization of decision making;
2. adoption of a short-term crisis mentality;
3. loss of innovativeness;
4. increased resistance to change;
5. decreased employee morale, commitment, and loyalty;
6. increased political infighting and politicized special interest groups;
7. risk aversion and conservatism in decision making;
8. loss of trust among customers and employees;
9. increased interpersonal conflict;
10. restricted communication flows and less information sharing;
11. lack of team work;
12. loss of accessible, forward thinking, and aggressive leaders.

Because the majority of the consequences for organizations are negative, it follows that the larger society is affected negatively as well.

Broader Societal Implications

The *New York Times* (1996) observed that after the economic recovery of 1990, more income was going to management and owners of capital (stockholders) than to workers. Corporate profits have risen dramatically while worker compensation, as a share of national income, has fallen. This raises the potential of increased employee anger when coupled with ongoing job losses, little hiring, stagnant or falling wages, and more money going to the wealthiest citizens of society (Murray, 1995).

Luttwack (1996) writes in a similar vein. On August 10, 1995, Boeing Company was so highly regarded by stock analysts and investors that a share earned $65 on the New York Stock Exchange, 77 times the earning of a Boeing share in the previous 4 months. In the same week, a survey of members of the International Association of Machinists and Aerospace Workers, a union representing Boeing's 32,500 workers, showed that just over 20% thought their jobs were "somewhat secure," while over 50% saw their jobs as "not secure."

Jobs of Boeing workers were indeed vulnerable. In November 1995, Boeing's machinists, then on strike, learned of a possible merger of Boeing and McDonnell Douglas, which would mean more job loss. Employees laid off from Boeing were likely to have a difficult time finding similar jobs at the same pay level. As a consequence, more and more Boeing workers, except those at the top, now go to work every day anxious about their jobs. The income gap widens. Those who are anxious vent their anger by wanting to punish someone or something. Some results of this attitude are the tougher treatment of criminals, less concern for the poor, and voting for conservative political candidates (Luttwack, 1996).

Picot, Myles, and Wannell (1990) used Canadian data to examine whether polarization in wages and earnings had occurred as a result of structural changes in the economy. Some have suggested that these changes create "good" jobs and "bad" jobs (high- and low-paying jobs). The shift in employment to the services sector, technological change, changing workforce demographics, and contracting out have produced more workers and jobs at the top and bottom of the earnings distribution and fewer in the middle. Picot et al. used data on employment earnings of full-time, full-year workers from 1967 to 1986. Taking demographics into account, they found that the earnings distribution had become more polarized in this population since 1967. A decline in the relative wages of young people accounted for much of the change. Changes in hourly wage rates and changes in hours worked contributed equally to wage polarization.

After the end of World War II, rising real wage rates and high levels of employment led to rising standards of living and to the emergence of the middle class. More good jobs were created than bad jobs. Harrison and Bluestone (1988) suggested that the recession of the early 1980s hastened and deepened the shift toward low-wage employment (e.g., growth in the unskilled consumer service industries, use of part-time workers, contracting out to low wage firms).

Akyeampong (1986), using Canadian data covering the 1975 to 1985 decade, noted a large increase in part-time workers who would have liked to work full-time. From 1975 to 1985, full-time employment grew by 15.2%, voluntary part-time employment by 41.0%, and involuntary part-time employment by 375.4%. The number of involuntary part-time workers exceeded half a million in 1985 (516,000) compared with 109,000 in 1975. Involuntary part-time employment was concentrated among women, youth, the less well educated, and industry and service workers. In 1975, about 1 in 100 workers were employed part-time involuntarily; in 1985, this number rose to 5 in 100.

Betcherman and Morissette (1994) found that due to a drop in the relative hourly wage, relative annual earnings of young workers fell during the 1980s. (*Young* workers refers to those aged 15 to 24.) They raised the issue of *scarring*, the effect of early labor market experiences on later employment outcomes, and indicated that considerable research supports the existence of this relationship. Their own data provided mixed results.

Rifkin (1995) wrote about the "jobless recovery," a state characterized by job insecurity, chronic unemployment, and systemic underemployment.

Rifkin suggested that technology is eliminating some of the best jobs and many of the worst jobs, downsizing the middle class out of existence. Similar sentiments have been observed by the *New York Times* (1996).

Lerner (1994) raised the question as to whether secure, full-time, adequately waged employment will be available to much of the North American workforce in the near future or whether jobless economic growth, underemployment, or temporary employment will become commonplace. This phenomenon has occurred in the United Kingdom and is now becoming increasingly widespread in other developed countries. Lerner reviewed various policy options for addressing these new realities. She first stressed the need to obtain accurate information about the rates of unemployment and underemployment to examine the implications of the new patterns of work on income distribution and education. She then considered five policy proposals: reduction of work time, redesign of jobs and workers' organizational roles, redefinition of work, increased employee self-sufficiency, and guaranteed annual income. She advocated a search for democratic approaches to these new realities which balance sociopolitical acceptability, economic viability, human development, and environmental capital.

In view of this evidence, we can conclude that the majority of the consequences of restructuring for individuals, organizations, and society are negative. Can there be a positive outcome from restructuring?

Is There a Healthy Side to MADness?

Marks (1994) contended that people are saturated with change and transition and that efforts must be made to help them deal with the pain of the past before they can move on to accept future changes. Most organizations in the 1980s and 1990s have gone through mergers, acquisitions, downsizing, restructuring, reengineering, culture change, and leadership succession. Many have gone through several of these, and often the changes were overlapping. These events not only have changed organizational systems but also have had a major and mostly negative effect on workers in them. The workforce is filled with victims, survivors, destroyed careers and career paths, cynicism, and a distrust of organizational leadership. Survivors work harder with fewer rewards. Multiple downsizings are seen over a few years. Those who lost their jobs may in fact be better off—they can now get on with different activities. Employees see no end to the changes, and they feel powerless to influence them.

Despite the negative outcomes, organizations must continue to change to remain competitive (Nolan & Croson, 1995). New technology and increased competition will hasten the rate of change (Marks, 1994). Senior managers are typically excited about opportunities, whereas middle managers are angry, depressed, and tired. The negative psychological, behavioral, and business consequences of these changes often weigh heavily on these middle managers.

There is a healthy side to MADness. Some organizations were bloated: They needed to rightsize by eliminating unnecessary work and employees and responding to the forces mentioned above. The point of Marks's book is the suggestion that transitions such as MAD can spur organizational renewal. This is easier said than done. Most organizations simply do not make these transitions well (Baumohl, 1993). But if organizations do not change, they will stagnate and decline. MADness is not a sign that organizations are deliberately malicious. Some MAD decisions are wise business choices. The merger of Molson's Breweries with Carling O'Keefe and the merger of two tobacco companies, Benson & Hedges, and Rothman's, are Canadian examples of such decisions. Many companies in the red may be wise to reduce their workforces. Companies can be revitalized, and individuals can be renewed . . . if the emphasis is rightsizing rather than downsizing.

There are some opportunities following downsizing and change. Downsizing can reenergize tired workers and heighten their aspirations, shift the organization's focus to futuure possibilities, strengthen the pay-for-performance link, increase investment in training and development, encourage innovation, improve communication, and produce a clearer mission (Cascio, 1993; Marks, 1994).

Heckscher (1995) interviewed over 250 middle managers from 14 firms. Each of the firms had gone through major changes and had reduced their managerial workforces. Ten of the organizations were troubled and four dynamic. In the troubled organizations, loyalty was racked by crisis. Although initially supporting the need to downsize and restructure, these managers retreated over time into an inward-looking paralysis. Three to 5 years after the changes had been undertaken, there was more bureaucracy than before the changes. There was also inadequate communication from the top down. The loyalty of the managers in the troubled firms prevented them from clearly seeing what the new situation demanded of them, delaying a proactive adaptive response.

Traditional loyalty was rejected by managers in the dynamic companies. Instead they took time to reevaluate their corporate values. They embodied what Heckscher termed a "community of purpose," a coming together of individuals with commitments and an organization with a mission. Individuals were committed to a personal set of skills, goals, interests, and affiliations. These commitments were also consistent with the emergence of a new employment contract. According to this contract, individuals must build their own identities and careers without subordinating their needs to the organization; organizations must take responsibility for helping employees maintain employability (Noer, 1993). In addition, the governmental societal infrastructure must change in ways supportive of the new employment contract. For example, service and insurance providers must work to permit benefit continuity during workplace transitions, and the government should scrutinize private sector organizations. Heckscher suggested that the breakdown of the organization be seen as positive and necessary.

Coping With Mergers and Acquisitions, Downsizing, and Privatization

Having examined these three trends and their effects, we turn now to an investigation of what individuals and organizations are doing to cope. Surviving these transitions will require the coping efforts of both parties.

Individual Coping

Armstrong-Stassen (1994) examined how layoff survivors coped with a workforce reduction involving permanent layoffs. Two dimensions of coping, control-oriented coping and escape coping, were investigated. Armstrong-Stassen considered both antecedents (i.e., those likely to use control coping and those likely to use escape coping) and the consequences or outcomes from the use of these two coping strategies. She found that survivors who perceived a higher threat to their job security were more likely to use both coping strategies. In addition, survivors using more control coping reported more favorable work outcomes (e.g., commitment, job performance, lower turnover intentions), and survivors using more escape coping strategies reported less favorable work outcomes.

Leana and Feldman (1992) suggested that for layoff survivors, problem-focused coping strategies are likely to be more effective than are symptom-focused coping strategies. Ashford (1988) reported that during an organizational transition, emotional expression reduced stress both before and after the transition.

Latack, Kinicki, and Prussia (1995) developed an integrative process model of coping with job loss. After job loss, an individual compares his or her status on four dimensions (economic, psychological, physiological, social) with a reference goal or standard. An individual appraises discrepancies between his or her actual and goal status in terms of harm, loss, or threat. This appraisal leads to a coping goal, moderated by one's perceived coping efficacy, which one tries to achieve through coping strategies (control, escape, seeking of social support).

Roskies, Louis-Guerin, and Fournier (1993) reported the results of two studies of the effects of personality on coping with job insecurity. One involved a sample of airline reservation clerks for whom the danger of job loss was clear and imminent, and the other involved managers and professionals for whom job insecurity was a long-term ambiguous threat. Measures of two personality constructs, negative and positive affectivity, were included. *Negative affectivity* refers to viewing one's environment in pessimistic ways; *positive affectivity* refers to viewing one's environment in optimistic ways. Let us consider some of the results. First, the personality measures of positive and negative affectivity were correlated more strongly with psychological distress than were any other variables. Second, in the airline reservation sample, objective job loss risk was the only predictor of perceived job insecurity. Third, in the managerial and professional sample, personality was the strongest predictor of perceived job insecurity.

Organizational Coping

To determine how organizations deal with restructurings, researchers contacted several Canadian organizations, to capture the perspective of managers in that country.

Maureen Hennessy, Wellesley Hospital's director of education and organizational development, set up a career center at Wellesley Hospital to help staff consider future directions and look for other jobs. The career center was staffed with trained counselors 4 days a week. Counselors also met with employees at night or on weekends to accommodate their shifts. When the provincial budget cut was announced, an open forum was held to permit staff to ask questions of the hospital's president. These sessions were taped and made available to staff who were unable to attend, as well as to patients in the hospital. Hennessy believes it is critical to communicate honestly and quickly and to give the staff all of the information available (M. Hennessy, personal communication, September 1995).

Janice Thompson, vice president and director of employment and staffing at North American Life Assurance Company, was part of a merger (announced in September 1995) with Manulife. Roles in the new organization were still being decided in December 1995, so employees were under a great deal of uncertainty. Thompson found that human resources (HR) staff had to keep a fine balance between representing the company, helping staff through their anger and grieving, and sharing their own uncertainties. She noted that when HR staff appeared tense, employees concluded that layoffs would soon be announced. In addition, the organization had to continue functioning through these trying times. Employees were especially tense when managers of the two about-to-be-merged organizations were meeting to integrate the two companies.

At Bell Canada, employee communications stressed that the company's restructuring was due to increased competition and reinforced the intention of the company to treat staff with dignity. Every effort was made to accommodate the wishes of those laid off as to date of departure. To address concerns by survivors about workload demands, Bell's communications to employees emphasized work simplification initiatives. Company successes (e.g., new contracts) were signaled via E-mail to all employees.

The Ontario government, in its efforts to assist about 2,000 executives who could lose their jobs, offered the executives training sessions on setting up public–private partnerships, sent them on site visits to private sector firms, and facilitated roundtable discussions between executives and outside experts. In addition, information on how to deal with nervous staff and what to do if they themselves lost their jobs was made available to all executives.

Having reviewed individual and organizational coping actions, we will now examine the research on what organizations should and should not do in managing the transition processes.

Mistakes to Avoid

Examining the research literature shows that much can be learned about actions that should be avoided in managing restructurings. Leana and Feldman (1992) studied about 1,000 laid-off workers at two sites: the space coast of Florida in the wake of the *Challenger* disaster (white-collar) and the Pittsburgh steel mills during the decline of "rust belt" industries (blue-collar). They noted that in both cases, aspects of the layoff process created difficulties for individuals and the organization. The layoffs were announced in a cavalier way, the criteria for layoffs were arbitrary, there were concerns among those who remained that the layoffs were handled fairly and honestly, and there were also questions about whether those laid off were handled with dignity. In both cases, layoffs were apparently implemented without respect or consideration of affected workers and caused disruption in the morale and productivity of surviving workers.

Despite this evidence, downsizing remains a strategy of choice for organizations with excess capacity, too many employees, escalating costs, and declining efficiency. Most managers cannot envision any other options. One recent survey (Greenberg, 1990) found that two thirds of companies that downsized did it again 1 year later. In Cameron's research on several hundred organizations (Church, 1995) that had engaged in downsizing, about two thirds did it poorly. That is, these companies were worse off at the end of the downsizing effort than at the beginning. Typically, human resources professionals not only were unhelpful but also were harmful. They caused harm by violating expectations, breaking commitments, bruising human dignity, and being secretive or political (Cascio, 1993).

Brockner et al. (1994) examined the connection between procedural justice—the perception of fairness in the methods used to make decisions—and employee reactions. Three studies in three different firms showed that employees were more negative and even hostile when they believed that procedures leading to the layoffs were unfair, when they were not given sufficient notice, and when they perceived unfair treatment during the downsizing efforts.

What Individuals Can Do

Individuals must take a proactive role in managing their responses to these transitions. There are several things they can do, including developing career resilience, self-reliance, and hardiness.

Resilient people can adapt best to organizational change. They see change not as an interruption in their work, but as the central focus of their work. Given the changes taking place in the employment contract, employees need to see themselves as entrepreneurs who are selling their skills and abilities to their employing organization (Atchison, 1991). As long as the organization needs these skills, employees have a job. But employees need flexibility in the event that their employers no longer need these skills. Some employers are already indicating to their staff that they can no longer offer job security; instead they hope to offer opportunities for growth, development, and acquisition of new skills and breadth of experience. This applies to all levels of employees. Employees learn to manage their careers to guarantee future employability by ensuring that they have portable professional knowledge and skills. Career resilience has benefits for organizations, whether employees remain or leave. Corporate goals are more likely to be met in the 1990s with flexible, adaptable, focused, and distress-free employees.

Waterman, Waterman, and Collard (1994) emphasized the importance of developing a career-resilient workforce. Such workers are committed to continuous learning, reinventing themselves to keep pace with change, taking responsibility for their own career management, and dedicating themselves to their company's success.

Another attribute that will help individuals navigate organizational transitions is self-reliance. *Self-reliance* is an attribute related to how people form and maintain supportive attachments with others. It is a flexible, responsive strategy of developing multiple diverse relationships that allow the individual to manage stress well (Quick, Joplin, Nelson, & Quick, 1992). Self-reliant people know when to ask for help from others and know when to handle a task themselves. They are interdependent individuals who develop egalitarian relationships and adjust to transitions well. Their two opposites—counterdependent individuals, who avoid supportive relationships, and overdependent individuals, who overrely on others—do not handle transitions successfully (D. L. Nelson & Quick, 1991). Self-reliance during times of restructuring can allow individuals to remain healthy while undergoing the stress of the transitions.

Hardiness is another attribute that will help individuals manage restructurings effectively. *Hardy* individuals are characterized by commitment, challenge, and control (Kobasa, Maddi, & Kahn, 1982). *Commitment* is an active curiosity about the environment that leads one to experience life as interesting and enjoyable. *Challenge* means that hardy individuals view change as a challenge rather than as a threat. *Control* is the ability to interpret events as personal choices. Hardy individuals engage in transformational coping; that is, they actively change an event into something subjectively less stressful by viewing it from a broader perspective, by taking action, or by achieving greater understanding of the process. Thus, hardy individuals will weather mergers and acquisitions, downsizings, and restructurings more effectively.

What Organizations Can Do

Successfully managing transitions such as mergers and acquisitions, downsizing, and other restructurings requires considerable commitment from organizations. The research literature provides guidance for managers who are leading such transitions.

Managing the Merger Process Successfully

Blake and Mouton (1984) provided a detailed case study of the application of their interface conflict-solving model to the merger of two organizations. In this merger, an American company had acquired a British company that had previously been its competitor. The intervention targeted top teams of both organizations and involved a series of daylong meetings. The process used perception sharing, identification of concerns and questions, and the development of a sound operating model by groups from both organizations. Qualitative data collected 2 years later suggested that the merger was a success. No senior personnel had left either organization.

A merger is a process rather than an event, and processes require planning, managing, and monitoring to prevent negative results. Communication and preparation are critical in this regard. Complete, open, and early communications are a necessity for all people involved (especially employees, but also managers and top executives) and in both the pre- and postcombination situations. Anxiety, uncertainty, and other negative feelings that result from the announcement of a merger, and ultimately help to create the merger syndrome, come from a lack of reliable information about the future (Marks & Mirvis, 1985b). Employees should know where they stand as early in the process as possible. If management is straightforward and honest with employees from the very beginning, employees are likely to in return give efficient levels of performance during the transition period. A good communications program should be developed before the merger is finalized. This should help to minimize problems in the postmerger situation.

In a pre- and postmerger situation, regular communication channels such as company newsletters, magazines, and formal meetings can be expanded to include such items as face-to-face sessions with top management. Daily news updates that detail the progress of the merger can be posted at coffee stations and bulletin boards. If employees are kept well informed in a rapid and candid manner, then communications should be instrumental in helping a merger to be successful.

Schweiger and DeNisi (1991) considered the impact of a realistic merger preview, a program of realistic information on employees of an organization that had just announced a merger. Employers from one plant received the merger preview while those in another plant received only limited information. Data were collected at four points in time: before the merger was announced, after the announcement but before the realistic merger preview program was introduced, and twice after the realistic merger program. The study extended for a 5-month period overall. Both objective and self-report data were obtained.

The following conclusions were drawn. First, the announcement of the merger was associated with significant increases in global stress; perceived uncertainty; absenteeism; decreases in job satisfaction, commitment, and perceptions of the company's trustworthiness, honesty, and caring; and no change in self-reported performance. There were no differences between the two plants after the announcement of the merger. The experimental plant was significantly lower on perceived uncertainty and significantly higher on job satisfaction, commitment, and perceptions of the company's trustworthiness, honesty, and caring after the realistic merger preview program. These same differences were also present 3 months later.

Reducing the Stress of Staff Reductions

Greenhalgh (1982) described and assessed an action research program that was intended to alter an organization's procedures for achieving workforce reductions in response to a declining need for its services. The organizations were state-supported hospitals that had followed state guidelines and had historically conducted workforce reductions through forced layoffs. A cost–benefit study compared two alternative workforce reduction strategies (layoffs and planned attrition) and found that the layoff strategy was less cost-effective.

An opportunity to use an attrition program arose when the state decided to consolidate three urban hospitals. An agreement was made to accomplish the consolidation through transfer and attrition rather than the simple use of layoffs. Thus potentially affected employees were guaranteed that they would not be summarily laid off. The consolidation plan provided that each employee was to be given at least one opportunity for continued state employment in an equivalent position within reasonable commuting distance. Such opportunities were arranged by coordinating the hiring by various state agencies within the urban areas. The timing of the consolidation plan was arranged to permit the orderly transfer of employees who did not retire or voluntarily leave state service. A mechanism to retrain some workers was also established (see also chapter 10 by Noer).

Government policies, particularly advance notification provisions, extended unemployment benefits, and worker retraining programs, have been helpful in supporting workers in difficult times. Advance notification gives workers more time to find new employment by decreasing the length of unemployment and emotional distress. Extended unemployment benefits lessen the economic distress. Retraining programs help the unemployed find new jobs. Company programs such as outplacement initiatives have also been of some help to those losing their jobs.

The large-scale survey of downsizing practices in Canada that was described earlier (Axmith, 1995) also investigated organizational efforts for survivors. Organizations that have downsized or restructured have undertaken a variety of initiatives to rebuild morale and commitment:

- 60% conducted employee meetings or focus groups
- 44% reevaluated jobs to better reflect new responsibilities
- 29% offered training programs to help employees adjust to the changes
- 22% conducted employee surveys to identify their concerns

- 9% developed new communication strategies, provided counseling and stress management assistance, and held morale-boosting events

According to Cascio (1995) and Cameron, Freeman, and Mishra (1991), effective downsizing has some common characteristics. In the companies studied, the following was observed:

- Downsizing was implemented by command from the top, with recommendations from lower level employees, based on job and task analyses of how work was organized.
- Both short-term (workforce reduction) and long-term (organization redesign and systemic change in the organization's culture) strategies were used, together with across-the-board and targeted downsizing.
- Special attention in the form of outplacement, generous severance pay, retraining, and family counseling was paid to those employees who lost their jobs. Those employees who did not lose their jobs received special attention through increased information exchange among top managers and employees.
- Through internal data gathering and data monitoring, firms identified precisely where redundancy, excess cost, and inefficiency existed. They then attacked these areas specifically. They treated outside agents (e.g., suppliers, distributors) as involved partners as well as potential targets of their downsizing efforts.
- Reorganizations often produced small, semiautonomous organizations within large, integrated ones. However, geographic or product reorganizations often produced larger, more centralized units (e.g., information processing) within decentralized parent companies.

Downsizing was viewed as a means to an end, that is, as an aggressive strategy designed to enhance competitiveness, as well as the targeted end.

Cascio (1993) also offered some guidelines for managing downsizing effectively. First, to downsize effectively, be prepared to manage apparent contradictions like those between the use of top-down authority and bottom-up empowerment and between short-term strategies (head count reduction) and long-term strategies (organization redesign and systemic changes in culture). To bring about sustained improvements in productivity, quality, and effectiveness, integrate reductions in head count with planned changes in the way that work is designed. Downsizing is not a one-time, quick-fix solution to enhance competitiveness. Rather, it should be viewed as part of a process of continuous improvement.

Marks (1994) also offered some guidelines to organizational leaders to facilitate downsizing: prepare for a high level of activity, rally people with a vision of a better organization, offer transition management training, acknowledge uncertainty and concerns, communicate plans and actions, tell all you can and tell the truth, involve people in managing the transition, visit with people and be visible, and establish a safety net for transition victims.

Conclusion

We believe that the contemporary organizational realities of transition, restructuring, and downsizing resulting in organizational MADness (Marks, 1994), merger syndrome (Marks & Mirvis, 1985a), and the survivor syndrome (Noer, 1993) continue to take their toll on employees at all levels. This results in both individuals and their employing organizations being less effective than they want and need to be to remain vibrant and competitive in an increasingly demanding global economy.

We also believe that individuals and their employing organizations can do a much better job in adapting to and changing these realities. Our sense is that organizations have a particularly critical role to play in averting the destructive pattern highlighted in the research studies we reviewed. This insight, coupled with action, is vital in improving the quality of work experiences and performance of these organizations.

Preparation of this chapter has been a sobering experience. It highlighted the pervasiveness of organizational transitions, with the toll being paid by individuals, families, organizations, and communities. In addition, it appears that downsizing, restructuring, and privatization will be facts of organizational life in the foreseeable future. These prospects may have a particularly devastating effect in Canada, given its high levels of current unemployment, huge deficits, and dependence on multinational organizations headquartered in other countries.

Church (1995) wondered if psychologists could make the downsizing experience better for all, should they? That is, if downsizing is an ineffective strategy, should psychologists get involved? If downsizing is an organizational evil, do psychologists have an ethical or moral imperative to try to prevent its practice? Downsizing may create short-term gain in profitability and long-term damage to the satisfactions, loyalty, morale, productivity, and health of survivors. Should we endorse its usage or argue against such initiatives? Organizations will continue to downsize in any event. Can't we, in the short run, make it as humane as possible while in the long run develop the case for limiting its use?

Psychologists, as experts in human behavior, have the training, skills, and experiences to make downsizing and restructuring processes more humane. Psychologists also have an ethical responsibility to make the experience less painful and damaging to those involved. How should we apply our skills, knowledge, and ethical responsibility to organizational transitions such as downsizing? Should we make the process as painless as possible and help those terminated find jobs? Or should we work with the survivors and help reestablish trust and loyalty to their employer? Should we argue for other methods of organizational change?

Psychologists have much to contribute to the success of these transitions, although they have been involved in only minor roles to date. Psychologists can contribute through counseling, consulting, research, and advocacy. Psychologists can assist individuals, families, and communities that have been devastated by job loss. Psychologists can help organizations to downsize and restructure in more humane ways, developing processes that afford dignity to those who must lose their jobs and revitalization to those that survive. In addition, consulting psychologists can work with firms to identify alternatives to downsizing. Psychologists with a research orientation can isolate elements of successful change, as well as document the benefits of such initiatives for individuals, families, organizations, and communities. Finally, psychologists need to communicate—with passion—the great potential damage that might be inflicted on individuals in all walks of life through the insensitive and sometimes brutal way in which downsizing, restructuring, and privatization are typically undertaken. The role for psychologists will not end there. Many writers (e.g., Hamel & Prahalad, 1994) have suggested that drastically downsized companies will suffer from "corporate anorexia," from overdoing their restructuring efforts. These companies are sacrificing innovation by neglecting to focus on inventing tomorrow's products and scoping out tomorrow's markets, both of which require the best efforts of the best people. Suppose these best people are downsized out of the company? Psychologists can help managers view restructuring in the longer term, to avoid potential corporate anorexia.

We need more research—both laboratory and field study. We need more case studies, more interventions, and more descriptions and evaluations of these. This is where psychologists—both academic and applied—have a role to play. Psychologists also need to show more leadership in the public arena and to alert organizational leaders to the downside of what Marks terms "organizational MADness."

People take for granted the notion that Canadian/American society exists to service the needs of the economy and not the other way around. The economy seems to be doing fine; society may be in bad shape. Psychologists can help to implement a change in attitudes that could lead to an economy that contributes to the psychological, social, and financial well-being of members of the workforce.

References

Akyeampong, E. B. (1986). "Involuntary" part-time employment in Canada, 1975–1985. *The Labor Force* (71-001).

Armstrong-Stassen, M. (1994). Coping with transition: A study of layoff survivors. *Journal of Organizational Behavior, 15,* 597–621.

Ashford, S. J. (1988). Individual strategies for coping with stress during organizational transitions. *Journal of Applied Behavioral Sciences, 24,* 19–36.

Atchison, T. J. (1991). The employment relationship: Un-tied or re-tied? *Academy of Management Executives, 5,* 52–62.

Axmith, M. (1995). *1995 Canadian Dismissal Practices Survey.* Toronto, Ontario, Canada: Author.

Baumohl, B. (1993, March 15). When downsizing becomes dumbsizing. *Time,* 55.

Berg, P. (1988). *Privatization of Air Canada.* Ottawa, Ontario, Canada: Research Branch, Library of Parliament.

Betcherman, G., & Morissette, R. (1994). *Recent youth labor market experiences in Canada.* Ottawa, Ontario, Canada: Statistics Canada.

Blake, R. R., & Mouton, J. S. (1984). *Solving costly organizational conflicts.* San Francisco: Jossey-Bass.

Blundell, W. E. (1978, August 17). As the axe falls so does productivity of grim U.S. workers. *Wall Street Journal.*

Brockner, J. (1987). The effects of work layoffs on survivors: A psychological analysis. In R. P. McGlynn (Ed.), *Interfaces in psychology* (Vol. 5). Lubbock: Texas Tech Press.

Brockner, J. (1988). The effects of work layoffs on survivors: Research, theory and practice. In B. M. Staw & L. L. Cummings (Eds.), *Research in organizational behavior* (Vol. 10). Greenwich, CT: JAI Press.

Brockner, J., Grover, S., Reed, T., & Dewitt, R. (1992). Layoffs, job insecurity, and survivors' work effort: Evidence of an inverted-U relationship. *Academy of Management Journal, 35,* 413–425.

Brockner, J., Konovsky, M., Cooper-Schneider, R., Folger, R., Martin, C., & Bies, R. (1994). Interactive effects of procedural justice and outcome negativity on victims and survivors of job loss. *Academy of Management Journal, 37,* 397–409.

Brown, J. (1991). Novatel announces lay-offs. *Computing Canada, 17,* 47–50.

Burke, R. J. (1982). Occupational locking-in: Some empirical findings. *Journal of Social Psychology, 118,* 177–185.

Burke, R. J. (1987). Managing the human side of mergers and acquisitions. *Business Quarterly, 52,* 18–23.

Cameron, K., Freeman, S. J., & Mishra, A. K. (1991). Best practices in white-collar downsizing: Managing contradictions. *Academy of Management Executives, 5,* 57–73.

Cameron, K. S., Whetten, D. A., & Kim, M. U. (1987). Organizational dysfunctions of decline. *Academy of Management Journal, 30,* 126–137.

Carson, K. D., Carson, P. P., & Bedeian, A. G. (1995). Development and construct validation of a career entrenchment measure. *Journal of Occupational and Organizational Psychology, 68,* 301–320.

Cascio, W. F. (1993). Downsizing: What do we know? What have we learned? *Academy of Management Executives, 7,* 95–104.

Cascio, W. F. (1995). Whither industrial and organizational psychology in a changing world of work? *American Psychologist, 50,* 928–939.

Catalano, R., Rook, K., & Dooley, D. (1986). Labor markets and help seeking: A test of the employment security hypothesis. *Journal of Health and Social Behavior, 27,* 227–237.

Champy, J. (1995). *Reengineering management: The mandate for new leadership.* New York: Harper Business.

Church, A. H. (1995). From both sides now. Organizational downsizing: What is the role of the practitioner? *The Industrial–Organizational Psychologist, 33,* 63–74.

Cobb, S., & Kasl, S. V. (1977). *Termination: The consequences of job loss* [Research report]. Cincinatti, OH: NIOSH.

Cunningham, B., & Mitchell, L. (1990). Privatization in British Columbia: What the experts say will happen. *Industrial Relations, 45,* 382–401.

Dekker, S. W. A., & Schaufeli, W. B. (1995). The effects of job insecurity on psychological health and withdrawal: A longitudinal study. *Australian Psychologist, 30,* 57–63.

Depolo, M., & Sarchinelli, G. (1987). Job insecurity, psychological well-being, and social representation: A case of cost sharing. In H. W. Scroiff & G. Debus (Eds.), *Proceedings of The West European Conference on the Psychology of Work and Organization.* Amsterdam: Elsevier.

Downside to the jobs upturn. (1994, November 14). *Business Week,* p. 26.

Feldman, D. C., & Turnley, W. H. (1995). Underemployment among recent business college graduates. *Journal of Organizational Behavior, 16,* 671–706.

Fraze, J. (1988). Displaced workers: Oakies of the 80s. *Personnel Administration, 33,* 42–51.

Galal, A., Jones, L., Tandon, P., & Vogelsang, I. (1994). *Welfare consequences of selling public enterprises.* New York: Oxford University Press.

Gill, J., & Foulder, I. (1978). Managing a merger: The acquisition and its aftermath. *Personal Management, 10,* 14–17.

Gottlieb, M. R., & Conkling, L. (1995). *Managing the workplace survivors: Organizational downsizing and the commitment gap.* New York: Quorum Books.

Greenberg, E. R. (1990). The latest AMA survey on downsizing. *Compensation and Benefits Review, 22,* 66–71.

Greenhalgh, L. (1982). Maintaining organizational effectiveness during organizational retrenchment. *Journal of Applied Behavioral Science, 18,* 155–170.

Greenhalgh, L., & Rosenblatt, Z. (1984). Job insecurity: Toward conceptual clarity. *Academy of Management Review, 9,* 438–448.

Greenwald, J. (1991, September 9). Permanent pink slips. *Time,* pp. 54–56.

Hallier, J., & Lyon, P. (1996). Job insecurity and employees' commitment: Managers' reactions to the threat and outcomes of redundancy selection. *British Journal of Management, 7,* 107–123.

Hamel, G., & Prahalad, C. (1994). *Competing for the future.* Boston: Harvard Press.

Harrison, B., & Bluestone, B. (1988). *The great U-turn: Corporate restructuring and the polarizing of America.* New York: Basic Books.

Hartley, J., & Klandermans, P. G. (1987). Individual and collective responses to job insecurity. In H. W. Scroiff & G. Debus (Eds.), *Proceedings of the West European Conference on the Psychology of Work and Organization.* Amsterdam: Elsevier.

Haugen, S. E., & Meisenheimer, J. R., II. (1991). U.S. labor market weakened in 1990. *Monthly Labor Review, 114,* 3–16.

Heckscher, C. (1995). *White-collar blues: Management loyalties in an age of corporate restructuring.* New York: Basic Books.

Herz, D. E. (1991). Worker displacement still common in the late 1980s. *Monthly Labor Review, 114,* 3–9.

Hirschhorn, L. (1983). *Cutting back.* San Francisco: Jossey-Bass.

Hunt, J. W. (1986). Alienation among managers—The new epidemic or the social scientists' invention? *Personnel Review, 15,* 21–26.

Jick, T. D. (1985). As the axe fails: Budget cuts and the experience of stress in organizations. In T. A. Beehr & R. S. Bhagat (Eds.), *Human stress and cognition in organizations: An integrated perspective* (pp. 83–114). New York: Wiley.

Jobs in an age of insecurity. (1993, November 22). *Time,* 35.

Kay, E. (1975). Middle management. In J. O'Toole (Ed.), *Work and the quality of life* (pp. 207–232). Cambridge, MA: MIT Press.

Kierans, T. E., & Stanbury, W. T. (1985). *Papers on privatization.* Montreal, Quebec, Canada: Institute for Research on Public Policy.

Kobasa, S. C. (1988). Conceptionizational and measurement of personality in job stress research. In J. J. Hurrell, Jr., L. R. Murphy, S. L. Savier, & C. L. Cooper (Eds.), *Occupational stress: Issues and development in research* (pp. 100–109). New York: Taylor & Francis.

Kozlowski, S. W. J., Chao, G. T., Smith, E. M., & Hedlund, J. (1993). Organizational downsizing: Strategies, interventions, and research implications. In C. L. Cooper & I. T. Robertson (Eds.), *International review of industrial and organizational psychology* (pp. 263–332). New York: Wiley.

Latack, J. C., & Dozier, J. B. (1986). After the axe falls: Job loss on a career transition. *Academy of Management Review, 11,* 375–392.

Latack, J. C., Kinicki, A. J., & Prussia, G. E. (1995). An integrative process model of coping with job loss. *Academy of Management Review, 20,* 311–342.

Leana, C. R., & Feldman, D. C. (1992). *Coping with job loss: How individuals, organizations and communities respond to layoffs.* New York: Macmillan/Lexington Books.

Lerner, S. (1994). The future of work in North America: Good jobs, bad jobs, beyond jobs. *Futures, 26,* 185–196.

Levine, C. H. (1980). *Managing fiscal stress.* Chatham, NJ: Chatham House.

Lipsey, G. (1985). Issues in privatization. In T. E. Kearns & W. T. Stanbury (Eds.), *Papers on privatization* (pp. 86–102). Montreal, Quebec, Canada: Institute for Research on Public Policy.

Luttwack, E. (1996). Does America still work? *Harper's, 292,* 35–47.

Marks, M. L. (1994). *From turmoil to triumph.* New York: Lexington Books.

Marks, M. L., & Mirvis, P. H. (1985a). Merger syndrome: Management by crisis. *Mergers & Acquisitions, 20,* 70–76.

Marks, M. L., & Mirvis, P. H. (1985b). Merger syndrome: Stress and uncertainty. *Mergers & Acquisitions, 20,* 50–55.

Marks, M. L., & Mirvis, P. H. (1986). The merger syndrome. *Psychology Today, 20,* 36–42.

Meyer, G. J. (1995). *Executive blues: Down and out in corporate America.* New York: Franklin Square Press.

Mirvis, P. H. (1985). Negotiations after the sale: The roots and ramifications of conflict in an acquisition. *Journal of Occupational Behavior, 6,* 65–84.

Murray, M. (1995, May 4). Thanks, goodbye: Amid record profits, companies continue to lay off employees. *The Wall Street Journal,* pp. A1, A5.

Nelson, A., Cooper, C. L., & Jackson, P. R. (1995). Uncertainty amidst change: The impact of privatization on employee job satisfaction and well-being. *Journal of Occupational and Organizational Psychology, 68,* 57–71.

Nelson, D. L., & Quick, J. C. (1991). Social support and newcomer adjustment in organizations: Attachment theory at work? *Journal of Organizational Behavior, 12,* 543–554.

The New York Times. (1996). *The downsizing of America.* New York: Random House.

Noer, D. (1993). *Healing the wounds: Overcoming the trauma of layoffs and revitalizing downsized organizations.* San Francisco: Jossey-Bass.

Nolan, R. L., & Croson, D. C. (1995). *Creative destruction: A six-stage process of transforming the organization.* Boston: Harvard Business School Press.

O'Neill, H. M., & Lenn, J. (1995). Voices of survivors: Words that downsizing CEOs should hear. *Academy of Management Executives, 9,* 23–34.

Organization for Economic Cooperation and Development. (1992). *Economic outlook.* Paris: OECD Perspectives of Employment.

Picot, G., Myles, J., & Wannell, T. (1990). *Good jobs/bad jobs and the declining middle: 1967–1986.* Ottawa, Ontario, Canada: Statistics Canada.

Quick, J. C., Joplin, J. R., Nelson, D. L., & Quick, J. D. (1992). Behavioral responses to anxiety: Self-reliance, counterdependence, and overdependence. *Anxiety, Stress, & Coping, 5,* 41–54.

Quinn, R. P. (1975). *Locking-in as a moderator of the relationship between job satisfaction and mental health.* Unpublished manuscript, Survey Research Center, University of Michigan, Ann Arbor.

Rifkin, J. (1995). *The end of work: The decline of the global labor force and the dawn of the post-market era.* New York: Putnam.

Robert Half International. (1991, September 9). [Press release]. New York.

Rosellini, L. (1981, December 16). Federal cuts increasing workers' stress levels. *New York Times,* pp. 107–133.

Roskies, E., & Louis-Guerin, C. (1990). Job insecurity in managers: Antecedents and consequences. *Journal of Organizational Behavior, 11,* 345–359.

Roskies, E., Louis-Guerin, C., & Fournier, C. (1993). Coping with job insecurity: How does personality make a difference? *Journal of Organizational Behavior, 14,* 617–630.

Sales, A. L., & Mirvis, P. H. (1984). Acquisition and collision of cultures. In R. Quinn & J. Kimberly (Eds.), *Managing organizational transitions.* New York: Dow Jones.

Schlenker, J. A., & Gutek, B. A. (1987). Effects of role loss on work-related attitudes. *Journal of Applied Psychology, 72,* 286–293.

Schweiger, D. M., & DeNisi, A. A. (1991). Communication with employees following a merger: A longitudinal field experiment. *Academy of Management Journal, 34,* 110–135.

Sorrentino, C. (1993). International comparisons of unemployment indicators. *Monthly Labor Review, 116,* 3–9.

Thurley, K., & Word-Penney, C. (1986). Changes in the roles and functions of middle management: Alternative survey of English language publications. In *Report to the European Foundation for the Improvement of Living and Working Conditions.* London: London School of Economics.

Volinn, E., Lai, D., McKinney, S., & Loeser, J. D. (1988). When back pain becomes disabling: A regional analysis. *Pain, 33,* 33–39.

Waterman, R. H., Jr., Waterman, J. A., & Collard, B. A. (1994, July–August). Toward a career resilient workforce. *Harvard Business Review,* 87–95.

Wolpin, J., & Burke, R. J. (1986). Occupational locking-in: Some correlates and consequences. *International Review of Applied Psychology, 35,* 327–345.

3

Learning From Outcomes: Financial Experiences of 311 Firms That Have Downsized

Wayne F. Cascio

Downsizing, the planned elimination of positions or jobs, has had and will continue to have profound effects on organizations, managers at all levels, employees, labor markets, customers, and shareholders. These are just the direct effects. They do not include the effects on families and communities. In the United States, 43 million jobs were erased between 1979 and 1995, according to a *New York Times* analysis of Labor Department data (Uchitelle & Kleinfield, 1996). Although far more jobs were created than lost over that period, with a net increase of 27 million jobs, the real story lies in the types of jobs that are disappearing. Increasingly, higher paid, white-collar jobs and, along with them, the careers of women and men, many of whom are in their peak earning years, are disappearing. According to the U.S. Department of Labor (1995), only about 35% of laid-off workers end up in equally remunerative or better paying jobs. Indeed, the torrent of downsizing companies has produced fundamental structural changes in our economy and has affected the minds and hearts of the workforce that drives it. Consider just five statistics that characterize the revolution that is taking place (Uchitelle & Kleinfield, 1996):

1. Nearly three quarters of all U.S. households have had a close encounter with layoffs since 1980. In one third of all households, a family member has lost a job, and nearly 40% more know a relative, a friend, or a neighbor who was laid off.
2. One in 10 adults—about 19 million people—acknowledged that a lost job in their household had precipitated a major crisis in their lives.
3. Permanent layoffs have been symptomatic of most recessions, but now they are occurring in the same large numbers even during an economic recovery that has lasted 5 years and even at companies that are doing well.
4. In the 1990s, better paid workers—those earning at least $50,000 per year—account for twice the share of the lost jobs (12%) that they did in the 1980s (6%).

5. Roughly 50% more people—about 3 million—are affected by lay-offs each year than are victims of violent crimes.

Downsizing often is a reactive response to organizational decline (Cameron, Sutton, & Whetten, 1988), although it may also be a proactive measure taken by organizations that perceive future competitive threats. For example, many banks are downsizing proactively because they perceive that their competitive position in the marketplace may be threatened by further deregulation of their industry and competition from a host of other providers of financial services, including insurance companies and brokerage firms.

The Lure of Downsizing

Many executives see downsizing as a compelling strategy to achieve their organizational and financial objectives. Although the "menu" of potential strategies to become more efficient and more productive is a long one, included on almost every executive's list is a reduction in head count. There are really only two ways for companies to become more profitable: either by increasing revenues or by cutting costs. Furthermore, most observers would agree that future costs are more predictable than future revenues. Human resources represent costs, so to become more profitable, it seems logical for a company to reduce those costs through decreasing the number of employees. Unfortunately, when confronted with the need to reduce costs, many of the same executives who tout people as their "greatest assets" see those assets as ripe opportunities for cutting costs.

Firms downsize to make the best possible use of their resources—human, capital, and physical. In theory, downsizing accomplishes this through gains in efficiency (e.g., speed, quality, reductions in the use of resources) and productivity, that is, output per employee. Firms may do this in a number of ways. For example, they may reduce the number of employees, invest in new technology, or eliminate functions, hierarchical levels, or units. They may also change the way that work is done through reengineering, redesigning jobs, or outsourcing noncore activities.

In the study described below, which I conducted along with two colleagues at the University of Colorado—Denver, James R. Morris and Clifford E. Young, our primary concern was with two indicators: changes in the number of employees over time and changes in the dollar value of assets. Negative changes in the former indicate employee downsizing, and negative changes in the latter (if they exceed the percentage of negative change in employees) indicate organizational restructuring. We examined the relationship between downsizing and financial performance over time, using a model and hypotheses that are described more fully below.

Company Performance and Downsizing

Figure 1 is a theoretical model of company performance and downsizing. Each variable in the model is listed below. Formulas for creating the measures were drawn from Standard and Poor's Compustat (1994a) database.

Predownsizing Company Performance Measures

We defined four measures of company performance prior to downsizing:

- *x1* Return on assets (EBDIT/Assets): earnings before depreciation, interest, and taxes (EBDIT) divided by total assets (Assets).
- *x2* Cost of Goods/Sales: cost of goods sold divided by total sales.
- *x3* SG&A expense (Expenses/Sales): selling, general, and administrative expenses (Expenses) divided by total sales (Sales).
- *x4* Profit margin (EBDIT/Sales): earnings (EBDIT) divided by total sales (Sales).

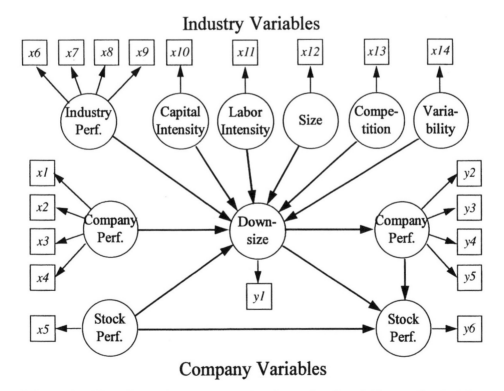

Figure 1. The effects of company- and industry-level variables on the decision to downsize (Perf. = performance).

Stock Performance Measure

> $x5$ Stock Return: A 3-year indexed total return on common stock, that is, a value of 100 would indicate no return, whereas a value of 105 would indicate a 5% return in 3 years.

Level of Downsizing

> $y1$ Downsizing: The measure of employment downsizing was the number of employees in year $t + 1$ divided by the number of employees in year $t - 1$, where t is a given year. This 2-year measure of employment downsizing is a ratio that is less than 1.0 for downsizing companies and is even smaller for companies that experience greater downsizing. As an example, if in 1997 ($t = 1996$, $t + 1 = 1997$), an organization had reduced its size to 7,000 employees from 10,000 employees in 1995 ($t - 1 = 1995$), $y1$ would equal 7,000 divided by 10,000 = 0.7.

Industry Measures

The data for industry comparisons were summed over the companies included in a four-digit Standard Industrial Classification (SIC) code. Standard and Poor's (Compustat) included a company in an SIC based on the product line that constituted its largest line of business.

For an industry group to be defined, it must meet four tests: (a) A qualifying group member company must report at least $50 million in sales in the most recent period; (b) there must be four or more qualifying companies for an industry group to be aggregated; (c) in a given year, at least 60% of the companies in the group must have data available; and (d) all dominant companies must have data available, where *dominant* is defined as having an asset percentage of the industry aggregate that exceeds the arithmetic mean percentage of the industry aggregate (Compustat, 1994b).

Industry Performance Measures

Industry performance measures were defined as the industry-aggregate equivalents for the same 3-year period as the respective company-level performance measures defined above. That is,

> $x6$ = return on assets for the industry aggregate,
> $x7$ = cost of goods sold for the industry aggregate,
> $x8$ = SG&A expense for the industry aggregate, and
> $x9$ = profit margin for the industry aggregate.

In addition, other measures of industry characteristics include

$x10$ Industry Capital Intensity: total industry sales divided by industry total capital assets.

$x11$ Industry Labor Intensity: total industry sales divided by total employment in the industry.

$x12$ Industry Sales: natural log of total industry aggregate sales (Sales).

$x13$ Industry Competition: number of companies contained in the industry aggregate.

$x14$ Industry Variability/Stability: ratio of standard deviation of yearly change in quarterly sales to the average of yearly change in quarterly sales.

The same four measures of industry performance—return on assets, cost of goods sold, SG&A expense, and profit margin—are shown in the model as $y2$ through $y5$. Postdownsizing stock performance is indicated as $y6$.

Specification of Sample, Variables, and Time Frame

We obtained the data for this study from Standard and Poor's (1994a) Compustat PC Plus database. Data were available from 1974 through 1993, and the sample of companies was chosen from the companies included in Standard and Poor's 500 average. A company was included in the sample if it experienced a decline in the number of employees of 3% or more in any year during the period 1980 through 1990. According to data from the American Management Association's (1994) survey on downsizing, the level of downsizing has been significant in recent years, at an average level within companies of 9.2% in 1994, 10.4% in 1993, and 9.3% in 1992. We arbitrarily chose 3% as the minimum level to be considered as significant downsizing. We then inspected the matrix of downsizing ratios, starting in 1990 and working back to 1981, for all companies in the Standard and Poor's 500 and defined time period t_0 as the most recent year in which the number of employees declined by at least 3%. Time period t_0 was selected separately by the three researchers. Checks of interrater reliability showed the reliability to be greater than .95, and all conflicts were resolved. This selection resulted in a sample of companies with base years from 1981 through 1990. Table 1 shows the average level of downsizing among the 311 companies in our sample over the time period from 1981 to 1990.

We defined the construct of performance in terms of a 3-year average both of predownsizing performance measures and of postdownsizing performance measures. We defined predownsizing performance measures in terms of periods t_{-2}, t_{-1}, and t_0 and postdownsizing performance measures in terms of periods t_1, t_2, and t_3. We measured industry variables as the same 3-year average prior to the downsizing base year, that is, t_{-2}, t_{-1}, and t_0.

Table 1. Average Level of Downsizing of Sample Companies

Base Year	No. Companies	2-year Average Ratio	Average Percentage of Downsizing
1981	11	.833	16.7
1982	20	.882	11.8
1983	9	.929	7.1
1984	16	.959	4.1
1985	30	.890	11.0
1986	41	.835	16.5
1987	31	.910	9.0
1988	35	.873	12.7
1989	61	.880	12.0
1990	57	.863	13.7
	311	.904	9.6

Hypotheses

Based on this model, and based on the results of a preliminary study of firms that used extreme downsizing in an effort to improve their financial performance (Cascio & Morris, 1994), we tested the following *null hypotheses* (hypotheses stating that there will be no differences in results for the chosen variables):

1. There is no difference between postdownsizing performance and predownsizing performance.
2. Level of downsizing is unrelated to predownsizing company performance and stock performance.
3. Level of downsizing is unrelated to predownsizing industry performance variables (in Figure 1, variables, $x6-x9$), as well as to industry variables of labor intensity, capital intensity, size, competition, and variability/stability.
4. Postdownsizing company performance is unrelated to the level of downsizing and industry variables.
5. Postdownsizing stock performance is unrelated to the level of downsizing, industry variables, and predownsizing stock performance.
6. The effect of variables predicting downsizing, postdownsizing company performance, and postdownsizing stock return will be no different for companies that experience organizational restructuring (a divestiture of assets at a percentage greater than the percentage decline in employees) than for companies that experience downsizing only (a decrease in number of employees).
7. The effect of variables predicting downsizing, postdownsizing company performance, and postdownsizing stock return will be no different for companies with higher levels of downsizing than for those with lower levels of downsizing.

To test Hypotheses 6 and 7, we used two different divisions of the sample. First, to distinguish between companies with higher levels of downsizing, we divided the sample into two groups based on the level of downsizing. We simply performed a split of the sample at the median downsizing ratio of .89. Thus, the two groups are defined as those with a "high level of downsizing"—companies with more than 11% downsizing in 2 years—and those with a "low level of downsizing"—companies with less than 11% downsizing in 2 years.

Second, to investigate the interaction between employment downsizing and divestiture of assets, we divided the sample into two groups based on whether assets declined along with employment. If assets declined at a percentage equal to or greater than the percentage decline in employment, we considered the company to have performed *organizational restructuring* in conjunction with downsizing, and we defined this as downsizing with divestiture of assets. If the percentage decline in assets was less than the percentage decline in employment, we considered the change to be *pure downsizing*.

To understand our measure of divestiture, consider a company with a number of divisions (*n*), all equal in terms of number of employees, plant size, and amount of equipment. If a division is sold, the number of employees, size of the plant, and amount of equipment should decline by the same relative amount. If there is a central headquarters in addition to the divisions, with headquarters personnel being retained, then the sale of a division should result in the company's plant size and amount of equipment declining proportionately more than the number of personnel. By considering companies whose plant size and equipment amounts decline proportionately more than their number of employees as the divesting companies, we are using a conservative screen for divesting companies. By our measure, divesting companies are those that engaged in the greatest degree of asset sales along with employment downsizing.

Analytical Approach

We proceeded with the analysis in three stages. First, we conducted an analysis of the entire sample to investigate global relationships. Second, we analyzed the two subgroups based on whether the downsizing was considered to be downsizing only or downsizing with divestiture. We used a two-group LISREL[1] analysis to test the null hypothesis that the *standardized regression coefficients* (those expressed in standard deviation units) between the groups were equal. Third, we examined separately the two subsamples that were created based on the median level of downsizing, to see if there were any differences between them.

---

[1]LISREL stands for linear structural relations. LISREL is a powerful statistical tool, which is used to perform confirmatory factor analysis, to examine partial regressions in models with multiple dependent and independent variables, and to study relations among constructs corrected for measurement error in the indicators. It also allows one to test the equivalence of variable relations between subgroups and over time.

Summary Statistics

Table 2 contains summary statistics for each of the measures for the entire sample of 311 companies. Inspecting the differences in means between the predownsizing and postdownsizing performance variables shows that after downsizing, income has declined, expenses have increased, and stock performance has fallen significantly. Thus, we concluded that in general, downsizing has not led to improved performance by the companies in our sample. We therefore could not reject null hypothesis 1.

Inspection of the significant differences between subsamples tabulated in Table 3 shows that pre- and postdownsizing income measures of performance were worse for the high-downsizing companies. High-downsizing companies experienced a significantly greater decline in stock performance than did low-downsizing companies. Patterns of significant differences between companies that downsized only and those that downsized with divestiture were unclear. However, we did notice that the decline in stock

Table 2. Summary Statistics

Variable	M	SD	Min	Max
Predownsizing				
EBDIT/Assets ($x1$)	.158	.064	.006	.494
Cost of Goods/Sales ($x2$)	.671	.151	.152	.944
Expenses/Sales ($x3$)	.199	.121	.005	.617
EBDIT/Sales ($x4$)	.160	.086	.004	.451
Stock Return ($x5$)	174.929	87.238	44.079	776.276
Industry EBDIT/Assets ($x6$)	.148	.043	.005	.287
Industry Cost of Goods/Sales ($x7$)	.683	.126	.317	.944
Industry Expenses/Sales ($x8$)	.181	.107	.016	.441
Industry EBDIT/Sales ($x9$)	.157	.077	.011	.368
Industry Capital Intensity ($x10$)	3.633	3.229	.356	30.258
Industry Labor Intensity ($x11$)	138.919	101.078	22.404	457.199
Industry Sales ($x12$)	9.980	1.533	6.634	13.217
Industry Competition ($x13$)	17.397	14.201	3.000	58.000
Industry Variability ($x14$)	.089	.074	.019	.401
Downsizing ($y1$)	.878	.169	.255	1.756
Postdownsizing				
EBDIT/Assets ($y2$)	.146	.064	−.033	.480
Cost of Goods ($y3$)	.666	.166	.174	1.031
Expenses/Sales ($y4$)	.212	.126	−.020	.632
EBDIT/Sales ($y5$)	.160	.096	−.031	.470
Stock Return ($y6$)	156.943	77.993	44.806	924.985
EBDIT/Assets ($y2-x1$)	−0.012	0.050	$p < .0001$	
Cost of Goods ($y3-x2$)	−0.005	0.057	$p < .1189$	
Expenses/Sales ($y4-x3$)	0.010	0.029	$p < .0001$	
EBDIT/Sales ($y5-x4$)	−0.001	0.048	$p < .8356$	
Stock Return ($y6-x5$)	−17.985	49.118	$p < .0001$	

Note: Min = minimum; Max = maximum.

Table 3. Significant Differences Among Subsamples

Variable	Mean High	Mean Low	p
High vs. Low Downsizing			
EBDIT/Assets (*x1*)	0.150	0.167	.015
EBDIT/Sales (*x4*)	0.142	0.177	.001
Industry EBDIT/Sales (*x9*)	0.142	0.173	.003
Industry Variability (*x14*)	0.100	0.078	.015
Downsizing (*y1*)	0.768	0.989	.001
EBDIT/Assets (*y2*)	0.136	0.156	.007
EBDIT/Sales (*y5*)	0.143	0.178	.001
Stock Return (*y6−x5*)	−24.980	−10.990	.012
Downsizing Only vs. Downsizing With Divestiture			
EBDIT/Assets (*x1*)	0.161	0.143	.045
Industry EBDIT/Assets (*x6*)	0.152	0.121	.001
Industry Sales (*x12*)	10.104	9.188	.001
Downsizing (*y1*)	0.866	0.947	.002
Cost of Goods (*y3*)	0.657	0.716	.029
Cost of Goods (*y3−x2*)	−0.008	0.014	.015
EBDIT/Sales (*y5−x4*)	0.002	−0.017	.010
Stock Return (*y6−x5*)	−20.453	−3.564	.032

performance was significantly greater in downsizing-only companies than in divesting companies. This finding is consistent with published studies indicating stock decline for companies that downsize only, and not for those that also divest assets (Worrell, Davidson, & Sharma, 1991).

Structural Equations

Tables 4, 5, and 6 display the results of the regression-formulated LISREL results. Table 4 contains the results of the analysis of the entire sample. Each entry in the table is presented as the standardized regression coefficient, and its corresponding *t* value is shown beneath it. Given the size of the sample, *t* values greater than 2.0 are significant at *p* < .05. The regression coefficient represents the standardized independent effect of the column variable on the row variable. For example, in Table 4, a change of 1 standard deviation in the return on assets (*x1*), yields an impact on downsizing (*y1*) of 0.065 standard deviations. This is a very small and nonsignificant change, as shown by the *t* value of 0.975. Table 5 contains the results for both high and low levels of downsizing. Table 6 contains the results for both downsizing only and downsizing with divestiture.

Interpretation of Coefficients

We concluded the following after inspecting the results of the entire sample (see Table 4). The level of downsizing (*y1*), that is, the magnitude

Table 4. Financial Performance Measures for the Total Sample

Dependent Variable	Independent Variables									
	x1	x2	x3	x4	x5	x10	x12	x13	x14	y1
Downsizing (y1)	.065[a]	−.119	−.212	.182	−.066	.018	−.166	−.051	−.165	
	.975[b]	−.680	−1.370	1.787	−1.176	.280	−2.245	−.565	−2.933	
EBDIT/Assets (y2)	.677					−.129	−.090	.063	−.109	.038
	16.428					−3.024	−1.757	1.210	−2.637	.908
Cost of Goods (y3)		.924				.094	−.017	.040	.038	−.005
		45.369				4.571	−.665	1.569	1.884	−.248
Expenses/Sales (y4)			.991			−.003	.088	−.079	.009	.004
			72.884			−.242	5.243	−4.727	.667	.273
EBDIT/Sales (y5)				.719		−.134	−.028	.118	−.085	.032
				18.862		−4.191	−.766	2.802	−2.966	1.084
Stock Return (y6)					.839	−.139	−.018	−.026	−.055	.012
					26.302	−4.197	−.466	−.632	−1.734	.360

Note: x1 = EBDIT/Assets; x2 = Cost of Goods/Sales; x3 = Expenses/Sales; x4 = EBDIT/Sales; x5 = Stock Return; x10 = Industry Capital Intensity; x12 = Industry Sales; x13 = Industry Competition; x14 = Industry Variability/Stability.
[a] Standardized coefficient. [b] t value.

Table 5. Financial Performance Measures for High-Downsizing vs. Low-Downsizing Companies

Dependent Variable	Independent Variables									
	x1	x2	x3	x4	x5	x10	x12	x13	x14	y1
High-Downsizing Companies										
Downsizing (y1)	−.001[a]	.662	−.681	−.135	.045	.052	.112	.004	−.314	
	−.006[b]	−1.001	−1.152	−.519	.435	.452	.815	.025	−3.243	
EBDIT/Assets (y2)	.617					−.219	−.215	.246	−.195	.079
	8.943					−3.207	−2.475	2.853	−2.735	1.105
Cost of Goods (y3)		.901				.153	.041	.003	.044	−.048
		19.431				3.444	.709	.044	.940	−1.009
Expenses/Sales (y4)			1.000			−.004	.070	−.088	.031	.022
			22.670			−.095	1.277	−1.663	.688	.471
EBDIT/Sales (y5)				.688		−.184	−.116	.189	−.119	.084
				10.257		−3.054	−1.622	2.441	−2.081	1.458
Stock Return (y6)					.862	−.148	.006	−.034	−.009	−.031
					14.666	−2.542	.085	−.452	−.152	−.514
Low-Downsizing Companies										
Downsizing (y1)	.037	−.052	−.194	.201	−.009	−.047	−.340	−.105	.048	
	.408	−.247	−1.048	1.397	−.110	−.479	−3.282	−.787	.608	
EBDIT/Assets (y2)	.731					−.097	−.062	−.037	−.021	−.030
	12.371					−1.477	−.798	−.481	−.363	−.483
Cost of Goods (y3)		.941				.038	−.046	.041	.025	.012
		32.401				1.203	−1.190	1.055	.864	.382
Expenses/Sales (y4)			.992			−.017	.106	−.073	−.004	−.002
			58.557			−.940	4.670	−3.222	−.233	−.141
EBDIT/Sales (y5)				.739		−.120	.006	.092	−.041	.001
				12.791		−2.514	.110	1.407	−1.018	.029
Stock Return (y6)					.825	−.119	−.060	−.004	−.104	−.005
					18.385	−2.402	−1.017	−.068	−2.273	−.104

Note: x1 = EBDIT/Assets; *x2* = Cost of Goods/Sales; *x3* = Expenses/Sales; *x4* = EBDIT/Sales; *x5* = Stock Return; *x10* = Industry Capital Intensity; *x12* = Industry Sales; *x13* = Industry Competition; *x14* = Industry Variability/Stability.
[a] Standardized coefficient. [b] *t* value.

Table 6. Financial Performance Measures for Downsized Only Companies vs. Downsized With Divestiture Companies

Dependent Variable	Independent Variables									
	x1	x2	x3	x4	x5	x10	x12	x13	x14	y1
	Downsizing Only									
Downsizing (y1)	.150[a]	-.109	-.153	.026	-.055	.037	-.134	.065	-.202	
	1.798[b]	-.475	-.760	.229	-.885	.513	-1.639	.645	-3.233	
EBDIT/Assets (y2)	.665					-.111	-.062	.063	-.091	.086
	14.454					-2.325	-1.107	1.098	-1.971	1.839
Cost of Goods (y3)		.922				.103	-.007	.031	.036	.032
		39.773				4.336	-.261	1.097	1.589	1.402
Expenses/Sales (y4)			.995			.007	.093	-.083	-.007	.005
			57.629			.383	4.338	-3.874	-.410	.297
EBDIT/Sales (y5)				.710		-.137	-.036	.144	-.072	.058
				17.122		-3.958	-.911	3.128	-2.276	1.831
Stock Return (y6)					.800	-.136	-.008	-.034	-.067	.051
					20.584	-3.340	-.158	-.691	-1.694	1.304
	Downsizing With Divestiture									
Downsizing (y1)	2.319[a]	-6.196	-7.224	-3.688	.973	-.801	-.647	-.334	-1.635	
	1.139[b]	-1.119	-1.164	-.974	1.073	-1.066	-1.110	-1.153	-1.273	
EBDIT/Assets (y2)	.677					-.270	-.221	.063	-.186	-.141
	4.879					-1.832	-1.031	.289	-1.333	-.968
Cost of Goods (y3)		.941				.107	-.012	.117	.008	.081
		9.632				1.071	-.083	.795	.080	.810
Expenses/Sales (y4)			1.028			-.026	.035	-.054	.106	-.012
			11.579			-.315	.298	-.452	1.185	-.133
EBDIT/Sales (y5)				.867		-.132	-.001	-.110	-.114	-.084
				5.038		-.970	-.008	-.538	-1.012	-.609
Stock Return (y6)					.948	-.109	-.129	.058	-.105	.090
					8.973	-1.000	-.819	.360	-1.008	.823

Note: x1 = EBDIT/Assets; x2 = Cost of Goods/Sales; x3 = Expenses/Sales; x4 = EBDIT/Sales; x5 = Stock Return; x10 = Industry Capital Intensity; x12 = Industry Sales; x13 = Industry Competition; x14 = Industry Variability/Stability.
[a] Standardized coefficient. [b] t value.

of the change in employment, does not appear to be a function of pre-downsizing company performance ($x1$ through $x4$). Thus, we could not reject null hypothesis 2. The only variables that were significantly related to downsizing were industry sales ($x12$) and industry variability ($x14$). Individual companies with larger sales (larger companies) experienced greater downsizing ($y1$, lower ratio of employees). Higher levels of industry variability ($x14$) resulted in greater downsizing. Thus, the level of downsizing is unrelated to industry characteristics and performance, so we rejected null hypothesis 3 for only two variables that described industry characteristics ($x12$ and $x14$).

We could not reject null hypothesis 4, which states that the level of downsizing has no effect on postdownsizing company performance. Predownsizing performance measures ($x1$ through $x4$) affected post-downsizing measures ($y2$ through $y5$), with highly significant and positive coefficients. Some industry variables (e.g., $x14$) were significant predictors of some postdownsizing company performance variables (e.g., return on assets, return on sales). Industry capital intensity ($x10$) was negatively related to EBDIT/assets and EBDIT/sales and positively related to cost of goods sold. Industry size ($x12$, sales) was positively related to expenses/sales ($y4$). The number of companies in the industry ($x13$, competitiveness) was negatively related to expenses/sales and positively related to EBDIT/sales ($y5$). Industry variability was negatively related to EBDIT/assets and EBDIT/sales. Thus, some industry-level variables did affect post-downsizing company performance, contrary to null hypothesis 4.

Looking specifically at the postdownsizing stock performance variable ($y6$), there was no significant effect from downsizing ($y1$). Thus, we could not reject null hypothesis 5 with respect to downsizing. Several small-scale studies have shown negative effects from large-scale downsizings on stock prices over time (Cascio & Morris, 1994; Dorfman, 1991), but this is the first large-scale study to demonstrate the lack of an effect over time on a broader sample of companies that downsized employees. One industry variable, capital intensity ($x10$), had a significant negative effect on stock return. Thus, we rejected null hypothesis 5 only with respect to capital intensity.

Test of Equality of Coefficients

We performed a two-group analysis using LISREL to test the null hypothesis that the set of coefficients for downsizing-only companies was no different from the set of coefficients for downsizing companies with divestiture (Hypothesis 6). Results of the nested chi-square from the two-group analysis versus the chi-square results of the independent one-group analyses yielded a chi-square value of 1,312.49 with 45 degrees of freedom and an associated probability of 0. Thus, the two groups are significantly different at an alpha level of $p < .001$. We therefore rejected null hypothesis 6 that there is no difference in the coefficients between the companies that downsized only and those that both downsized and divested assets.

We then performed a second two-group analysis using LISREL to test the null hypothesis that the set of coefficients for high-downsizing companies was the same as the set of coefficients for low-downsizing companies (Hypothesis 7). Results of the nested chi-square test from the two-group analysis versus the chi-square results of the independent one-group analyses yielded a chi-square value of 62.55 with 45 degrees of freedom and an associated probability of .045. Thus, the two groups are significantly different at an alpha level of $p < .05$, so we rejected Hypothesis 7 that the effect of downsizing on company performance will be no different for high-downsizing companies than for low-downsizing companies.

High- Versus Low-Downsizing Companies

When we inspected the coefficients in the high- versus low-downsizing subsamples, we found that the pattern of relationships among coefficients was quite similar between the low- and high-downsizing companies. In neither subsample was predownsizing company performance ($x1$ to $x4$) a predictor of downsizing ($y1$), nor was downsizing ($y1$) a predictor of post-downsizing company performance ($y2$ to $y5$).

Table 6 shows that the coefficients predicting downsizing in the downsizing-with-divestiture subsample were much larger in absolute magnitude than those in the downsizing-only subsample. Although the t values were low because of the small size of the downsizing-with-divestiture subsample (45), and thus the power of the statistics was quite limited in that subsample, many of them were higher than in the downsizing-only subsample.

As an example, consider the prediction of return on assets ($y2$). In the downsizing-only companies, the regression coefficients for industry capital intensity ($x10$), industry sales ($x12$), industry competition ($x13$), and industry variability/stability ($x14$) were $-.111$, $-.062$, .063, and $-.091$, respectively. In the downsizing-with-divestiture sample, the corresponding coefficients were $-.270$, $-.221$, .063, and $-.186$. In this example, with the exception of industry competition ($x13$), where the coefficients were identical in size in the two samples, coefficients in the downsizing-with-divestiture sample were roughly twice as high as those in the downsizing-only sample.

Because of the small number of companies in the downsizing-with-divestiture subsample, results regarding it must be viewed with caution. But it is clear that this subsample's results are different from those of the downsizing-only subsample. The coefficients for predownsizing company performance as well as industry variables predicting downsizing are all large. More studies looking at a larger sample size of companies that had both downsized and divested are needed.

Because we did not have direct information about divestiture, we used an arbitrary and conservative formula based on the percentage decline in assets versus the percentage decline in employees. We considered a company to be divesting only if the percentage decline in assets was greater than the percentage decline in employees. It is certainly possible that several of the companies reduced assets at some lower percentage and so were not considered to be divesting.

Summary and Conclusions

Based on our analysis of 311 companies that downsized employees by more than 3% in any year between 1980 and 1990, we concluded the following:

1. Across all companies in the sample, the percentage decline in employment was not related in a systematic manner to pre-downsizing financial performance.
2. Predownsizing industry performance variables, as a set, did not predict the level of downsizing for companies in that industry. However, individual companies with larger sales volume, and those in industries characterized by high levels of variability, experienced greater downsizing.
3. The level of downsizing in any given company did not affect post-downsizing company financial performance. However, several industry-level variables did affect postdownsizing performance. These included industry capital intensity, sales, variability, and competitiveness (number of companies in the industry).
4. Level of downsizing did not affect a company's postdownsizing stock performance.
5. Between companies that downsized only and those that both downsized and divested assets, there were major differences in the effects of the independent variables on downsizing, post-downsizing company performance, and postdownsizing stock return.
6. There were also differences in the relative strength of predictor variables among companies with high levels of downsizing versus those with low levels of downsizing. These differences, however, were minor.
7. As a general conclusion, employee downsizing per se did not appear to lead to improved company financial performance, nor did it have a detrimental effect on company financial performance.

These results might serve to advise companies to consider reorienting their thinking from a pure downsizing strategy to that of responsible restructuring. Pure downsizing asks, "What is the minimum number of people we need to run our operations?" Responsible restructuring focuses on a different question, namely, "How can we use the people we currently have more effectively?" Such an approach views employees as assets to be developed rather than as costs to be cut. It requires top managers to articulate a vision of what they want their organizations to achieve, to establish a supportive corporate culture that views retraining and redeployment of surplus workers as an investment, and to recognize that employees are unlikely to contribute creative, ingenious ideas for cutting costs if they think their own employment security will be jeopardized as a result.

Responsible restructuring represents an attempt to derive a competitive advantage from the more effective use of employees' skills and abilities. An increasing body of evidence (U.S. Department of Labor, 1995) indicates that companies can derive sustained competitive advantage from restructuring without employee cutbacks. Such evidence makes responsible restructuring an approach well worth considering.

References

American Management Association. (1994). *1994 AMA survey on downsizing and assistance to displaced workers.* New York: Author.

Cameron, K. S., Sutton, R. I., & Whetten, D. A. (1988). Issues in organizational decline. In K. S. Cameron, R. I. Sutton, & D. A. Whetten (Eds.), *Readings in organizational decline* (pp. 3–19). Cambridge, MA: Ballinger.

Cascio, W. F., & Morris, J. (1994). *Impact of downsizing on the financial performance of firms.* Unpublished manuscript, University of Colorado–Denver, Graduate School of Business.

Compustat. (1994a). Compustat PC Plus for Windows, Standard & Poor's Compustat. Englewood, CO: McGraw-Hill.

Compustat. (1994b). *Compustat PC Plus user's guide* (Appendix D, pp. D1–D2). Englewood, CO: McGraw-Hill.

Dorfman, J. R. (1991, Dec. 10). Stocks of companies announcing layoffs fire up investors, but prices often wilt. *Wall Street Journal,* pp. C1, C2.

Uchitelle, L., & Kleinfield, N. R. (1996, March 3). On the battlefields of business, millions of casualties. *New York Times,* pp. 1, 14, 15.

U.S. Department of Labor, Office of the American Workplace. (1995). *Guide to responsible restructuring.* Washington, DC: U.S. Government Printing Office.

Worrell, D. C., Davidson, W. N., III, & Sharma, V. M. (1991). Layoff announcements and stockholder wealth. *Academy of Management Journal, 34,* 662–678.

Part II

Case Studies of Organizational Restructuring

Introduction

Economic changes have had a major impact on organizations in the private and public sector. Some have had to downsize and terminate staff because of budgetary considerations. Others have reorganized and revitalized themselves in order to meet expected future requirements. The five case studies in this section represent these issues. The case studies follow models of best practice. Each organization looked to the future as it planned for immediate actions that it needed to take in order to survive. Each example shows the compassionate involvement of staff in decision making and the concern of top executives, managers, and supervisors for their staff's well-being. Each shows the importance of open and complete communication of information to the employees. No blame for errors or lack of foresight are necessary when everyone is informed as to what is happening and why it is happening. Each organization showed compassion and interest in its employees and worked to quickly reemploy any workers who were displaced.

In chapter 4, Graddick and Cairo describe the decision process and the results of those decisions in the splitting up of AT&T into three strong, focused, and independent multi-billion dollar new corporations: AT&T, Lucent Technologies (which includes Bell Laboratories), and NCR. This was done after AT&T carefully looked at the future prospects for the corporation. This was an unprecedented happening. The authors discuss the impact of the announcement to downsize 40,000 jobs in the process of restructuring. They discuss the processes of helping employees become adjusted to the new organizational structures. Finally, they include a "lessons learned" section and a checklist for other organizations facing restructuring. AT&T followed known best practices planning initiatives to accomplish this task. In breaking up into three corporations it also found humane ways to downsize its staff. AT&T was able to place a large number of the 40,000 displaced employees in new positions in the three new corporations. It also provided generous severance pay for those who might want to retire early or take part in some other career transition. All in all, only a fraction of the targeted total number of employees were terminated.

Gordon discusses in chapter 5 the history and present condition of the Chaparral Steel Corporation. This progressive learning organization has been in the forefront of innovation since its beginning. This chapter describes the knowledge-building activities of shared problem solving, integration of new technologies and methodologies, constant formal and informal experimentation, and pulling in of expertise from the outside to aid the corporation. Chaparral Steel began as an innovative start-up company. When the steel industry, except for very small specialty steel mills, was no longer thought to be viable in the United States, this corporation asked its employees for suggestions for improving itself. Corporate management also listened to the best and brightest academics from American universities. As a result, Chaparral Steel is in a process of continuous improvement, following the best of W. Edward Deming's theory of quality management. This case study shows how management's compassionate listening to employees positively affects the bottom line.

In chapter 6, Adkins presents an important transactional–ecological model and applies it to the base closure process at Williams Air Force Base, Arizona. This case study examines contextual factors (e.g., environmental, psychosocial, and organizational), stress hazards, buffers and coping strategies, signs of strain, and intervention and facilitation strategies. The chapter finishes with a set of lessons learned. Base closures are a relatively new phenomenon. When a base or other organization is slated for closure, employees can suffer mental and physical health problems as well as financial losses. The stress caused by base closure can also show up in increased accidents and employee absenteeism. Adkins shows how to assess this distress and how to help employees and their families deal with it. Studying the issue of distress is important. In the case of base closures, the organization has to continue operating until the termination date. This means that essential employees must stay on board. A balancing act ensues that must be directed from the top of the organization. Adkins' model is an excellent one for studying stress in any organization.

Chapter 7, by Grant and Kraft, presents a three-year case study of the United States Office of Personnel Management (OPM). The authors discuss the strategic planning involved in the downsizing effort and examine in detail the program implementation and follow-up program evaluation. They discuss reengineering the organization after the downsizing. The chapter concludes with a lessons learned discussion. Events often occur that are beyond the knowledge or control of an organization. This was the case for OPM. OPM has what is called a *revolving fund*. This fund was used to pay employee salaries and expenses as well as other costs. OPM would be reimbursed for its services performed for other government agencies. Unfortunately, other agencies' requests for OPM services suddenly stopped as a result of a major downsizing of the federal government. OPM was faced with a large permanent staff without income to pay their wages. Faced with this dilemma, OPM was forced to reduce its staff. This chapter discusses how OPM was able to manage its work while losing approximately 40% of its staff.

In chapter 8, Hardy and Rodela discuss the use of the Future Search conference planning method to develop, decide, and deploy strategies for restructuring and "reinventing" the Environmental Protection Agency's (EPA) Office of Human Resources and Organizational Services. This case study describes how customer involvement and employee empowerment energized and sustained the planning process. Although the chapter's emphasis is on how the planning and preparing for change took place, the lessons learned may be quite helpful to organizations in meeting the challenges of implementing a new way of doing business. These lessons are likely to have real and substantial impact on the future of organizations.

These case studies are examples of what some industrial psychologists consider state-of-the-art practices. Every reader should find something useful in them.

4

Helping People and Organizations Deal With the Impact of Competitive Change: An AT&T Case Study

Mirian M. Graddick and Peter C. Cairo

On September 20, 1995, AT&T announced plans for a strategic restructuring that would separate the corporation into three publicly traded, global companies. This bold strategic move was designed to take full advantage of changes in the fast-growing global information industry. Each new business could focus its resources more sharply on individual market opportunities. In addition, the restructuring would serve to eliminate strategic conflict among the businesses and accelerate decision making by greatly simplifying the corporate structure. Overall, the move was designed to create even stronger businesses and position each to add greater value to its customers, employees, and investors. "Changes in customer needs, technology and public policy are radically transforming our industry," said AT&T chairman Robert E. Allen. "We now see this restructuring as the next logical turn in AT&T's journey since divestiture."

The scope and scale of the restructuring were unprecedented. The task was to split AT&T—a company with $79 billion in revenue and 300,000 employees—into three companies, Lucent Technologies, NCR, and AT&T, in 15 months. The new AT&T, operating under the AT&T brand name, is now a global company focused on providing the best "anytime, anywhere" communications services in the world with $51 billion in annual revenue and about 127,000 employees. It is positioned to compete in a rapidly changing industry with new and powerful competitors. The newly named Lucent Technologies is one of the largest communications systems companies, with annual revenues in excess of $20 billion and about 131,000 employees. Bell Laboratories, a major competitive asset, will be the research and development engine for this new company. Lucent will now be better able to sell its technology to the new AT&T competitors (such as the regional Bell companies) as well as compete for AT&T's business. NCR will now be a stand-alone business providing computer systems and services, with $8 billion in revenues and about 38,000 employees. This organization will refocus its business on three industries in which it has a leading position—retailing, financial services, and communications.

The time frames for the breakup (commonly referred to as the "trivestiture") were extremely aggressive. By the end of 1995, each new company had to have established its new structure, including the types of corporate support functions that it would require as a stand-alone company. By March 1996, Lucent wanted to be in a position to make an initial public offering of 15% of its stock. Distribution of the remaining stock was scheduled for September 1996. All separation transactions had to be accomplished by January 1, 1997. Key success measures for the business included achieving the restructuring milestones while meeting customers' needs and maintaining financial commitments.

AT&T has had a long history of transformational change since it divested in 1984, when its status as a regulated monopoly ended. Since that time the company has been forced to respond to key forces in a dynamic industry involving continuous technological breakthroughs, increased competition, changes in government regulation, and global expansion. AT&T's response to these forces has been to transform the business through (a) mergers and acquisitions (e.g., the acquisition of McCaw—the nation's largest wireless communications company); (b) downsizing and reallocating its workforce (more than 100,000 positions have been eliminated since 1984); and finally, (c) restructuring into three independent companies.

In planning this trivestiture, AT&T leaders drew on lessons learned from their own previous restructurings as well as models of organizational change that had helped other companies design effective interventions. In particular, it was apparent from the outset that the human resource issues in this restructuring were enormous and unique. The aggressive time frames, scope of the effort, and the need to divide the corporate support workforce of 16,000 people among three new businesses all contributed to making this one of the most significant challenges in the company's history. Consequently, human resource professionals partnered with the business leaders during every phase of the restructuring. The partnership involved helping to design the new organizations, developing career transition programs and practices, building communication strategies, and establishing approaches for revitalizing the entire company.

AT&T had learned from its past. Among the most important lessons which influenced the design of the transition plan were (a) the need to engage employees throughout the restructuring by communicating frequently and creating shared ownership of the actions required to manage the change; (b) the need to create a process where people could compete fairly for positions, which would also meet legal requirements; (c) the need to establish support systems to help people transition to new careers within or outside AT&T and to assist leaders in managing employees throughout the change process effectively; and (d) the need to form a dedicated team of individuals responsible for planning the staffing and movement of people throughout the restructuring.

Our intent in this chapter is to share approaches, experiences, and insights regarding how to help individuals and organizations effectively navigate through transformational change. Although the recent trivestiture will be the focal point of the chapter, we will also incorporate observations from other AT&T experiences with downsizing and restructuring, to provide the reader with our most recent set of lessons learned.

Restructuring AT&T Into Three Publicly Held Companies

The restructuring of AT&T will be described in three phases: Planning, Execution, and Revitalization. While the activities across the various phases often occurred in parallel, this framework provides a useful way to describe the initiatives as they unfolded.

Phase I—Planning

While the time available for planning was limited, past experience had shown us that investing up front in the establishment of transition teams, principles, deadlines, and the development of a strategy for meeting our business needs would be critical to success. Below are the key elements of the planning process from the perspective of human resources personnel.

Structure of transition teams. The business objectives and deadlines for the transition were well articulated at the time that the restructuring was announced. Many of these were dictated by market forces that required AT&T to move quickly and aggressively. For example, the most important deadline was the need to make an initial public offering (IPO) for Lucent Technologies in March 1996. Coordinating all of the restructuring activities across the company within the required time frames while still running the existing business was a significant challenge.

First, Chairman Bob Allen appointed a senior officer to lead a dedicated restructuring project team. This team consisted of representatives from the corporate support departments; that is, Human Resources, Public Relations, Finance, Law, and Operations. The Project Team also included representatives from each of the three new companies. The role of this team was threefold: (a) to define implementation policies, principles, and guidelines for each company to use to redistribute assets and to realign operations; (b) to design and guide the processes necessary for the new companies to carry out the restructuring; and (c) to deliver the legal documentation necessary to establish the companies as separate units, including documentation for the IPO, spin-off, and sale efforts to support the Project Team. In addition, the AT&T Steering Committee, composed of the Chairman and the Senior Vice Presidents of Human Resources, Public Relations, Finance, and Law and Government Affairs, was established. Any issues that could not be resolved by the Project Team were forwarded to the Steering Committee for resolution. This governance process was critical to ensure decisions could be made within the required time frames.

Concurrent with the above-mentioned restructuring activities, the senior leaders in each of the new companies created teams and used the transition as an opportunity to reevaluate and redefine each company's strategy, structure, and governance processes in response to current and anticipated business needs.

   Development of human resources guiding principles. An initial activity of the Project Team was to establish a set of guidelines and principles within each functional area, designed to facilitate decision making during the restructuring. The human resources principles were quite extensive, covering general staffing guidelines, support for employees whose jobs were being eliminated, and the approach for placing support staff in new jobs. (Exhibit 1 includes a summary of the human resources vision and objectives and examples of key principles.)

   Two important business decisions influenced the development of these Human Resources principles. First, the company decided to assess all employees in the support departments and determine if their skills and experiences qualified them for jobs with the new companies. Thus everyone in the support departments was subject to the same review. Important principles were developed, such as requiring equitable distribution of talent across the new companies and ensuring that selection decisions were based on the skills required for the new organization design. Second, each new company used the transition as an opportunity to reduce costs. This

Exhibit 1. Human Resources Guiding Principles

The Vision: Create exciting and successful high-performing businesses where people are valued and valuable.

The Objectives:

  1. Design, size, and staff each new company to meet its future business requirements and strengthen its ability to compete successfully.
  2. Oversee the equitable distribution of talent among the entities and discourage unilateral "talent raiding."
  3. Retain critical skills and key talent throughout the transition.

Examples of Human Resources Principles:

  • The AT&T Redeployment and Staffing Project Team will tightly manage employee movement into and across the entities in sequence with key business events (such as the IPO).
  • Honor all existing collective bargaining and labor agreements.
  • The skills and performance of members of the functional communities (including those in business units and divisions) will be reviewed to ensure the best talent is identified and assigned to the new companies.
  • Employees in the support departments will have the opportunity to express their entity preferences.
  • We are committed to providing employees whose jobs are at risk a standard set of resources and tools that enable them to move to new careers either within or outside AT&T.
  • We will give supervisors the information and tools that enable them to support their employees and manage key events related to the transition.

---

led to organization designs that required fewer people than were currently employed by the company. The businesses therefore had to be prepared to address the anticipated surplus of employees.

To summarize, the unique human resources challenges during this restructuring included developing a process that would allow us to simultaneously (a) assess the talent within each support function across the company, (b) assign people to positions based on the skill requirements and the needs of the new companies, (c) determine those who were going to be left without job assignments, and (d) design appropriate career transition and employee support programs to facilitate their transitions.

The company also determined early on that the surplus of employees could be significant and that our ability to support them would be different from past restructurings. AT&T had a track record of being able to place large numbers of surplus people from one business elsewhere in the company. This time the circumstances were anticipated to be different. This meant that we had to encourage people to focus immediately on finding opportunities outside AT&T rather than searching for new jobs internally. One outcome was the decision to offer a voluntary separation package to everyone in a support position and many other individuals in the business. Although there were no differences in the financial elements of the voluntary and involuntary packages, the rationale was simply to give people an opportunity to volunteer to leave and thereby create openings for others. More than 7,000 employees took the voluntary offer. Organizations outside of common support departments had the option not to give the voluntary offer to those employees with special skills that would be critical to the business in the future. While the company lost some talented people by offering the voluntary separation package, this approach allowed more individuals to make their own choices and minimized the number who had to leave involuntarily.

The human resources redeployment and staffing project team. To effectively design and implement a plan that would be responsive to these complex human resources issues, a transition team was created within the Human Resources department. This team was led by the Human Resources representative on the AT&T Project Team to ensure alignment with the overall corporate direction. Several subteams were created to capitalize on the lessons learned from previous restructuring efforts regarding the type of support required throughout the transition. The subteams were as follows:

- *People Movement Team*—The subteam that designed the selection process and force management programs and established all policies and practices that guided any job transitions of employees throughout the restructuring.
- *Stakeholder Engagement Team*—The subteam that designed support tools for leaders to help them to manage employees effectively throughout the restructuring. Written guides for leaders, for example, were distributed to middle and senior managers in support

functions on a monthly basis to encourage face-to-face discussions with their teams. These guides contained information about the restructuring, resources available to help individuals affected by downsizing, etc. This team also developed and administered a bi-weekly survey to assess employees' reactions to the restructuring. The most critical issues raised by the survey results were then addressed in shaping the leaders' guides.

- *Deployment Control Center Team*—This control center was established to clarify company policies and practices so they could be applied consistently and quickly across the operating units. The members of this team consisted of individuals who were assigned to the control center full-time and a hub of staffing representatives from each of the operating units who had 24-hr telephone access to the center. They provided a hot line service so questions could be addressed in real time, monitored and tracked the movement of people throughout the restructuring (e.g., provided weekly reports), and served as a focal point for addressing and resolving problems. This communication was especially important in the light of the aggressive time frames driving the transition. The team rapidly uncovered the need for a new policy, the need to change an existing one, or a request for an exception based on a critical business need. This team enabled us to create and implement human resources policies quickly and consistently across the business.
- *Communication Team*—This team, working with the corporate Public Relations team, provided information to employees on the restructuring, including highlights of major policy issues. A key challenge in the area of employee communication was to determine how best to direct messages to particular audiences. For example, the roundtable selection process was designed primarily for the support department employees, whereas the voluntary separation package was targeted toward a larger group of employees across the company. The Communication Team needed to determine who should know what and by when to ensure that the restructuring deadlines could be achieved, while avoiding disruptions of workers who were responsible for meeting critical customer commitments. Public Relations was also responsible for communicating important messages to other key stakeholders such as the financial community and customers.

Time line for implementing the People Plan. A time line for the People Plan was established, to align activities with the overall restructuring time lines. Exhibit 2 highlights the major milestones. In order to meet the restructuring deadlines, we had to offer the voluntary separation package at the same time we were implementing the selection process. This posed some unique challenges, such as not knowing until the end of December how many people would take the voluntary separation offer. This will be discussed in more detail in the next section. By mid-January, we had to account for every person (i.e., specific assignments had to be known, as

Exhibit 2. People Plan Time Line

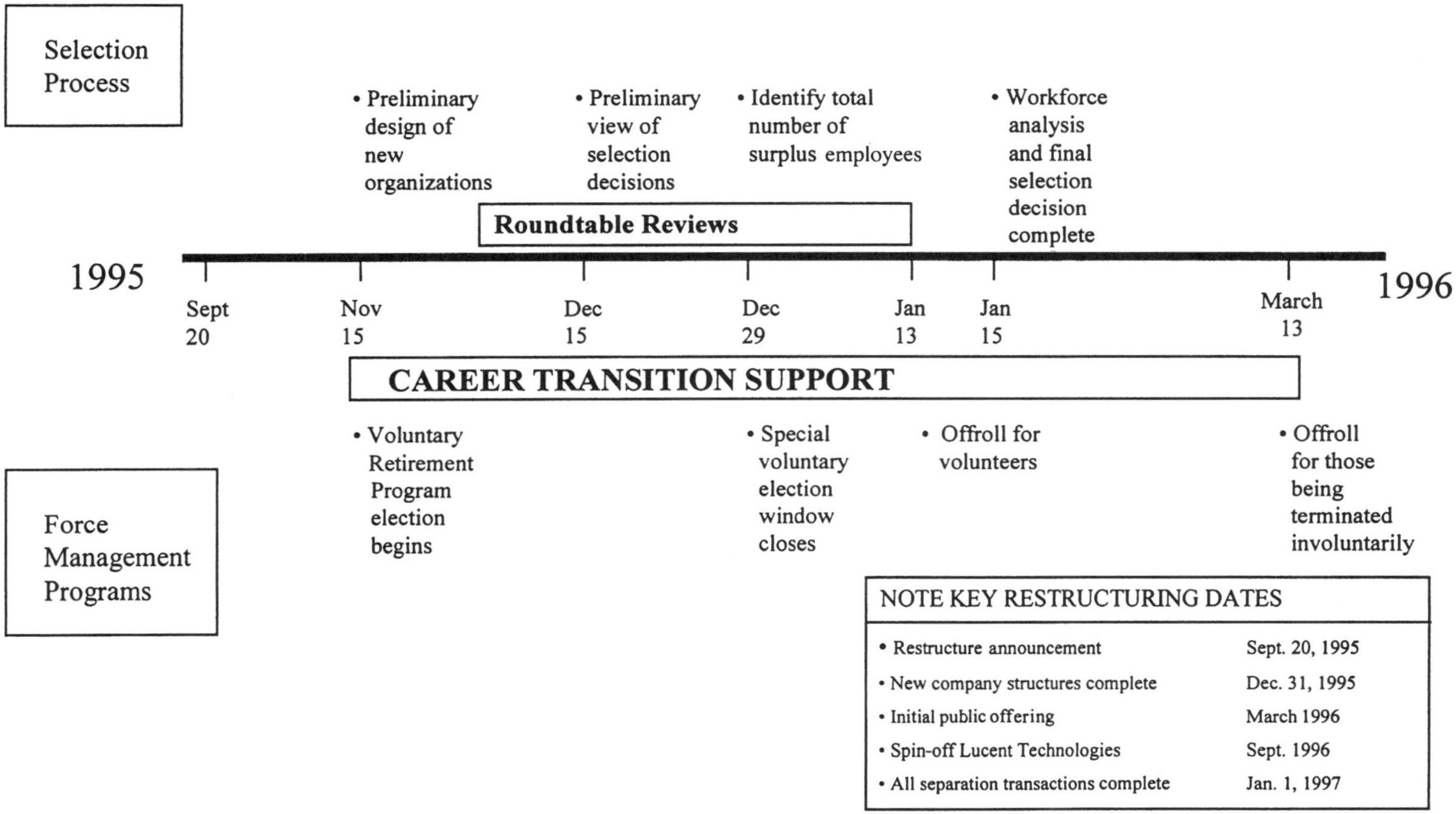

well as the number of positions that would be declared surplus) so that the financial community would have sufficient time to prepare for the Initial Public Offering of stock.

Retention of talent. An important part of the planning process involved making sure the company retained critical talent both during the restructuring and several years beyond. Because of the uncertainty about the future during a transition, people are more likely to seriously consider external offers. Careful consideration was given to identifying those individuals with critical and unique skills or experience, as well as those who were potential successors to key positions. Special incentives were established to retain these people and, most important, encourage them to improve the performance of the new companies.

Phase II—Execution

The major activities during the execution phase involved implementing the selection process, the force management programs, and other transition support initiatives.

Selection process. The goal of the selection process was to enable the rapid assessment of the skills of about 16,000 employees in support positions, allowing us to determine which employees could be targeted for specific job assignments and which employees' jobs would be at risk. Three objectives were established in designing this process: (a) development of a methodology that was legally defensible, (b) establishment of a process in which people had a fair chance to compete for positions, and (c) creation of the capacity to move people into available jobs while simultaneously downsizing the workforce.

The roundtable methodology used in the selection process and described below pertained only to management employees. Although a fairly large number of employees in bargained-for positions were affected by the restructuring, the job transitions of these individuals were guided by the 1994 labor agreement. A team of labor relations experts oversaw this process and monitored the transition of employees to ensure that it complied with the company's labor contracts.

Also, very few employees transferred to NCR from AT&T or Lucent Technologies. NCR had already gone through a downsizing process that had affected support employees. Therefore, NCR did not participate in the roundtable process, although many of their staffing policies and support programs were the same as those of the other two companies.

Roundtable structure. A series of roundtable reviews within each support department (e.g., Public Relations, Human Resources, Finance) was designed to select people to support the new AT&T and Lucent Technologies. Discrete roundtables for the different management levels and subfunctions were established to ensure that the number of people being discussed at any given roundtable was manageable. The total number of roundtables within each function depended on the number of subfunctions that were identified (e.g., Human Resources subfunctions included compensation, staffing, leadership development, and organizational effectiveness; Public Relations subfunctions included media relations and employee communications; Finance subfunctions included comptrollers and taxes). Each department was responsible for identifying all appropriate subfunctions.

Individuals were represented at the roundtable by their current supervisors or others knowledgeable about their skills and experience. The number of supervisors at a given roundtable ranged from 3 to 25, and the number of people reviewed ranged from 3 to well over 100. Roundtable meetings were led by facilitators who had attended a 1-day facilitation training workshop.

PREROUNDTABLE ACTIVITIES. Several activities were completed prior to conducting a roundtable. First, the size of the new organizations and the specific skills required were determined. Second, structured resumes were completed by employees, indicating both the particular subfunction position for which they wanted to be considered and their related skills and experience. Although gathering this information was time-consuming, it gave employees the opportunity to state their skills and experience (either within or outside the company) that were relevant to the requirements of the new positions. It was also a way to involve people in the transition process. In addition, supervisors rated each individual on a set of generic skills determined by previous research to be important to all management positions and the skills unique to a subfunction. Exhibit 3

Exhibit 3.   Information Gathered for the Roundtable

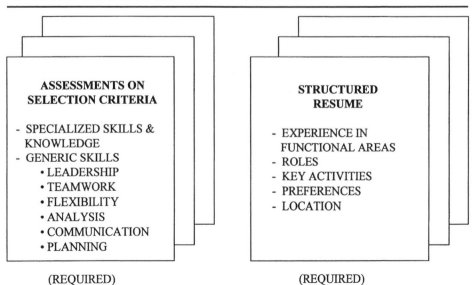

ASSESSMENTS ON
SELECTION CRITERIA

- SPECIALIZED SKILLS &
  KNOWLEDGE
- GENERIC SKILLS
  • LEADERSHIP
  • TEAMWORK
  • FLEXIBILITY
  • ANALYSIS
  • COMMUNICATION
  • PLANNING

(REQUIRED)

STRUCTURED
RESUME

- EXPERIENCE IN
  FUNCTIONAL AREAS
- ROLES
- KEY ACTIVITIES
- PREFERENCES
- LOCATION

(REQUIRED)

shows templates of the information gathered on each person prior to the roundtable.

ROUNDTABLE SESSION. There was a structured format for each roundtable. Attendees included a team leader, a facilitator, supervisors of the individuals being discussed, and a person from each new company who could describe the new organization designs. First, the new organization designs were presented, so people understood the skill requirements of the positions. Next, people were carefully matched to positions based on their skills and experience and the need to distribute the talent equitably across the new companies. If, for example, only two people had a specific background in benefits, then one was assigned to Lucent and one to AT&T. If the new job required a person to have compensation experience in mergers and acquisitions and international business and the two compensation specialists competing for the job were equally strong, the one with the skills and experience most relevant to the new job was selected. In some cases, it was determined that a person did not possess the required skills for any available position, and that was duly noted.

Three scenarios were possible within each roundtable: (a) There were more jobs than people, in which case vacancies existed after people were matched to jobs; (b) an equal number of people and jobs existed; and (c) there were more people than jobs. In the first two scenarios, the roundtables focused exclusively on placing the right people in the right jobs and making sure the talent was fairly distributed. There were occasions when vacancies remained and current employees were designated as at risk, rather than being transferred into these positions. In those situations, the team agreed that the individuals being placed at risk did not have the skills appropriate for the positions. In the third scenario, it was necessary to place some people in jobs and to declare others at risk. While team consensus was generally used to govern decision making, the team leader was empowered to resolve conflicts, if necessary.

Because the roundtable process and the voluntary separation option were happening concurrently, the roundtables had to develop an alternate list of people who could serve as a backup if the individual originally slotted for the position decided to leave the company. As individuals volunteered to take the early separation package, alternates were assigned to open positions. At the end of each roundtable, the team of supervisors agreed on what they would communicate to others about the results of the meeting. Facilitators were responsible for taking notes and compiling minutes as a record of decisions made during the session.

POSTROUNDTABLE ACTIVITIES. At the end of each roundtable, people whose qualifications for new jobs had been assessed were told the results of the job placements by their supervisors. This relieved some anxiety for employees and allowed those who were at risk to begin participating in the transition support programs that were available to them. Roundtable representatives also explained that no decision would be final until the middle of January, because a workforce analysis was required to ensure equitable distribution of talent and overall adequacy of the workforce plan in meeting AT&T business imperatives. As some individuals decided to take the early voluntary separation package, others on the alternate lists could be considered for resulting vacancies if their skills were consistent with the needs of the jobs being discussed.

Overall, 939 roundtables were conducted, and 15,342 employees' qualifications were discussed. At the conclusion of this process, 49% of the employees had been assigned to jobs at AT&T, 35% had been assigned to jobs at Lucent Technologies, and 7% were left unassigned. The balance were people who had taken the voluntary package.

Force management programs and career transition support. The voluntary separation program and the transition support initiatives were being implemented at the same time that the roundtables were being conducted. As mentioned above, AT&T leaders assumed that fewer internal placement opportunities would be available than were available after earlier restructurings. The focus was to help people find jobs outside of the company. Support programs were intended to achieve the following:

- Create innovative workforce plans to transition people outside the company compassionately but swiftly
- Minimize organizational immobility
- Prepare incumbents for the shock of change and the realization that AT&T's business would never be the same again
- Encourage as many people as possible to leave voluntarily before moving to a phase of involuntary separation
- Focus at-risk employees on external opportunities

As shown in Exhibit 2, the voluntary termination phase began on November 15 and ended on December 29. The involuntary termination phase began on January 15 and ended with employees' jobs being terminated by March 15. Some who took the voluntary offer were asked to stay on for several additional months to complete assignments related to short-term business needs. The transition support provided to employees is summarized in Exhibit 4.

Compared with past force management programs, several features were unique to this restructuring, including (a) doubling the duration of company-paid medical benefits; (b) introducing a bonus of up to $10,000 transition assistance for people who wanted to go back to school, start up their own businesses, or move to new jobs; (c) extending resource center services to people who took the voluntary offer; and (d) establishing a special "Transition to Retirement" provision.

Another opportunity provided for employees whose jobs were involuntarily terminated was the option of applying to remain in a staffing database for up to 6 months after employment termination. Individuals in this database could compete for job openings identified by operating units for up to 6 months from their off-payroll date.

Career Transition support for employees was quickly up and running. For example, in December the company provided financial workshops to individuals who were trying to decide whether to take the voluntary pack-

Exhibit 4. AT&T Career Transition Support

Lump sum payments, ranging from 5 to 35 weeks of salary based on age and years with the company

An additional 20% signing/release bonus

Up to 1 year of company-paid benefits

A Special Transition to Retirement provision—a way for managers within 2 years of pension eligibility to bridge the remaining time

Preferential consideration for open AT&T positions for up to 6 months after termination

Up to $10,000 transition assistance—for up to 2 years reimbursement for education, training, relocation to take a job elsewhere, and/or for costs for an individual to start up a new business

Seven primary resource centers (Career Transition Centers) and satellite locations, which provide a broad array of career transition services to support employees who leave the firm in their external job search

---

age. In the resource centers, people had access to numerous workshops (e.g., resume preparation, career transition, self-employment, interviewing skills, career counseling with trained professionals, and the use of equipment such as personal computers and fax machines). The resource centers also provided access to job leads. AT&T published an 800 number so other companies could call with job openings, which were then posted at the resource centers. On any given day, the system would have up to 10,000 job leads. Between January and August 1996, over 6,000 people had registered in one of the seven resource centers located across the United States.

Employee surveys. This restructuring was such a challenge because so many activities and programs were implemented simultaneously. Policies, decisions, and process changes had to be made quickly. Employee surveys were one important source of information during this period. They became an important barometer for determining what was working and highlighting additional support requirements. Several themes emerged during the course of the transition:

- Early on, employees were confused and apprehensive about the roundtable process and how it would work. The redevelopment and staffing team made greater efforts to help people understand what would happen during a roundtable review and how information would be used. The result over time was an increased understanding of the process.
- People reported not feeling as if they had input into decisions about the transition. Given the speed with which decisions were being made, these results were not surprising. The company responded by increasing efforts to help people understand the rationale for various decisions.
- Minorities expressed concern about the three companies' continued

commitment to diversity during the transition. The Redeployment and Staffing Team addressed this by keeping leaders within various minority organizations informed about the progress of various initiatives and decisions. Thus the leaders could be more responsive to questions they were getting from their constituents. Senior leaders also continued to reinforce the company's commitment to diversity as a business imperative.

- Throughout the restructuring, survey results indicated that people were concerned about the future of the new companies and their ability to retain talent. This loss of confidence was clearly triggered by the uncertainty about the future. Initiatives designed to create excitement and engage "survivors'" interest in the future of the new companies were therefore identified as important to our success.

- Finally, the need for our leaders to communicate more frequently to their subordinates surfaced repeatedly as a key issue. Not surprisingly, for example, a strong connection was found between frequency of leadership communication and perception of equity in the selection process and whether AT&T's values and principles were being upheld. Also, although people were appreciative of the written materials they received, these were no substitute for visible, frequent, face-to-face communication by the senior leaders.

The career transition support services were very comprehensive. AT&T has a long history of providing the necessary tools and programs to help people find assignments both within and outside the company. Although the decision to downsize is never easy, the impact on individuals can be minimized by making support services available and encouraging employees to take advantage of them.

Phase III—Revitalization

A critical component of any restructuring is the instilling of a sense of confidence, commitment, and excitement among those individuals who remain with the company. This is often difficult when the restructuring involves people losing their jobs, the severing of long-standing work relationships, and the changing nature of the employment contract.

Both Lucent Technologies and NCR designed initiatives to revitalize their workforces and provide clarity about the future. The remainder of this section will focus on examples of revitalization initiatives in the new AT&T that were occurring during the transition.

During the fall of 1995, a team of senior leaders worked almost full-time crafting AT&T's strategic direction and recommending a new organization structure designed to support the execution of the strategy. A new governance process was created to guide how the company would operate and make decisions. The new strategy and structure were rolled out in January 1996.

To engage employees and create a sense of excitement, each senior leader was assigned to visit a few field operations over a period of several months. The visits were primarily with the frontline employees (e.g., customer service, sales) who spend a significant amount of time communicating with AT&T's customers. The purpose of the visits was for leaders to listen to ideas, share the new organization's strategy, and solicit employee input on barriers to executing the strategy. Another important objective was to shift the focus from cost cutting to focusing on ways to grow the business. The feedback from people in the field was extremely positive; senior leaders listened to various problems and gave people an opportunity to talk about ways to improve the business. Many of the issues were subsequently addressed at senior leadership team meetings.

A strategy forum was designed for the company's executives and officers (top 700 leaders). This 2-day session focused on helping people better understand the strategic direction of the business and how best to implement the strategy. Discussions also focused on the new operating environment (i.e., culture and leadership) that was necessary to succeed in the marketplace. Each leader received a package of support material to distribute to their teams within a certain period of time after the forum. Leaders also provided feedback to the Chief Operating Officer about the approach they used to distribute the information and engage their team.

In September 1996, the launch of the new AT&T began. This involved engaging employees, customers, and investors by introducing new products and services, showcasing existing ones, and creating excitement about the new direction of the business.

Other critical initiatives required to move the business forward were identified. Results of the following work effort will help shape the business of the future.

- *Operating Environment.* Top leaders were involved in identifying skills and culture change requirements necessary for business success and ways to assess their own capabilities in these areas.
- *New Employment Relationship.* Reexamining the new employment contract between individuals and the company becomes particularly important in the context of new and emerging workplace models (i.e., virtual offices, flexible work arrangements, contingent workers, "boundaryless" organizations). At the same time that companies are redefining relationships and expectations among themselves and their employees, they are also challenged with finding ways to retain intellectual capital. As the number of knowledge workers increases, retaining intellectual capital will clearly be a source of competitive advantage. This suggests that despite this new contract, companies will still have to find ways of encouraging employee commitment as relationships are redefined.
- *Alignment of Human Resources Programs.* Another important initiative is the reexamination of various human resources programs and activities (e.g., compensation, recognition, performance management, hiring and staffing, leadership development, training and

education) to align them with the new strategic direction of the business, reengineer work processes, and leverage technology to operate more efficiently and effectively.

- *Workforce Planning Process.* The companies will put a robust people planning process in place to determine the staffing needs (number of people and skill requirements) of the various operating units over the next several years. This includes looking at ways to redeploy talent and hire contingent workers to handle peak workloads.

- *Enhancing Worker Security.* The examination of innovative ways to address worker security (e.g., pension portability; collaborating with other companies to increase the visibility of job opportunities and accelerating the placement of workers affected by downsizing) is also imperative.

Much of this work is ongoing and focused on (a) aligning processes with the business direction, (b) being nimble and flexible to shift as the needs of the business change, and (c) creating a climate in which people can add value to the business and feel valued by the companies.

Up to this point, the focus of this chapter has been on describing the approach we used to address the September 20, 1995, restructuring of AT&T. We recognize that every corporate restructuring is unique. Most important, however, any approach used must support the business objectives and take into account the external and internal environments.

In the remaining sections of this chapter, we will shift from being descriptive to being reflective. By capturing our collective experiences across a variety of restructurings, we will (a) show how organizational change models can help highlight relevant issues and questions and (b) offer lessons learned.

Reflections and Observations

Relevance of Organization Change Models

Models of organization change are sometimes regarded as too academic to have "real-world" applications. We found them relevant, however, not only for understanding the changes taking place at AT&T but also for anticipating the issues that would loom as important in developing interventions to manage the transition. In particular, open systems models (Burke & Litwin, 1992; Katz & Kahn, 1978), which depict how factors in the external environment affect organization performance and how the performance of organizations can in turn influence their environment (e.g., markets, customers, stakeholders), had particular relevance because the AT&T restructuring was prompted largely by dramatic changes in the marketplace. Federal legislation permitting AT&T to enter local telephone markets at the same time the local operating companies were preparing to compete for long-distance service required a more sharply focused business strategy. Competitors' (including the local operating companies) increasing reluctance to buy telecommunications products from the same company with which they were competing for long-distance services imposed barriers to the successful performance of AT&T's equipment business.

AT&T's response to these external forces required changes in major elements of the organization. One framework for understanding these elements is described by Burke and Litwin (1992), who refer to *transformational elements*, namely mission/strategy, leadership, and culture, which they suggest most dramatically influence an organization's performance. We have already described how AT&T developed a new business strategy in response to external forces. Changes in leadership behaviors were also required to provide direction for the new business and to manage the transition during restructuring. Leaders were asked to serve as role models for the organization and to continue to monitor and respond to the external forces having the potential to further influence AT&T's performance. AT&T's culture, especially its history in managing other restructurings, influenced significantly the guidelines, principles, and support systems established for employees. The company frequently judged elements of the transition plan in the light of what had been provided in other restructurings, that is, "how things had been done around here in the past." Strategy, leadership, and culture, of course, were not the only organizational elements requiring change. The Burke–Litwin model also includes other elements, such as structure, systems, management practices, climate, individual skills, and motivation, which are also important in understanding and simulating change and were essential for AT&T to address during the transition. A full description of the model and its application to the AT&T restructuring is beyond the scope of this chapter. Furthermore, there are other models which may be equally relevant, for example, the Nadler–Tushman (1977) model, which emphasizes the need for congruence or alignment among organizational elements. Nevertheless, we do believe that the AT&T experience supports the usefulness of models as a way for practitioners to identify those elements that must be understood if positive change is going to occur. Models can serve as diagnostic frameworks for determining the requirements for change, posing such questions as

- What are the external forces in the environment which require us to change, and what impact will our actions have on our markets?
- How widely understood and accepted is the organization's strategy?
- How well equipped are leaders to manage change?
- In what ways must the culture change? How difficult will these changes be?
- To what extent is the organizational structure well understood and consistent with the needs of the business?

- Are the right systems (e.g., management, information, compensation) in place to support employees?
- Do the skills and competencies of the organization match current and future needs of the business?

Experienced practitioners would probably agree that the answers to such questions are vital not only to understanding the condition of an organization but also to identifying the actions required to bring about change.

Lessons Learned From the Restructuring

Although AT&T continues to undergo significant changes in connection with restructuring, reflection on all that has taken place since September 20, 1995, has led us to several observations. We refer to these as "lessons learned." Some of them are deceptively simple and could be found in nearly all "recipes" for managing major organizational change. Others, however, are less common, although they reflect many of the changes that are occurring in large corporations everywhere and the workplace in general. In describing our lessons learned, we hope to help practitioners anticipate challenges in managing their own organizational changes.

Investment in planning. Few would argue with the value of planning. In the case of AT&T, the up-front investment paid special dividends. Despite the aggressive time frames established for the restructuring, leaders of the business, including those in Human Resources, established goals and objectives for the restructuring that guided the actions taken throughout the trivestiture. Key deadlines were established to monitor progress against the goals and adjust accordingly. Equally important was the establishment of principles. All significant decisions and actions were judged against these principles to ensure consistency with intentions and integrity of the process.

Transition teams. Establishing a dedicated group of leaders to guide the transition was one of the first actions taken after the restructuring was announced. The capacity of these individuals to work with great intensity over long periods of time and achieve high levels of performance was remarkable. Although the term *high-performing team* is overused, in this instance, it describes these transition teams. Many of the characteristics associated with high-performing teams (e.g., complementary skills, mutual accountability, meaningful work, clarity of purpose, ability to be decisive) were evident on the transition teams. While the establishment and composition of transition teams were clearly important, their success raised a troubling question for us: Why can't this same level of performance be stimulated in "noncrisis" situations? Part of the AT&T culture has been to describe itself as capable of responding to any and all crises, whether it is a network failure or the divestiture of a major business. An important challenge that many companies face is maintaining high performance standards in the absence of a crisis.

Open communication. Communication issues were prominent throughout the restructuring. Although many of these lessons learned may seem obvious, they are worth mentioning because they often get lost in the turmoil of change:

1. Candor. Too often mistakes are made by ill-conceived efforts to protect employees from knowing what is happening. We found that candor in communication worked better than "whitewashing" or silence.
2. Repetition. Important messages need to be repeated time and time again. Employee anxieties interfere with understanding. Problems occur when assumptions are made about what people hear and understand.
3. Multiple methods. Some people are comfortable receiving information through memos or E-mail, whereas others prefer town meetings. Some read newsletters, and others do not. We found that people's preferences for receiving information required that multiple methods be used. At the same time, our experience suggests that there is no substitute for face-to-face communication between leaders and employees.
4. Consistency. Alignment of messages across organizations, departments, and levels had two positive outcomes. First, it provided clarity, and second, it increased employee confidence in the alignment of AT&T leadership. Problems occurred when people in one part of the organization received a different message from those in another. This led to confusion and feelings of unfair treatment.
5. Frequency. An AT&T leader reflecting on an earlier AT&T restructing put it best: "The amount of communication should be directly proportional to the magnitude of change or uncertainty people are experiencing, not the amount of information available to share."

Handling management versus occupational differences. Real differences exist between management and nonexempt employees at AT&T with respect to the types of support that can be provided to each group. Constraints on what can be done for occupational employees relate to labor laws and contractual obligations with the unions. Nevertheless, we found that managers were not always fully informed about the union contract and how it influenced what would happen to occupational employees throughout the transition. This led, in some cases, to confusion about how to support occupational employees. Consequently, many of these employees' questions and concerns were not addressed in a timely manner. The lesson learned here was that supervisors should provide employees with timely and accurate information. Furthermore, the needs of occupational employees must be handled with the same degree of intensity as the other groups of employees, regardless of the contractual constraints.

Aggressive time frames. We recognized that there were both advantages and disadvantages to the aggressive time frames established for the transition. The advantages included accelerated decision making, establishment of a sense of urgency, and limiting the time of uncertainty for employees. On the other hand, the compressed time frames limited the amount of time available to engage employees in the process. On balance, however, sacrificing some precision to achieve goals and objectives and to meet deadlines was viewed as important to success.

Methods for downsizing. The roundtable process was extremely labor-intensive. It provided an excellent opportunity for employees' qualifications to be reviewed in a consistent manner and for leaders to determine the best way to distribute talent equitably. If, for example, the skill sets remain unchanged in the downsizing scenario, it is appropriate to use existing performance appraisals and band employees by performance categories. On the other hand, if different skills are required, then assessments on skills needed in the future will need to be gathered. In each case, the selection methodology should be legally defensible and based on the business objectives. An additional consideration is the extent to which the company can afford to disrupt the workforce by using a laborious selection process.

Corporate responsibility. AT&T's announcement of its intention to eliminate 40,000 jobs created an avalanche of media attention. It drew attention to the issue of job security in a rapidly changing environment and added fuel to the rising public debate about stagnation and inequality in wages, the growing income gap, and business downsizing. With 1996 being an election year, AT&T's downsizing also became a lightning rod for politicians to gain attention and support.

Because of the nature of competition, many business leaders believe that downsizing is inevitable but that corporations have a responsibility to help employees cope with the personal impact of change. AT&T has been committed strongly to helping individuals affected by downsizing make the transition to new jobs within or outside the company. The company has also embraced the concept of lifelong learning and spends $1 billion a year on employee education. Another lesson learned, however, was that a company may have difficulty solving the problems associated with a corporate restructuring on its own. Therefore, AT&T is taking the lead in forming partnerships with other businesses and finding creative ways to address the issue of worker security (e.g., creating a national job bank, exchanging talent).

Transition checklist. Our lessons during the AT&T restructuring have led us to create a checklist of actions and activities that should be taken by organizations facing similar challenges. The list below is not intended to be inclusive but suggestive of issues that must be addressed during organization transitions. It is organized according to the three phases of AT&T's transition.

PLANNING

- Clearly define goals, objectives, and deadlines and the methods for tracking them.
- Ensure that senior leadership is clear about the purposes for change, actively supports them, and is focused on planning for the future (i.e., creating new strategies, structures, cultures, skill/experience requirements, and operating environments).
- Establish dedicated teams with clear roles and responsibilities that are accountable for managing all aspects of the transition and, when necessary, closing down operations.
- Create a governance structure for making timely decisions and agree on principles to guide decision making.
- Identify key stakeholders and anticipate their needs (i.e., employees affected by the transition, senior leaders, supervisors, investors, and customers).
- Establish incentives for retaining critical talent.
- Create delivery channels for getting information and support materials to employees, especially supervisors.

EXECUTION

- Monitor and address the various emotions employees experience during times of change and be especially sensitive to signs of stress and burnout.
- Engage employees in communication to determine their understanding and acceptance of the changes taking place and the methods for managing the transition.
- Establish a method for responding quickly and clearly to issues as they arise, including adherence to principles.
- Communicate frequently using multiple channels (e.g., written, face-to-face, E-mail).
- Ensure visibility of senior leadership.
- Provide career transition support for people whose jobs are being eliminated.
- Ensure that critical customer and financial commitments are being met throughout the transition.

REVITALIZATION

- Avoid ignoring past accomplishments and qualities, but emphasize why changes are required for future success.
- Ensure that employees understand the new business direction, opportunities for growth, and how they can contribute to these.
- Clarify requirements for change, including new skills and competencies, culture changes, and leadership behaviors.
- Celebrate and recognize important accomplishments.
- Drive process improvements so that the smaller, downsized work-

force does not end up doing the same amount of work as the pre-downsizing workforce had done.

- Communicate the new employment contract between employees and the company (i.e., clarify mutual expectations).
- Align goals throughout the organization and clarify roles and responsibilities.
- Realign human resources processes and programs (e.g., compensation, workforce planning, education and training, performance management, leadership development) with the new business direction.

The challenges that AT&T confronted were not unlike those other companies face as dramatic changes continue to occur in the workplace. These changes have been well documented. Handy (1989) describes the organization of the future as a shamrock consisting of three parts: (a) core managers, technicians, and professionals, (b) contract specialists, and (c) a contingent workforce whose size will vary according to an organization's needs. This new organization will require a more flexible workforce in which individuals possess a portfolio of skills enabling them to move easily from assignment to assignment and where a premium is placed on lifelong learning (Mirvis & Hall, 1996). With these changes in the workplace comes a shift in the social contract between employers and employees. Altman and Post (1996) described three significant changes involving a shift from long-term company commitment to employment based on performance; from corporate responsibility for career development to employee responsibility for his or her career; and from job security to employability whereby corporations take responsibility for enhancing employees' abilities to get jobs elsewhere, if necessary.

Our experience at AT&T is a vivid example of these forces at work. The magnitude of the restructuring, the need to reduce the workforce across the business, and the utilization of skill-based assessments to determine job suitability sent a message to AT&T employees that their employment contract had changed. While changes in the contract had been evolving for the past decade, the trivestiture was the most dramatic confirmation yet that AT&T's relationship with its employees had been irrevocably altered. The challenge now for AT&T is to find more and better ways to enhance its workers' employability and provide opportunities for workers to develop skills that are transportable to other companies in the event that workforce dislocations occur in the future. The goal is to find ways of enhancing career self-reliance to reduce employee vulnerability during times of significant change.

References

Altman, B. W., & Post, J. E. (1996). Beyond the "social contract": An analysis of the executive view at twenty-five large companies. In D. T. Hall & Associates (Eds.), *The career is dead, long live the career: A relational approach to careers* (pp. 46–71). San Francisco: Jossey-Bass.

Burke, W. W., & Litwin, G. H. (1992). A causal model of organizational performance and change. *Journal of Management, 18,* 523–545.

Handy, C. (1989). *The age of unreason.* Boston: The Harvard Business School Press.

Katz, D., & Kahn, R. L. (1978). *The social psychology of organizations* (2nd ed.). New York: Wiley.

Mirvis, P. H., & Hall, D. T. (1996). New organizational forms and the new career. In D. T. Hall & Associates (Eds.), *The career is dead, long live the career: A relational approach to careers* (pp. 72–101). San Francisco: Jossey-Bass.

Nadler, D. A., & Tushman, M. L. (1977). A diagnostic model for organization behavior. In J. R. Hackman, E. E. Lawler, & L. W. Porter (Eds.), *Perspectives on behavior in organizations* (pp. 85–100). New York: McGraw-Hill.

5

Creating a High-Performance Work Culture at Chaparral Steel

John Gordon

Chaparral Steel Company, located in Midlothian, TX, owns and operates a technologically advanced steel mill, which produces bar and structural steel products by recycling scrap steel. The plant commenced operations in 1975 and more than doubled its capacity in 1982. In 1992, a large beam mill was completed, which further expanded Chaparral's capacity and product range. The company now has two electric arc furnaces with continuous casters, a bar mill, a structural mill, and a large beam mill, which enable it to produce a broader array of steel products than traditional minimills. Chaparral follows a market mill concept, which entails the production of a wide variety of products ranging from reinforcing bar and specialty products to large structural beams at low cost, and is able to adapt its product mix to changing market conditions or customer requirements.

Chaparral's steel products include beams, reinforcing bars, special bar-quality rounds, channels, and merchant-quality rounds. These products are sold principally to the construction industry and to the railroad, defense, automotive, mobile home, and energy industries. Chaparral's principal customers are steel service centers, steel fabricators, cold finishers, forgers, and original equipment manufacturers. The Company distributes its products primarily to markets in North America and, under certain market conditions, in Europe and Asia. Chaparral is listed on the New York Stock Exchange and is 81% owned by Texas Industries, Inc.

Although marketing and technological strategy appear to have played a major role in the success of Chaparral Steel, the key factor from management's perspective has been the role of their human resource strategy. Starting with the concept of participative management derived primarily from the work of Douglas McGregor, President Gordon Forward has developed an operating culture based on trust and the development of the individual. Captured in large part in the dictate "push decision making to the lowest competent level and make the lowest level competent," the organization embodies empowerment and training at all levels. Individuals and teams are encouraged to experiment on the floor and make mistakes—as long as they don't repeat the same mistakes. Sabbaticals to visit competitors, attend conferences, or take courses are the norm. All employees are part of the sales force and regularly visit customers, to understand firsthand in what applications their products are used and thus what the key concerns of the customer are, in terms of quality, performance, and delivery. Everyone is part of a work-focused team as well as a cross-functional task team. Profit sharing and employee ownership are a significant part of the compensation package. When asked about the relative importance of technology versus people, Gordon Forward states categorically that "good people can make any technology work but the reverse is not necessarily true." There are valuable lessons to be learned from the story of Chaparral because of its inseparable and synergistic coalition of technological process and management philosophy.

Background

Chaparral Steel was founded in 1973 as a joint venture between Texas Industries of Dallas and CoSteel International of Toronto, Ontario, Canada. To appreciate the existing technological capabilities of Chaparral as well as its organizational culture, it is useful to understand the history of CoSteel International and its founder, Jerry Heffernan.

The minimill process, which forms the basis of Chaparral's technology, owes much of its development to Jerry Heffernan, who has been characterized by many as "father of the process." Although individual components have their origin with steel pioneers like Bessemer, Heffernan ultimately put together the components of scrap, electric arc furnace, continuous casting, and a basic rolling mill into a total process with a competitive advantage. Born in western Canada, where he grew up on a farm in the interior of British Columbia, Heffernan studied metallurgy at the University of Toronto, graduating as gold medalist in 1943. Shortly after graduation, he found himself in charge of a platoon of soldiers in Europe in World War II, assigned the task of constructing a bridge across a river. With no experience in the science or art of bridge building, Heffernan intuitively turned to his platoon members and solicited their ideas and experience in bridge building. This resulted in the successful execution of their task and marked the beginning of Heffernan's addiction to participative management.

At the end of the war, he returned to the West Coast of Canada to become a teaching and research assistant for Professor Frank Forward at the University of British Columbia in the Department of Metallurgical Engineering. Very quickly he found himself working more than full-time, as he also assisted Professor Forward in his extensive consulting practice and took courses in industrial management, including cost accounting, which he credits for much of his financial success in the steel industry. This experience led to employment as a superintendent at Westland Iron and Steel Foundry and then as general superintendent at Western Canada Steel. It was at this time that he gained his first direct exposure to electric arc steelmaking and exhibited his lifelong drive to constantly change and improve processes. Engaging a friend who was an electrical engineer, he set to work to increase the power of the furnace and thus increase its output. By 1954, he was anxious to start a new steel plant on the West Coast. He found no takers within his existing company, however, so he set out with some local financial support to establish a "green field" plant in Edmonton, Alberta, to produce sucker rod for the burgeoning oil and gas developments in western Canada.

Premier Steel Works was established in 1954 in Edmonton as a small plant based on an electric arc furnace and traditional ingot casting, which was then rolled. About this time, Atlas Steel in Welland, Ontario, was beginning to experiment with continuous casting, which had caught Heffernan's attention a number of years earlier. By 1959, he had decided to install continuous casting at Premier and recruited one of Welland's engineers to come to Edmonton to help. By the early sixties, Premier had become a major success and had gained the interest of a number of companies worldwide. Not to be outdone by an offshore competitor, the Steel Company of Canada (Stelco) made a significant offer to buy the company, which was accepted by Heffernan and his private investor consortium.

Within 2 years, in 1964, Heffernan's group opened a new plant in Whitby, Ontario, called Lake Ontario Steel, based entirely on what had become known by then as *minimill technology*, recycling scrap steel by electric arc furnace, continuous casting, and the rolling of rebar. Three years later, they opened North Star Steel in Minneapolis-St. Paul. By 1968 they had assembled a strong group of steel engineers and decided to establish Ferrco Engineering to harness this talent to build future plants, as well as to upgrade existing plants. At the same time, Heffernan ventured into a new steelmaking technology based on the use of iron ore and natural gas to produce pellets for direct feeding into electric arc furnaces. In 1972 the investor consortium opened Sheerness Steel in Kent, England, just outside London, and quickly made inroads into the construction industry in London, to the dismay of the British Steel Corporation.

The Founding of Chaparral

CoSteel was established in 1970 to coordinate the activities of the growing number of companies that were built around minimill technology and employed the unique Heffernan style of management.

In the early 1970s, CoSteel and Ferrco became aware of the growing market for construction materials in the south-central United States, fueled in part by the oil and gas boom, as well as the migration of population to the region. Sheerness was past the planning stage, and the investor consortium was once again in search of a new challenge. As it turned out, Texas Industries in Dallas was also aware of this market through its direct involvement in construction; steel had to be imported from other parts of the country to support this growth, so the company was looking at ways to enter the industry. A friend in a New York financial institution put Jerry Heffernan in touch with Ralph Rogers of Texas Industries, and that became the beginning of a joint venture between the two companies.

It was clear to CoSteel that the south-central region of four core states—Texas, Oklahoma, Louisiana, and Arkansas—represented a growing market that was poorly served locally. In addition, the construction boom meant a ready market for reinforcing bar, which was the bread and butter at the time for minimills. The work ethic of the population and an essentially nonunion environment combined naturally in establishing a high-performance culture and a partnership with the workforce. The essential raw material for a minimill steel scrap was readily available. Coupling these factors with a local joint venture partner in the construction business made the location a natural, in spite of or perhaps because of the absence of a steelmaking tradition. With a joint venture partner in the cement business, CoSteel began planning in earnest in 1971, and construction of the Chaparral Steel Company of Midlothian, TX, began 2 years later. Located just outside Dallas, the original plant was completed in 1975; it was followed in 1978 by Raritan River Steel in Perth Amboy, NJ. During the 1980s, new capacity and products were added at all of the minimills. (North Star Steel of Minneapolis-St. Paul was sold in 1976 after protracted negotiations with joint venture partner Cargill; similarly, Chaparral was sold to Texas Industries in 1985.)

The initial configuration of the Chaparral plant consisted of an electric arc furnace and a 250-kt/y concaster together, referred to as the *melt shop*, and a rolling mill with double that capacity. Hiring and training began in 1974, and the first steel was poured in 1975. In 2 years' time, the company was making money and by 1979 had a workforce of 450 employees. The initial technology and capital requirements were modest, and with moderate additional investment, Chaparral was able to make incremental improvements in capacity and operating procedures, which led to a doubling of rated capacity. The geographic area served was expanded to 10 states and the product line extended to higher margin products. The plant's productivity began to attract attention throughout the industry.

Two of the key aspects of the company were its management philosophy and its human resource practices. These derived originally from Jerry Heffernan, who has a natural capability to identify and attract the right people. His vision and leadership greatly influenced the development of minimill steelmaking around the world, as well as the human resource practices found in many of the CoSteel family of companies. Although he is no longer directly associated with CoSteel, he remains on the board of Chaparral Steel and is actively involved in a number of new and growing technology-based companies, including National Rubber of Toronto, which is engaged in the recycling of tires.

Frank Forward had a major influence on Heffernan early in his career, and Heffernan turned out to have the same effect on Frank's son. Gordon Forward graduated from the University of British Columbia in metallurgy in the early 1960s and achieved a doctorate at Massachusetts Institute of Technology, ultimately ending up as a senior research scientist at Stelco. After 6 months at Stelco, Gordon realized that research and development was far removed from operations and that many of the ideas generated in the laboratories in Burlington would never see the light of day. To his great relief, Jerry Heffernan emerged on the scene and offered him a job as melt shop superintendent at Lake Ontario Steel in Whitby. After a few years in an office located 100 feet from an electric arc furnace, Gordon Forward was ready for the challenge of starting a new minimill deep in the heart of Texas.

Essentially based on participative management, practices at Chaparral under Forward's leadership were to encourage employees to experiment and learn from their mistakes. Incentives were based on profit, and business and competitive information was widely shared throughout the organization. Management levels were limited to four; formal lines of communication were nonexistent. Teams were related both to work centers, such as the melt shop, and to special projects, such as the design of a company-wide information system. Formal training was reinforced by multiskilling and a salary policy geared to skill level rather than seniority. The basic philosophy was commitment to the customer, with all employees expected to be part of the sales force. The culture was not only one of "can do" and pressure for constant improvement but also one of having fun. The culture functioned by the credo, "Push decision making to the lowest competent level and make the lowest level competent."

The First Expansion

After a successful start-up and 2 years of operating at a profit, the senior management team led by Forward as vice president of operations began considering a major expansion that would double the 1979 capacity of the plant within 3 years. This would entail adding a second electric arc furnace and concaster, as well as a new rolling mill capable of rolling midsized structurals up to 18 in. This planned expansion would move Chaparral into higher end products, as well as state-of-the-art technology, which would be a move away from its traditional niche and strategy. Although the basic financial analysis of this proposed expansion was not positive, it became apparent that the business risk of not doing it was considerable, given the growing competition in the region and also in the industry. The expansion included installing the largest electric arc furnace in the world, as well as doubling the size of the workforce. These actions were likely to affect the organization's culture. Selling all the resulting product would mean expanding the geographic market to at least 20 states, but this in turn would increase the potential catchment area for the necessary scrap to feed the plant. In spite of the many apparent risks, Chaparral management decided to proceed with the expansion, which was on line by 1981; additional rolling capacity for junior beams for mobile homes was added in 1982. The market then took a downturn, and interest rates rose to unprecedented levels. This created major pressure on cash flow because of the high leverage used to finance the expansion. Fortunately, the involvement of a financial institution in the financing made it possible to refinance the debt. Chaparral thus survived a short-term cash crisis and by 1984 was again generating a positive cash flow.

Continuous Improvement

During the rest of the eighties, Chaparral made constant improvements to its facilities, technology, and workforce, and its performance reflected these efforts. In 1984, the Company was recognized by *Fortune Magazine* as one of the 10 "best managed plants in the United States," and in 1988 Gordon Forward was named CEO of the Year by Tom Peters. Following a public offering in 1985, Texas Industries (TI) bought out CoSteel's share in Chaparral, although no changes took place in the board or the management following this change in ownership. The infusion of cash from the buyout permitted CoSteel to clean up its heavily debt-ridden balance sheet and then to go public in 1986. By 1988, 20% of the shares owned by TI were converted into Chaparral shares, which, in turn, were listed on the New York Stock Exchange; each employee was given one share for each year of service. As a result, over 80% of the employees became shareholders in the company. In 1989, Chaparral became a certified supplier to Japanese industry, the only nondomestic steel supplier so recognized. By this time, the Company was shipping steel to 44 states, as well as a number of offshore countries, including Russia and South Africa.

Throughout this period, continuous improvements and experiments were conducted on the floor to improve the operational practices and processes used in the mill. Bottom tapping (as opposed to tilting the furnace to empty the contents) was developed and implemented for both furnaces, thus reducing the tap-to-tap time (time to process a batch) and increasing overall capacity. The ladles which carried molten steel between the furnaces and the concasters were modified to act as furnaces themselves; this provided greater temperature control and also further reduced the tap-to-tap time, as some of the refining could be done in the ladle. An experimental caster was built and molds developed with outside suppliers to begin testing the concept of casting beam blanks, as opposed to billets, thus beginning to approach the development of a "near net shape" casting product. The resulting dog bones would require considerably less rolling and reduce the labor cost and the energy requirements. By the end of the decade, the combined capacity of the melt shop had reached a total of 1.7 million tons per year, more than double its design capacity of 750,000 tons per year. This was achieved not by massive infusions of capital and new equipment, but rather by new and better ways of operating and experimenting on the floor. As a result, Chaparral's labor productivity was approaching "one man hour per ton of steel," making it the most efficient steel mill in the world—two or three times as efficient as northern integrated steel producers and appreciably more efficient than Japanese mills. In addition to these process improvements, the Quality Control Department developed new products based on microalloys, an achievement which was recognized by the American Metals Institute's award of a medal to Peter Wright, the Vice President of Quality Control.

The Second Expansion

Chaparral's original product line had been broadened from its early focus on basic construction products. In 1990, the company began building a large section mill which would further extend its range of higher margin products by including 24-in.-wide flange beams. This added capacity was achieved by 1991 at a cost of $100 million and put the company clearly in the structural business. Meanwhile, Nucor, its major competitor, chose to move to a flat-rolled product. By 1992, Chaparral was well positioned to respond flexibly to market changes in product needs as well as volume, thus honoring its pledge to be customer-driven and the easiest steel company with which to do business. By this time, Chaparral aspired to be on the leading edge of technology and to do this by acknowledging and nurturing the human side of enterprise. The mission to be "the international low-cost supplier of quality steel products" was enunciated. In 1992, Gordon Forward was named "Steelman of the Year" by *Iron Age* magazine.

Although Chaparral's process innovations had positioned it well, slow growth and declining prices in the steel market in the early 1990s left Chaparral with a $2 million loss for 1993. This loss occurred in spite of increased volumes and was indicative of the sales department's traditional price discounting that was necessary to deal with increased competition. As a result, Forward decided that the time had come for a major change in marketing policies, as well as for a general "wake-up call" to address high costs. At a meeting with senior management, he placed on the table the challenge of cutting $5 million from operating costs by reducing everyone's salaries unless they could come up with other ways of achieving the same savings, and then he left the room. Within a day, management conceived a plan to cut outside contracting and to do the work with existing resources, ultimately realizing savings of $8 million. At the same time, management decided to break with the traditional sales strategy of discounted prices and rebates and stick with a posted mill price plus freight for all customers. This then began to shift the emphasis within the sales department to a marketing approach to determine what other variables were the keys to winning and maintaining customers. Finally, a restructuring of the organization led to a product/market orientation instead of the traditional process-based organization.

The outcome was the creation of three business units: a recycling department responsible for shredding and the two electric arc furnaces produced the basic material for separate operations, manufacturing bar and structurals. These two operations competed with each other for the hot metal they needed, on the basis of their willingness to pay for it from the recycling department. This shifted some of the traditional sales activities to the business units, which became profit centers responsible for production and marketing. The effect was a reduction in the sales force of approximately 25% and the elimination of the position of Vice President of Marketing. The three casters were configured in a manner which made it possible to switch their outputs among the three mills, depending on the market demand and margins, with the exception of 70% of the output from the newest caster which was "hot-linked" to the large structural mill. This restructuring, which effectively created three operating vice presidents of the three profit centers, together with the cost cutting and the new pricing policy, resulted in a $12 million profit in 1994.

During this period, technical developments continued at the usual pace, resulting in significant improvements in the casting of near net shape beams, in particular the bantam beams which established Chaparral as a major player in the residential and light commercial building systems market. A related process, whereby a beam was cut and welded to produce a structural member of equivalent strength but half the weight, created the castellated beam, a potential rival to wooden joists. The bar division continued to expand its capability to supply a wider range of products in smaller lot sizes, thus approaching the concept of "mass customization." The number of engineered bars was nearly 3,000 by 1995. At the recycling end, where Chaparral had the largest shredding capacity for automobiles in the world, a major project was under way to achieve virtually 100% recovery of all inputs, hence eliminating disposal to landfill. Because of their intensive heat, the electric arc furnaces can treat all the different materials of which automobiles are built. The resulting furnace emissions were collected and separated (for use as raw materials in future products) in a joint project with Mexican collaborators. At the same time, the company purchased 3,500 acres adjacent to the original mill site in anticipation of creating Eco Park, an industrial park devoted to value-added products produced by customers of Chaparral.

Discussions were by then under way with National Steel Rolling of Singapore for the creation of a joint venture in Southeast Asia. In 1995, Chaparral was named by American Metal Market as the steel company highest in customer satisfaction and by A. D. Little as the "best of the best in manufacturing management."

Human Resource Management

Although Chaparral's most visible aspects are its technological achievements, its management credits the human resource practices and resulting culture as the keys to the company's success. Most noticeable at the outset was the emphasis placed on participation at all levels in recommending and implementing changes to improve operational performance. The credo of "pushing decision making to the lowest competent level and making the lowest level competent" may well be the underpinning of empowerment. Following from this is the dedication to training at all levels. Over 85% of employees are involved in continuing education, which is captured by the theme of "K to 90" (kindergarten to age 90) and the dedication of more space to classrooms than to offices. The notion of employees taking sabbaticals to visit and study the competition and new process developments has led to technology transfer without any resistance associated with the "not invented here" syndrome.

The practice of multiskilling, backed up by compensation geared to the number of skills mastered in the classroom and on the floor, has created a flexible workforce without any concern for job descriptions or individual accountability. Employees share the attitude that "we're all in this together." Akin to multiskilling in the technical functions, Chaparral uses cross-functional teams, both work related and special project oriented. These teams have led to a broader perspective of the whole, rather than a territorial prerogative, by providing each team member with exposure to different functional views.

This team-based mentality, of course, is further reinforced by profit-driven incentives whereby 8% of before-tax profits are distributed to all employees and over 90% of employees are shareholders. The relatively flat structure of four levels means that information sharing, including financial performance and competitor information, is the norm, occurring mainly on a face-to-face basis. The steady employment level, which is at odds with traditional steelmaking, has created an environment of stability and long-term commitment. The significant technological achievements have been accomplished without the help of a formal research and development department but rather through experimentation in operations by line personnel. Learning from mistakes is the order of the day, and it occurs in a culture in which risk and curiosity are expected. Cooperation is encouraged, and confrontation seems to have taken a back seat to openness and learning.

The values of the organization have been summarized by management as

- trust and responsibility,
- risk and curiosity,
- knowledge and expertise,
- networking and information exchange,
- humor and humility.

Gordon Forward himself likes to talk about "mentofacturing," as opposed to manufacturing, based on

- competence, not authority,
- capability, not position,
- mindedness, not manualness,
- unity of effort, not division of labor,

and Dorothy Leonard-Barton has characterized the knowledge-building activities of Chaparral as

- shared problem solving,
- the integration of new technologies and methodologies,

- constant formal and informal experimentation,
- use of expertise from the outside.

Overall, the culture developed and nurtured over two decades may be the explanation for the Company's sustainability. Much of the human resource strength of Chaparral is captured in Jeff Pfeffer's (1994) "Sixteen Practices" (see Exhibit 1), as enunciated in his book *Competitive Advantage Through People*.

The Challenges Ahead

In early June of 1996, Gordon Forward received an honorary doctor of science degree from his alma mater, University of British Columbia, and took the opportunity while in British Columbia to spend a week at his newly purchased retreat on the Sunshine Coast. As always, he used the time to reflect. He reflected less on the history of Chaparral than on future challenges.

In the last few years, Forward had been talking with his management team about spending less time at the plant and more time traveling or becoming involved in the many charitable efforts he enjoyed. He had proposed the idea of giving up his office at the plant and only visiting from time to time, when he would use the office of someone who was away on business. In Forward's own words, "This place runs better when I'm not around, so maybe I should be learning something from that."

Now that the company had achieved the capability to recycle over 80% of an automobile, its next aim was to recycle 100%, leaving no disposable waste. This led naturally to the concept of Eco Park on the property next to Chaparral Steel, where all materials entering a plant would be used to produce downstream products of economic value. The structural

Exhibit 1.   Pfeffer's Sixteen Practices
_____

- Employment Security
- Selectivity in Recruiting
- High Wages
- Incentive Pay
- Employee Ownership
- Information Sharing
- Participation and Empowerment
- Teams and Job Redesign
- Training and Skill Development
- Cross-Utilization and Cross-Training
- Symbolic Egalitarianism
- Wage Compression
- Promotion From Within
- Long-Term Perspective
- Measurement of the Practices
- Overarching Philosophy
_____

market was growing, and bantam and castellated beams were now proven products well positioned to exploit this opportunity. In fact, these products led to the formation of a subsidiary called Castellite Inc., the first occupant of Eco Park. Situated beside the Chaparral mill, this company would take wide flange beams, cut and weld them for buildings based on designs produced by proprietary software to meet the specifications supplied by architects/engineers, and deliver them to the construction site. Similar plants might now be established throughout North America, close to major construction sites, to provide responsive service as building systems.

A recent new product idea involved cutting a beam longitudinally down the web to create two "T" sections which would then be used as railroad ties. This idea was inspired by the difficulties railways were having replacing old pressure-treated wooden ties, which then had to be collected and disposed of, causing a potential hazardous waste problem. Forward sat on the Board of such a railway, and listening to this problem being aired, he realized the potential market for such a product represented over 1 million tons of steel a year. On the bar side of the house, another opportunity existed in the large-diameter special bar quality market if a company could master the technology necessary to produce bars more than 3 in. in diameter. Forward realized that these challenges were the very diet which Chaparral had grown up on, and he felt confident that the organization which he had established could hardly wait to tackle them.

Implications

The fundamental lesson to be gained from the Chaparral situation is the role of trust in developing a high-performance work culture. Regardless of the fact that Chaparral started as a green field site and therefore had the opportunity to develop its culture from a clean slate, many similar organizations have established trust between management and labor and achieved similar results. Empowerment coupled with training and development creates an environment conducive to continuous improvement and thus a significant competitive advantage. Some have observed that Chaparral is a nonunion plant and thus has had an advantage in creating a high-performance culture, but Gordon Forward has always maintained that the key is labor–management relations, not union–management relations, and that this culture is not union versus nonunion. In addition to the fundamental role of trust, some other key aspects affect the culture. With trust comes responsibility on the part of employees. With the acceptance of risk on the part of management, in terms of encouraging learning through mistakes, comes a natural expectation of curiosity on the part of employees. This expectation of curiosity leads to the fostering of continuous learning and thus the development of a learning organization. The sharing of information inside the organization through "open book management" leads to a network of contacts and sources outside the organization. And finally, "why shouldn't people have fun at work?" The notion of a balance between humor and humility is experienced throughout the plant. Maybe this is best expressed by one of Gordon Forward's many catch phrases, "management by adultery"—treat employees as adults, and they will reciprocate!

Reference

Pfeffer, J. (1994). *Competitive advantage through people.* Boston: HBS Press.

6

Base Closure: A Case Study in Occupational Stress and Organizational Decline

Joyce A. Adkins

Rapid, sweeping change has become a part of our everyday culture. It permeates the public, private, and international environments. World events, coupled with the desire to cut federal spending, brought the era of change to the U.S. Department of Defense (DOD). Along with change came the corporate processes of downsizing, reorganization, and reengineering, as well as DOD-specific processes associated with "reinventing" federal government (Gore, 1993) and desegregating the defense and commercial industrial base (Allen, Gutmanis, & Rockey, 1996). The processes associated with change within the DOD impact the military organizational structure, personnel and their relationships with each other and the organization, and the surrounding communities. Change also brings with it increased occupational stress and the associated impact on individual and organizational health and safety.

The purpose of this chapter is to examine occupational stress and related psychosocial factors associated with organizational decline—the downsizing and ultimate closure of an operational unit within the context of a larger, ongoing organization. It begins with a general backdrop of details describing the base closure and defense drawdown process, to provide an informational foundation in support of the example presented. A case study follows, embedded within a transactional–ecological theoretical framework. Although this case is drawn from the DOD, the lessons learned may be effectively applied to both public and private civilian organizations experiencing significant organizational change and transformation.

The Base Closure and Drawdown Process

Downsizing the DOD has involved reducing both personnel and infrastructure. Reducing military infrastructure includes completely closing some

The views presented are those of the author and do not necessarily reflect the policies or position of the United States Air Force or the Department of Defense.

military installations and agencies, streamlining others, and realigning or moving functions from installations selected for closure to locations selected to receive those functions. The current process of base closure began in 1988 through Public Law (PL) 100–526, and the first list of closure bases was approved that year. Included on that list were recommendations of 86 bases for closure, 54 bases for realignment, and 5 bases for partial closure. In 1990, PL 101–510 redefined the Base Realignment and Closure (BRAC) Commission and allowed for three waves of base closures, one in every odd year beginning in 1991. In 1991, recommendations called for closing 31 major bases and realigning another 48; 1993 involved 28 major base closures and 13 realignments; 1995 involved closure (in conjunction with privatization where feasible) of 79 bases and realignment of 26 others (Department of Defense, 1995). Military installations have closed throughout our nation's history; for example, between 1961 and 1988, 97 bases were closed within the last major round of closures occurring in the mid-1970s. However, the current amount of change within the DOD is unprecedented (Cliatt & Stanley, 1994).

Reductions in personnel have affected both active duty and federal civil service workers. Overall, from a high of 2.2 million federal civilian positions in 1990, a total of 160,000 jobs had been cut government-wide as of December 1995, going toward a presidential goal for year 2000 of 1.8 million remaining federal civilian jobs. Current congressional thought would involve even deeper cuts (Reischl & Koca, 1995). Personnel reduction goals associated with the DOD multiyear downsizing efforts, originally projected to end in 1997, have varied based on presidential and congressional decisions. The original reduction goals required cutting approximately 25% of the military population and 22% of the civilian workforce within the DOD, based on 1987 end strength numbers. These goals equated to a decrease of 561,000 military personnel and 249,000 civilian personnel (General Accounting Office [GAO], May 1993, September 1993). Actual cuts have exceeded those goals. As of May 1997, the U.S. Air Force had reduced active duty personnel by 36% with additional reductions expected to reach 44%.

Actions to reduce personnel have included both voluntary an involuntary separation initiatives. In an effort to entice voluntary separation from government service short of regular retirement, the federal government implemented strategies similar to those used in private industry (General Accounting Office, March 1995; Holliman, 1993). Direct actions included introducing severance packages with offers of incentives (cash buyouts) and early retirement options. Indirect actions involved significant curtailment in promotion opportunities and reduction to lower pay grades through realignment processes in addition to regular attrition and periodic hiring freezes.

Voluntary separation incentives alone were considered insufficient to achieve the reductions needed within the established time frame, prompting DOD leaders to pursue an involuntary reduction in the workforce. For active duty military personnel, involuntary separation came through mandatory retirement for selected groups and individuals and mandatory separations for individuals who failed to progress in rank and responsibility. Within the federal civil service workforce, involuntary reductions in force (RIF) were implemented. Outplacement specialists with the DOD Office of Economic Adjustment reported that as of March 1996, the federal government had been required to involuntarily separate only 20,000–25,000 (S. Holliman, personal communication, March 1996) civilian personnel, with primary reductions coming from attrition and voluntary separation incentives. Complex procedures were implemented to ensure fairness and procedural justice in selecting personnel for RIF and realignment actions. However, because the employment contract and associated promise of job security assumed by many employees was broken, employees may have perceived the process as inherently unfair.

The third wave of BRAC-related base closures introduced a new concept of privatization. Privatization involves contracting out DOD workload to private industry. In the process of privatization, much of the infrastructure of the closed military installation is maintained—it is merely transferred to a local reuse authority (LRA), generally a local governmental entity. The LRA, in turn, negotiated with private industry for the use of the physical plant and equipment to accomplish the contracted workload. Jobs are retained in the local area but are no longer public service positions. Individuals who desire to remain with the workload and are hired by the new process owner leave the rolls of public service and become employees of private industry.

Closure of a military installation is a lengthy, dynamic process. Although a military installation on the 1995 list for closure actually completed privatization in a record 9 months, progression from announcement until final closure typically runs from approximately 2 years up to a legislatively mandated maximum of 6 years. During that time, downsizing is accomplished through a series of RIFs combined with voluntary separation incentives. Nevertheless, the original mission continues for some time, coupled with the added mission of closing the physical plant and transferring resources to a new owner.

A growing volume of information has been produced about the economic impact of base closure on the federal government, DOD, and surrounding communities (Defense Conversion Commission, 1992) and the environmental impact on the local community (General Accounting Office, February 1995). In addition, increasing attention has been given to issues related to outplacement and job transition (Day & Vance, 1996; Wanberg & Hough, 1996). However, surprisingly little effort has been devoted to describing or quantifying the psychological and psychosocial impact of base closure or the effectiveness of change management processes designed to mitigate that impact. The following case study focuses attention on those neglected issues. The theoretical framework used to guide the change facilitation process in this example, along with the organizational health principles related to leadership, assessment, supervision, and support practices extracted from these experiences, provides direction for future change management efforts.

Williams Air Force Base: Closure of an Operational Military Installation

Williams Air Force Base was a small pilot training installation located in the southwestern United States. Personnel consisted of 2,000 active duty military personnel, 1,500 civilian employees, and 350 military student pilots completing undergraduate pilot training (Williams Air Force Base, 1991). Williams was originally placed on the list for consideration for closure in July 1990. The final closure decision was announced in April 1991. (Time line for base closure events is included in Figure 1.)

Contextual Factors

Environmental context. PRECLOSURE ENVIRONMENT. Before the announcement of base closure, each organization has a preexisting culture and system of operating which has been in existence for some time. The level of preexisting organizational health impacts the effectiveness of managing the upcoming changes. In addition, concurrent events that are extraneous to the closure process may influence the progress of closure activities.

Williams was a comparatively small base with a single mission of training Air Force pilots. The task of maintaining the aircraft used in training was contracted to a private corporation that provided 100 on-site technical maintenance personnel. The base's organizational structure in-

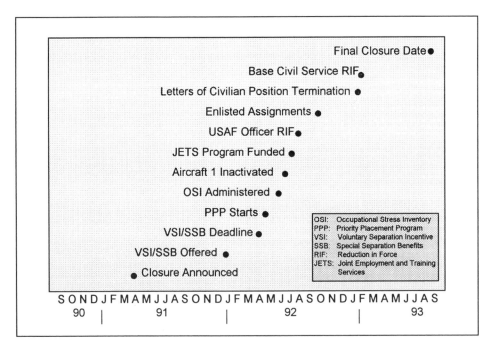

Figure 1. Time line of events during Williams Air Force Base Closure.

cluded eight primary operating units, referred to as *groups* and *squadrons*. The operating units reported to a central leadership function referred to as a *wing*.

A military installation is much like a small town. It provides its own educational facilities, health care, social and community services, and maintenance agencies. Many personnel live with their families in houses on the base; unmarried enlisted personnel live in dormitories and have a central cafeteria for meals. The installation or wing commander, in addition to being the CEO of this organization, is the "mayor" of the community. The commander is responsible for all support services and for maintaining safety, security, and quality of life of all personnel and their families. In the event of base closure, the commander ensures closure not only of the operations of the base but also of the community aspects of the base.

Before the base closure announcement, operations on Williams had been stable and routine. Fortunately, the base community had not previously experienced significant reorganization or downsizing efforts. Mission effectiveness and productivity were high based on routine Operational Readiness Inspection criteria.

ANTICIPATION, ANNOUNCEMENT, AND INITIATION. The process of closure for Williams began with DOD's announcement of installations recommended as candidates for closure. The announcement began an independent BRAC evaluation designed to examine and verify the costs and benefits associated with each installation staying open compared with the costs and benefits associated with its closure and transfer of workload to another location. Community involvement is typically high during this process (Cliatt & Stanley, 1994). Local, state, and national congressional representatives, along with labor groups, lobby to maintain the feasibility of the base in their area and make associated, although perhaps premature, promises of maintaining jobs to anxiously awaiting base personnel (Day & Vance, 1996).

If the decision is made to continue with closure, a grieving period begins in both the organization and the community. Generally, the community remains involved and provides continued support and resources to the base population. For example, following a recent closure announcement at a large military installation, the surrounding community responded with pro bono counseling for all base employees. This community support is essential to employees' successful transitions, as base support agencies diminish with closure-related downsizing.

At Williams, the community remained involved in providing support and served as a primary job relocation site for many of the civilian personnel transferring to both private and alternate federal positions. Williams was located near a large metropolitan area that was minimally impacted by the loss of employment opportunity and loss of resource contribution to the surrounding community. However, a large retiree population in the community was significantly affected by the loss of base services (especially medical care), the loss of camaraderie, and the symbolic death of an institution and artifacts associated with a way of life.

The announcement of closure did not immediately stop operations. Pilot training classes continued for the first year after the closure announcement. Although the base's mission was changing, the original workload continued along with the need for safe and effective operations in this high-risk environment of pilot training.

CLOSURE FLOW. A plan for closure, including a detailed time line, was prepared by base leadership in conjunction with input from the various base occupational groups and was communicated to the base and community population. Although the evaluation and decision-making process associated with selecting bases for closure is clearly specified (General Accounting Office, April 1995; Office of the Assistant Secretary of Defense, memorandum, Dec. 1994), guidance in closure processes has been slowly developed. With Williams being a part of only the second round of closures, little guidance from the experience of other similar bases was available.

At Williams, a 2-year closure period was established. During that 2-year period, the newly defined mission for base personnel included gradually scaling down mission operations, sequentially closing operating units (squadrons) and moving realigning units, reducing personnel, cleaning up the environment, and disposing of property and resources related to operations and to the base community functions (Department of Defense, 1995).

FINAL DAYS. Pilot training is conducted in two phases. Once the final class of students completed the first phase of training, two of the five aircraft squadrons were inactivated. This event brought many employees to the realization that the base would really close. Despite closure of these operating units, administrative and support functions continued to be required. Nevertheless, personnel reductions began to accelerate at this point, resulting in multiple formal functions and ceremonies to recognize the loss of departing personnel. As the number of personnel decreased, those employees remaining were often redeployed to new jobs or to multiple job areas to accomplish the remaining workload.

A formal military ceremony is conducted to commemorate the final inactivation of a wing. This ceremony marks the end of operations; remaining thereafter are members of the base caretaking staff, composed of the minimum number of personnel needed to watch over the remaining property and resources until final transfer to the new owner.

Psychosocial context. An organization is a vital system with interconnected parts and subsystems that are essential to its functioning. Although each person and group within the system has independent meaning, they all function interdependently—they all function in relationship to one another and in relationship to the internal and external environment (Mink, Esterhuysen, Mink, & Owen, 1993). The experience of and adaptation to the change process vary depending on the perspective of the individual, group, or organizational element observing or participating in that change. Thus, base closure involves ramifications of varying levels for each subsystem, the surrounding community, and the organization as a whole.

OCCUPATIONAL GROUPS—INDIVIDUAL AND GROUP PERSPECTIVES. Active duty military members move on the average every 3 to 5 years. Therefore, it is typically assumed that this group would perceive the closure of a military installation as less traumatic than would their civilian counterparts. However, although military members generally have a high degree of control in the normal reassignment process, base closure removes the element of control in terms of both timing and choices, especially when large groups of individuals are relocating at the same time.

While Williams was preparing for closure, overall active duty personnel reduction efforts also were initiated Air Force-wide. Specific initiatives included voluntary separation incentives, involuntary separations based on future potential (defined by promotability), and decreased promotion opportunities. Military members have no incremental retirement fund; they receive benefits only upon normal retirement. Downsizing efforts introduced new special separation benefits (SSB) and voluntary separation incentives (VSI), which offered personnel the opportunity to leave government service before retirement in exchange for monetary compensation based on accumulated years of service. The window of opportunity for selection of this option was finite and without promise of a similar opportunity in the future. Decisions were required before notification of the next assignment. Influencing the military members' decision was the possibility of involuntary separation for individuals who failed to receive promotions in the future. Involuntary separations for cause also appeared to be increasing and did not offer the compensation associated with a voluntary separation. The separation incentive options were offered to enlisted members in most career specialties and to some specialty areas for officers.

Officers. The process of reassignment of officers at Williams followed the general Air Force procedure involving use of a computerized "want ad" system. Individuals read computerized listings of Air Force-wide positions available in their career field and indicated to the personnel manager their desires to be reassigned to particular positions. Although no one is ever guaranteed their choice of assignment, attempts are made to fill open positions with qualified volunteers. During the closure process at Williams, selections were limited because of time constraints; nevertheless, the officers' amount of control over assignments during base closure was similar to the normal process.

Enlisted Personnel. The reassignment plan for enlisted personnel at Williams was significantly more constrained than the process for officers. Enlisted personnel generally outnumber officers on a ratio of approximately four to one (General Accounting Office, Sept. 1993), so relocation of this greater number of enlisted personnel was necessarily more complicated. Thus, enlisted personnel at the closure base had significantly reduced control over their job and career goals than did officers. Enlisted personnel also experienced increased conflict with peers associated with competition for limited assignments.

Federal Civil Service Personnel. Federal civil service employees may remain at the same job location for an entire career, which can span over 30 years. Historically, the federal government has been a very stable and dependable employer, and compensation rates, especially for technical work, have been very competitive. Announcement of base closure brings to federal workers at the base decreased control over their employment situation, a forced choice between relocating or entering into an employment contract with a private firm (which often involves starting at a lower salary in an entry level position with the new organization), loss of the civil service retirement package, job uncertainty and insecurity, loss of professional identity and feelings of competence, loss of social support from long-time colleagues, a new job environment with the possibility of a decrease in position, or retraining into a new career field altogether. Family concerns arise as well, such as school changes for children, spouse employment considerations, and financial realities of relocating. Decisions must be made in a time-constrained, option-constrained environment. Decision making is hampered by emotional responses. Reacting both to the anticipation of and to actual job loss, employees of the closing base are likely first to experience fear and disbelief along with strong denial of personal impact. Shock and anger, along with resentment of the perceived disloyalty of the system, may follow. In addition, the employee may feel a sense of powerlessness, depression, and an underlying uncertainty about future job prospects outside the government system (Carey, 1996; Flint, 1988; O'Hare & Vilardi, 1994).

The reduction-in-force system for DOD employees requires notification in writing to each employee competing for job retention no less than 120 days before the effective date for the RIF action when a significant number of employees are being separated (5 CFR 351.801 [a][2]—Title 5, Code of Federal Regulations, Part 351.801). Decisions concerning the disposition of individual employees in RIF situations are made based on a complex formula of criteria. Employees selected for RIF are notified of either separation, a change to a lower grade, or job reassignment. Employees receiving termination notices are eligible to participate in federally funded job search and job retraining programs. They may also register for the DOD worldwide Priority Placement Program (PPP), which is a list of DOD employees affected by the reduction in force who receive preference for alternate government jobs that become available. A Certificate of Expected Separation may be made available to employees 180 days in advance to provide them an opportunity to be considered for eligibility to participate in dislocated workers' programs (5 CFR 351.807). The Defense Authorization Act of 1993 also allows for commanders of closing installations to petition for DOD approval of early employee enrollment in dislocated federal worker services, such as the PPP, up to 24 months before the established date of closure or realignment. In addition, presidential electives require all federal agencies to give a special selection priority to qualified displaced federal workers who apply for a job within their current geographic area. At closure bases, all civilian personnel eventually receive separation notices, perhaps after being reassigned multiple times as part of the RIF process.

Contractors. Contractors are not entitled to the same benefits as civil service employees; therefore, at Williams, employees in the contracted maintenance organization were not protected by federal personnel policies. Although managers of the contract organization reported that every effort was made to provide a 60-day warning notice of job termination, it was not uncommon for employees to receive their termination notice at the end of the day effective immediately. Furthermore, the contract with the base did not include support agreements for base services; so, contract employees were not eligible to participate in base-supported change management and transition assistance programs. Individual employees could participate in stress management programs through their health care plan and did have access to commonly provided services in the civilian community such as state and local employment and unemployment agencies.

WORK UNIT/SQUADRON PERSPECTIVE. Base closure affects work units differently depending on the nature of their particular function, the time line for dissolution of that function, and the availability of jobs in the DOD and the local community. For example, civil engineering squadrons are responsible for closing down the physical plant and conducting the inventory and disposition of property while also continuing to maintain functioning of the base before complete closure. Support service personnel have a heavy workload throughout the process, although they are subject to the same rate of downsizing as other personnel. Military health care facilities are responsible for continuing care as well as the transfer of patient care responsibilities to other health care services (Bales, 1993).

ORGANIZATIONAL PERSPECTIVE. The base closure process, coupled with the overall federal drawdown, shifts personnel throughout the federal government. Within the civilian personnel system, approximately three employees are displaced for every position abolished (Holliman, 1993). In a 1994 survey of 1,500 personnel at a large, nonclosure military facility, all respondents reported that they had been affected by downsizing and reorganization in some way, either through new coworkers, new supervisors, or transfer to new jobs altogether (Adkins, 1995). Therefore, the process of change ripples through the entire organization. Furthermore, military installations with different missions tend to have different organizational cultures and different stress hazards (Adkins, 1995), making adjustments required for transferring personnel more than just geographic.

Organizational context. High levels of stress within organizations have been linked to high accident rates, poor work atmosphere, general job dissatisfaction, increased absenteeism and turnover, lower job performance and motivation, carelessness and mistakes, bad humor, tardiness, forgetfulness and irritability on the job, and increased stress-related health problems (Bray et al., 1995; Deits, 1988; Hurrell & Murphy, 1993; Yaverbaum & Culpan, 1989). At Williams, primary personnel-related operational concerns during base closure revolved around the impact of stress on personnel safety and health and organizational effectiveness and productivity.

SAFETY AND HEALTH. The impact of occupational stress and organizational change on individual health and well-being has been widely discussed (e.g., Quick, Quick, & Horn, 1986). Research specific to organizational decline has also focused on the negative effects on individual health of anticipated and actual job loss and subsequent short- and long-term unemployment (Grayson, 1985; Helgerson, 1988; Kasl & Cobb, 1982; Morris & Cook, 1991). In addition, the negative impact of turbulent change extends to employee behaviors related to safety. In an inherently dangerous operation such as flight training, safety concerns at Williams were high from both a flying and a maintenance perspective. Pilot flying high-performance aircraft must maintain continuously high levels of situational awareness. Stress-related distractions or preoccupation with issues outside the cockpit can be disastrous. Anomalies of attention and perception can lead to slowed reaction time or poor decision making in an environment measured in seconds. The ability to extract information from environmental cues is also negatively affected by high stress levels (Wickens & Flach, 1988); perception, information processing, and task prioritization are impaired, creating an operational safety hazard.

The base closure process is continuous and prolonged, leading to increased time for exposure to a high-stress environment and resultant increased probability of behavioral and emotional symptoms including anxiety, fear, depression, grief, and anger (Miner, 1985). Intense affective states can lead to errors in visual perception, difficulty in learning new things, slower work, and diminished memory and reasoning capacity both for the pilots in the air and for the maintenance crews on the ground, increasing risks for errors and mishaps.

Historically, Williams had a remarkably positive record both for ground and flight safety. The last Class A aviation mishap (involving fatalities or aircraft damage exceeding $1 million) occurred in 1986. Despite ongoing closure activities, Class B and C flying mishaps (minor accidents) and maintenance-related mishaps actually decreased. Ground, industrial, miscellaneous, sports and recreation, privately owned vehicle, and military and civilian lost-time accidents were at lower rates than ever in recorded base history (Olson, 1992). Military organizations record both on- and off-duty accidents, so this was a remarkable safety record during this time of turbulent change.

PRODUCTIVITY AND ORGANIZATIONAL EFFECTIVENESS. Threat of unemployment is associated not only with stress, safety, and personal health but also with diminished productivity (Helgerson, 1988; Theorell & Karasek, 1996) and employee resistance to change (Yaverbaum & Culpan, 1989). Survivors of the change process, even those who feel their personal job is secure, are less likely to be cooperative and hardworking if they perceive that management does not at least attempt to avoid layoffs (Wright, 1989). Survivors are also subject to affective, behavioral, and physical consequences of the grief process, which can lead not only to decrements in productivity but to dysfunctional behavior and organizational delinquency. At one end of the continuum of behavior, aggressive actions rooted in anger may include theft, sabotage, and aggressive acts toward people (Jones & Boye, 1992). At the other end lie apathy, decreased commitment, and lack of direction (Jeffreys, 1995; Noer, 1993). It is not surprising, therefore, that federal productivity as calculated by output per employee hour declined for only the second time in recorded history in the fiscal year following announcement of the overall federal reduction in force (Carnes, 1991).

A good match between employee skills and job characteristics is important to job success and to decreased occupational stress (Harrison, 1978). When workers are rotated to other jobs without adequate training, which happens frequently during RIF and closure processes, they often are destined to fail (Miner, 1985). This leads to decreased productivity and organizational effectiveness and declining morale. Motivation to produce also decreases when the job no longer presents opportunities for success or advancement (Flach, 1988; Miner, 1985). For successful transitions during times of change, the organization as a whole must be flexible, and employees must be confident enough to accept changing positions and responsibilities (Krantz, 1985). Building terms with shared responsibilities toward new mission requirements may contribute needed confidence as employees relate to being members of a team rather than identifying with a specific job series (Madique & Hayes, 1989).

Because of the strong connections among bases throughout the DOD and because of the mobility of personnel both during and outside times of drawdown, closure of one base affects other bases as well. At the closure base, grief over job loss, loss of friends and coworkers, and loss of an institution is continual. Grief is coupled with anger related to perceptions of a lack of control over the process which is dictated by external pressures. Personnel leave the installation incrementally and continually throughout the closure process. Individuals who remain are subject to the repeated experience of loss. In addition, just as a fatal crash of an aircraft affects the entire flying community in that weapon system, the "fatality" of a base affects the broader Air Force community. The entire system feels the impact of survivor-related grief, insecurity, and uncertainty. Individuals may be relocated to new bases which in turn are targeted for closure. These employees must repeatedly relocate and readjust. Repeated experiences of loss that are outside the control of the individual employee and the organization also occur for personnel who do not relocate. In response, throughout the broader DOD organizational system, an atmosphere of "learned helplessness" (Seligman, 1992) can begin to permeate the work environment, reducing innovation, creative problem solving, and overall organizational effectiveness.

FORCE SHAPING. Downsizing strategies typically are intended to reduce excess capacity, not just the number of personnel. Effective projection of and comprehensive planning for future objectives require organizations to balance the loss of personnel with the need to maintain essential skills and experience. Voluntary separation incentives do not always achieve that balance. Military personnel systems attempt to shape the force through offers of separation incentives only to specified career areas and promotion year groups along with continued personnel acquisition to meet projected future personnel and experience needs. Because of a number of external and internal constraints, civilian personnel systems have relied extensively on attrition and periodic hiring freezes to reduce personnel.

This practice can result in a skills imbalance. If job training does not keep pace with employee redeployment, workload for those employees who are trained and overall job ambiguity will increase (General Accounting Office, May 1993).

Change Facilitation Strategies

Integrated Systems Approach

As the process of change progresses through various stages of closure, responses of individuals and groups change, and the system itself changes. Furthermore, intervention by a change facilitator creates new dynamics. The unfolding of events in the local community and the organization as a whole creates a changing environmental context with new external pressures that influence resources and coping strategies of the multiple players. To be effective in this environment, intervention and facilitation must be multifaceted, dynamic, and systems-oriented.

Prevention and Systems Intervention

The intervention process at Williams included aspects of organizational development (Beer & Walton, 1990) and clinical intervention along with both organizational and individual health promotion. This multifaceted system of intervention allowed for change management at the individual, group, organizational, and community level (Ivancevich, Matteson, Freedman, & Phillips, 1990).

Change management team. Making the transition toward base closure required a change in corporate culture and function, with the base shifting its focus away from values and goals based on operational readiness to an emphasis on organizational divestiture and transfer of personnel and property. To facilitate the overall change process, a multidisciplinary, cross-functional change management team (CMT) of major stakeholders in the change process was created. The team included representatives from base service-related agencies, senior leadership, and enlisted personnel from each of the eight primary squadrons, on a rotating basis. The purpose of the team was to coordinate the psychosocial aspects of the change process through the joint efforts of support agencies, management, and labor, to ensure actions taken would promote the physical, emotional, behavioral, and organizational well-being of the base and its workforce. Rather than serving solely as a stress management or stress reduction committee (Murphy & Hurrell, 1987) and by actually including representatives of both management and labor, this group could take direct action rather than forwarding recommendations for management discussion and action. The CMT created a solid partnership between change leaders and change facilitators, facilitated communication among those involved in managing change from different organizational levels, and instituted a method of sharing problems and effective solutions across work units as well as a means of planning rather than crisis management. Change facilitation and intervention strategies flowed through this organizational working group, which also monitored the change process and the impact of interventions and made adjustments as needs changed.

Organizational Level Intervention

Focus on leadership. To effectively facilitate change, top management must demonstrate a commitment to action in support of people. Leadership participation in the CMT began the process followed by quarterly meetings specifically focused on education, consultation, and support of the base leadership as a group.

LEADERS' LUNCHEON. A Commanders' and First Sergeants' luncheon was held quarterly and focused on a specific organizational health content area including education about that content area and associated services available, group solving of commonly observed problems, and identification of best practices. An important and explicitly stated facet of this forum was peer support for leaders in the organization—an often neglected group. The luncheon format provided an opportunity for senior management to engage in informal discussions with colleagues, which often did not happen in other contexts given the high-paced, task-oriented environment of base closure.

Focus on information and communication. The method of information distribution and communication chosen within a system is highly dependent on the organizational context and structure. Methods of communication chosen at large closure bases have included such processes as town hall meetings, call-in talk shows broadcast over closed-circuit television, personnel hotlines, anonymous drop boxes, distribution of newsletters and handbooks, and dedicated information clearinghouse functions (General Accounting Office, March 1995). Williams selected formats for communication based on the technology available and the relatively small size of the installation, which allowed frequent personal communication with management. All communication media were used, including weekly base newspapers and newsletters, information on the base television channel, and regularly placed articles in the local community newspapers and television stations. Personnel met regularly with management at all levels for face-to-face information and question-and-answer sessions. A telephone action line was continuously available for personal and anonymous questions. Answers to frequently asked general questions were published in the base newspaper. Informational and instructional videos were played in waiting areas such as in the hospital and personnel areas.

Focus on awareness, education, and training. Education and training activities were primarily tailored to individual groups within the organizational context. However, the potential for suicide received overall organizational focus.

SUICIDE RISK REDUCTION. Suicide rates among active duty Air Force members consistently remain significantly lower than national rates (Office for Prevention and Health Services Assessment [OPHSA], 1996). However, at downsizing has progressed, suicide rates within the Air Force have increased (Adkins, 1996a). At Williams, prevention efforts were put into place to ensure continued well-being of all base personnel, family members, and retirees. A comprehensive suicide risk reduction program was implemented including components of education, support, referral, crisis response, and postcrisis stress debriefings. High-risk groups were discussed at CMT meetings, and specific organizational interventions were made based on the needs of those groups. Work unit interventions ranged from increased peer support to increased training in supportive supervision and early recognition and referral techniques. No suicides occurred among base personnel during the closure period, despite an increase in suicides among other training bases during this time period.

FOCUS ON SOCIAL SUPPORT. Social support has been identified as an important buffer for stress in the workplace and in changing perceptions of stress (Lieberman, 1982; LoRocco, House, & French, 1980). Professional, supervisory, and peer support were considered important aspects of reducing a potentially negative increase in stress at Williams during the closure process.

PEER SUPPORT. Volunteers representing the total workforce were trained in peer counselor skills specifically tailored to base closure and job loss (Schore & Atkin, 1993). In addition to providing effective listening to their colleagues, these peer support volunteers provided information and referral assistance and facilitated the flow of accurate information to curtail rumors. They also were able to bring forward issues from their coworkers to the CMT, and thus to management's attention, providing a timely and effective method of two-way communication.

Individual and Group Level Intervention

Intervention at the group and individual level focused on facilitating transition while maintaining personal well-being and was tailored to the needs and perceptions of the different occupational and community groups to increase effectiveness.

Transition and relocation assistance. Job security was a primary concern for most base personnel. Based on a September 1995 presidential memorandum, career transition assistance services are now required for all federal agencies. Within the DOD, traditionally available services were expanded by the 1991 National Defense Authorization Act (Schroetel, 1993). Choosing, finding, getting, and making the transition to a new job required counseling, education, job search training, job retraining, and a database of available jobs. Employment and career counseling, geographic relocation assistance, and other outplacement services were provided to military members and their families, civilian employees, and retirees. Automated database systems, including the Transition Bulletin Board and the Defense Outplacement Referral System, were also available to all employees. In addition, civil service employees participated in a number of civilian-specific outplacement services including the DOD Priority Placement Program, the DOD Reemployment Priority List, and a locally developed Joint Employment and Training Services program, which provided expanded resources for transition training, job retraining, general education, and job searches.

Organizational health. Organizational strain was evidenced primarily by an increase in interpersonal conflict and reports of personal distress from multiple work team members within specific work units. Two initiatives were introduced to intercede in this process. First, a conflict mediation process for all base personnel along with supervisor consultation in personnel and behavioral management concerns was continuously available. Second, organizational assessments of distressed work units along with skill-building, supervisor coaching, and teambuilding activities were provided based on the assessed needs of the team or work unit.

Wellness initiatives. Corporate health and wellness programs have consistently proven their effectiveness in assisting individuals to cope more effectively with job- and non-job-related stress. Various methods of stress inoculation (Meichenbaum, 1985), hardiness development (Kobasa, 1979), and overall health and fitness improvement (Gebhardt & Crump, 1990) have been used effectively to produce employees resistant to the negative implications of associated stress. By changing individual perceptions and behavior, the stress process is necessarily changed as well. Therefore, at Williams, a comprehensive health and wellness program was implemented and continually refined throughout the closure process.

NEEDS ASSESSMENT. Formal pen-and-paper needs assessments were conducted annually. The resulting data were tabulated for the base as a whole, for the individual occupational groups, and for individual work units and were used by the base Health Promotion Committee and the CMT in planning change facilitation activities and in monitoring satisfaction with those activities.

WELLNESS AND FITNESS COORDINATORS. Both a wellness coordinator and a fitness coordinator were designated for each work unit and given the responsibility for communication within their work team regarding interest in and opinions of the base wellness program. They served as the primary point of distribution for health and wellness information and for coordination and promotion of wellness activities for their squadrons.

WORK SITE WELLNESS WORKSHOPS. Wellness workshops, encompassing multiple tools for stress and change management, were conducted at the work site for individual base units with natural work teams attending together. Attendance was considered part of normal job duties. Workshops were conducted in module format allowing employees to attend modules they perceived most relevant. Unit supervisors introduced and endorsed the process, encouraged active participation, and attended along with the team.

HEALTH RISK APPRAISALS AND LIFESTYLE SEMINARS. Health risk appraisals (HRAs) were available at work site wellness seminars. In addition, a random sample of employees was selected each quarter for a complete HRA conducted through the base hospital. Individuals received confidential feedback and attended a quarterly lifestyle seminar that included a mini health fair, awareness classes for modification of identified risk factors, and an enrollment process for more comprehensive training and behavioral modification procedures. The Health Promotion Program Manager discussed composite data from the HRA process with unit commanders during quarterly meetings to target unit wellness goals; aggregate organizational data were used by the CMT for overall planning purposes. HRAs were repeated for each individual, on a voluntary basis, every 6 months for tracking, monitoring, and program development based on changing needs of individuals, groups, and the organization.

GROUP RECREATIONAL EVENTS. Basewide recreational events made health and fitness more enjoyable. Quarterly events such as fun runs and other sporting events were well attended.

PARTICIPATION INCENTIVES. A potential weakness in corporate health and fitness programs is that the participants often become involved because of ongoing interests and those who need them most seldom participate—at least not without incentives that are personally meaningful. The Wellness Initiative, therefore, incorporated a number of incentives to encourage participation.

Time off. Activities were conducted during regular work hours, and employees were allowed to participate without change to annual or sick leave. Activities scheduled for after-duty hours received less participation.

Social support. Employees participated in activities with their work team, receiving support from their buddies to attend and participate.

Individual awards. Participation and achievement awards such as medals, trophies, and T-shirts were presented at recreational events.

Team awards. Squadron members accumulated points for participation in wellness activities. Squadrons with the most accumulated points received team awards.

Management support and visibility. Base leaders and managers attended events with their team. They were routinely briefed on the wellness status of their organization so they could develop unit-appropriate incentives to encourage participation. Maintaining wellness was considered a leadership challenge by wing leadership so unit supervisors paid attention.

DISTRIBUTION OF WELLNESS INFORMATION. To supplement the wellness activities, general health and wellness information was distributed in a variety of contexts. Wellness packets were provided to incoming and outgoing personnel. Comprehensive health and wellness literature displays were constructed at the hospital and at work sites. Literature was also distributed through quarterly lifestyle seminars, recreational events, and at the annual health fair.

COMMUNITY INITIATIVES. The base community, including families and retirees, was invited to participate in many wellness activities and classes. In addition, special events were held for these groups to cover topics of interest to them. Retirees were provided with their own lifestyle seminars since their health and wellness needs differed from general workforce issues. A suicide by a retiree in a base facility before the closure announcement spurred attention to training health care providers in identifying risk factors in the elderly population to prevent future occurrences.

Family assistance. Families were considered an integral part of the employees' lives that affected their work performance and stress levels. Programs of intervention were designed specifically for family-related issues, such as family health care, family violence prevention, and relocation issues. A unique program designed for families at Williams was the Youth Sponsor Program. Employees are routinely assigned a sponsor at their training base to assist with transition. However, the needs of children during transition have often been overlooked. Through the Base Youth Center, sponsors were selected for young people. They were encouraged to correspond with their sponsors to find out about the area and to form a relationship with someone with similar interests.

Occupational Stress Assessment

To counter the negative impact of occupational stress associated with organizational change at Williams and to target and measure the effectiveness of the change facilitation strategies, it became important to clearly define and quantify the stress process. Occupational stress associated with organizational decline or drawdown involves a complex set of phenomena. Processes required to understand and intervene within this context of change and transformation grow out of the underlying theoretical model subscribed to by the observer or intervening agent. Unfortunately, much of the work in the area of occupational stress has been atheoretical, providing little in the way of a foundation on which to build effective research and intervention strategies. Although lessons can be learned from examining specific individual techniques used by others in managing change and stress, a more effective method is to come to an understanding of the underlying process and to build a plan of intervention strategies out of that understanding rather than merely linking diverse activities together without a uniting framework and purpose. Of the models surrounding the growing field of inquiry associated with occupational stress and dynamic organizational change, the most pertinent to the complex contextual environment that encompasses the DOD, including the closure environment at Williams, is the transactional–ecological model.

Transactional–Ecological Model of Occupational Stress

Within the transactional–ecological philosophy, process and relationship are seen as transcending units for examining and understanding our human situation (Dewey & Bentley, 1949). Transactional–ecological theory considers objects or events to be known through dynamic configurations or patterns; events co-occur in reciprocal relationships (Hinman, 1996), with each element affecting and being affected by others in the situation or constellation. Instead of a cause–effect interaction, events are related in a nonseparable, continuous process of mutual influence referred to as a *transaction*. Also important to the transactional–ecological worldview is the significant connection between the elements of an event and the observer of those elements (Dewey & Bentley, 1949). One comes to know an event only as an active part of perceiving it. Likewise, language plays an important part in our percepts. Dewey and Bentley suggest that "naming is knowing." Knowing, or gaining knowledge of an event, is an active and cooperative process and is interrelated with our communication of it. Thus, the words we select to define and describe occupational stress actively influence our intervention strategy decisions.

Leonard (1978) expanded the concept of the "wholeness" of events through the use of holographic theory. When two sets of light beams intersect, a hologram can be produced of the universe from that particular vantage point. If holographic film is divided into smaller parts, each part, even the smallest portion, contains all the information of the whole. As the pieces get smaller, resolution or clarity of detail is diminished, but the entire image can still be reproduced; the relationships among the elements remain intact.

This concept of reproducible patterns in both simple and complex phenomena is also at the core of chaos theory (Gleick, 1987). The study of chaos moves science away from reductionism and specialization toward examining universal behavior of complex systems. Order emerges from disorder, revolutionizing our thinking that lack of predictability is simply a matter of random "noise" or absence of vital precise variables. Rather than the whole being seen as a sum of its parts, the whole is seen in each of its parts. The science of chaos parallels the transactional–ecological worldview and holds great relevance to the complex dynamics associated with organizational change.

Similar ideas are seen in writings which look at organizations through a systems view (e.g., Cummings & Schwab, 1973; Katz & Kahn, 1966; Lewin, 1951; Miller & Rice, 1967), an ecological, environmental health view (Levi, 1992), a public health model (Sauter, Murphy & Hurrell, 1992), a safety culture view (Geller, 1995), a personal–environment fit model (Harrison, 1978), a social interaction model (Schlossberg, 1984) and a transactional, process view (Barone, 1995; Lazarus, 1995; Lazarus & Folkman, 1984). Lazarus (1995) postulates a metatheory which holds that understanding, researching, and intervening in aspects of occupational stress necessitate a transactional, process-focused, meaning-based orientation that takes into account the individual within the work context. The key to Lazarus's transactional model lies in the individual's appraisal of threat, harm, or challenge and associated adaptation or coping efforts to manage contextual demands that exceed personal resources. This appraisal and adaptation process changes continually across time and situation for the same individual and across individuals in the same context. Thus, he advocates a more psychologically, phenomenologically based approach to the issues involved with occupational stress. Critics of this approach argue that by taking an individual–environment perspective, overarching environmental triggers that affect large numbers of individuals will be omitted from review and intervention (Brief & George, 1995). However, the transactional approach does not preclude examining such overarching elements within the transaction. Rather, it holds that the mutual influence of the context and personal frame of reference must also be considered. Chaos theory would further support the concept that the process can in fact be seen in its elemental parts, depending on the level and method of looking.

Taken from the perspective of transactional–ecological theory, organizational change and decline can be seen as a naturally occurring, continuing process of connections and relationships rather than discrete or compartmentalized objects or events. This contextual fabric of experience is of even greater importance in the highly political and international environment of the DOD. In this context, base closure is not viewed as an isolated event but as a part of an overall process of change within the DOD system. Just as in a private organization, the DOD has its own culture, accepted operating procedures, and means of measuring and tracking productivity, health, and safety. Unlike the private corporate world, however, DOD does not have full control over its procedures and assets which are under civilian political control as specified in the United States Constitution. Therefore, current and future operations are strongly tied to the national and international environment (Sargeant, 1996). As with any change process, environmental conditions and personal adaptation strategies change throughout the various phases of the closure process and across the organization.

Naming Occupational Stress

The paradigm surrounding the newly emerging field of occupational health psychology is dynamically developing (see Kuhn, 1962). Perspectives about and definitions for occupational stress are numerous, each competing for widespread acceptance. Following the transactional–ecological model, *occupational stress* is the perception of threat, pressure, demand, or challenge requiring change and adaptation associated with psychosocial work hazards posed within the broad context of the occupational environment including the interface between work and non-work issues in living. Strain is associated with a negative imbalance in the transaction between environmental hazards and individual or organizational vulnerability and resources that influences overall health, well-being, and productivity of the system.

Within this naming, *stress* denotes the transaction, process, or relationship between environmental elements or subsystems, commonly referred to as hazards or stressors, and individual elements including both vulnerabilities and resources available for interfacing or coping. This process or transaction between environmental and individual subsystems takes place through an experimental process. This process involves a perception or appraisal on the part of the individual as well as an environmental element or trigger to that perceptual process. *Strain* is used to name the negative imbalance that can be associated with that transaction and can be associated with the individual or the organization (e.g., personal strain, organizational strain). Because the elements, or subsystems, are all interrelated, intervention at any point can change the balance within the transaction.

Measuring Occupational Stress

Planning intervention strategies at Williams required identifying psychosocial hazards and employee coping resources to assist in targeting change facilitation efforts effectively. Thus, the CMT undertook an effort to quantify elements of the stress transaction using the Occupational Stress Inventory (Osipow & Spokane, 1992), an instrument originally developed out of a transactionally based model. The Occupational Stress Inventory (OSI) measures stress hazards within the environmental context, personal resources of coping strategies, and indicators of strain. The three primary domains are further delineated into 10 subscales. Although initially developed as an individual assessment instrument, the OSI has been used in studies of both the organizational environment and effectiveness of organizational interventions (Mangelsdorff et al., 1995; Osipow & Spokane, 1992; Spokane, 1995).

The OSI was administered to a random, stratified sample of personnel at Williams, including civil service employees, rated officers (pilots), support officers, enlisted personnel, and contract maintenance personnel. The OSI was administered concurrently at a nonclosure base similar in mission, demographics, and geographic location. (Overall measures obtained from this administration of the OSI are depicted in Figure 2.) All responses were anonymous and voluntary. The combined response rate for both bases was 74.6%; consistent with military demographics, 78% of the respondents were male. The OSI was initially administered in June 1992, approximately the midpoint of the base closure process, to supplement information from other assessment techniques. (For complete study details, see Olson, 1992.) The aspects of the stress transaction measured by the OSI were examined for differences between the closure and nonclosure bases and between groups sampled. Figure 3 provides graphical displays of relevant scores obtained from the respondents at Williams and the nonclosure base compared with the 50th percentile ratings for males from the OSI normative group.

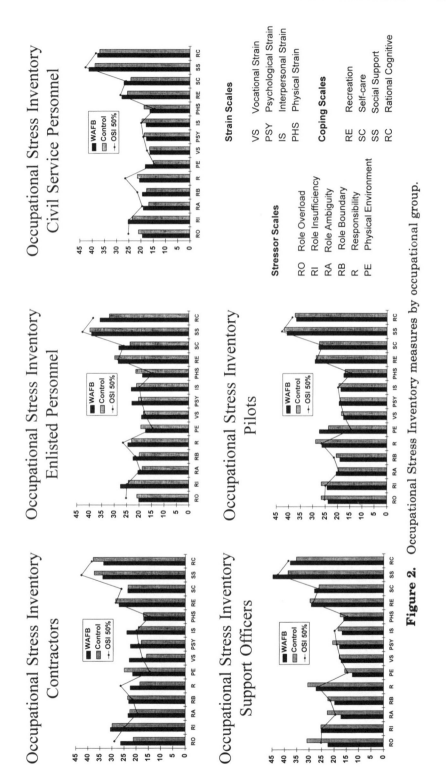

Figure 2. Occupational Stress Inventory measures by occupational group.

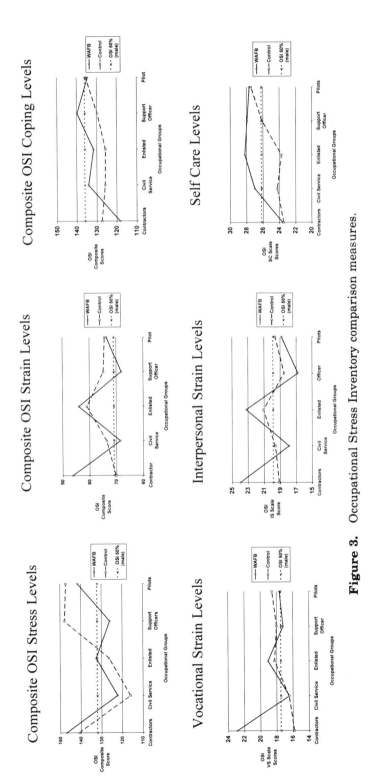

Figure 3.   Occupational Stress Inventory comparison measures.

Organizational differences. Both stress and coping composite scales revealed no significant differences between bases. Looking at the stressor subscale of responsibility, officers at both bases—both rated and support officers—reported perceiving a greater sense of responsibility than other groups, as was expected given their designated positions of responsibility for both personnel and mission accomplishment. The strain composite scale identified a significant difference between the contractor groups at the two bases. The only significant base effect was found within the domain of coping in the subscale of self-care, with Williams, as a whole, reporting significantly higher levels of self-care than the control base— the set of behaviors specifically targeted by the base wellness initiative.

Group differences. CONTRACTORS. The most consistently significant differences were found with the contract maintenance personnel. In terms of composite scales, contractors at Williams experienced significantly more strain than their control base counterparts and more strain than civil servants, pilots, and support officers at both bases. According to the stressor subscales, Williams contractors experienced more role overload than contractors at the control base and civil servants and enlisted members at both bases. They also reported a greater perception of responsibility than did their control base counterparts. In terms of strain subscales, Williams contractors reported significantly higher levels of vocational strain than did all other groups at both bases. They also reported significantly higher levels of interpersonal strain than did all other groups at both bases with the exception of enlisted personnel. In terms of coping subscales, control group contractors reported significantly higher use of rational/cognitive coping strategies than did the Williams contractors. The reported levels of self-care for the contractors at both bases were similar.

These findings suggest that contractors may have been the real victims of this base closure process. Compared with OSI interpretative data, the level of strain experienced by Williams contractors indicated a level of mild maladaptive strain which may include a negative attitude toward work, propensity for errors and accidents, concentration problems, and absenteeism (Osipow & Spokane, 1992, p. 5). The contractor group was the first to experience layoffs, beginning with the initial drawdown of the Phase I training aircraft. Contractors either received termination notices or were transferred to other jobs. This displaced coworkers, shifted relationships, and perpetuated perceptions of job insecurity regardless of aircraft assignment. Strain might also be related to the fact that Williams contractors had the lowest coping skills of all other groups and were not included in the basewide wellness and change facilitation initiatives.

These results were distributing given the high need for safe behavior from this group as sole maintainers of the aircraft and surprising given that there were no manifestations of problems in terms of maintenance-related safety mishaps. One recommendation resulting from this measurement was to pursue facilitation efforts with contractor groups, which might include renegotiating contracts to include specific support agreements for contract employees in sensitive positions.

CIVIL SERVICE PERSONNEL. OSI results for civil service personnel are also surprising. Popular opinion held that this group would experience significant distress as a result of the threat of job loss related to base closure. However, no significant differences were identified between civil service personnel scores at the closure and nonclosure bases on any scale of the OSI. Interestingly, civil servants produced a raw score on the composite stress scale that was slightly lower than the 50th percentile OSI normative group and the means of other occupational groups at both bases. The civil servants at Williams reported average coping skills (equivalent to the 50th percentile), and although the differences did not reach significance, they reported a higher level of self-care than their control base counterparts. They also were among the lowest of the groups sampled on the composite strain scale, a value lower than the normative 50th percentile for this measure. These findings were contrary to conversational reports from this group during the base closure period. Perhaps change facilitation strategies designed to assist this group supported them through the transition, reducing negative effects. Timing may also have been a factor in that this measurement occurred prior to the actual distribution of RIF notices for civil servants (January through February 1996). Or, perhaps it is wrong to assume that stressors and associated strain are inevitable products of the base closure process. However, it is interesting to compare this group with the civilian contractor group at Williams. Both civilian occupational groups were facing job loss, but through different processes. The civil servants were protected by specific federal regulations, had a longer notification period, and had greater access to change facilitation strategies. Subsequently, the Williams contractors displayed a configuration of distress expected of the civil servant population.

ENLISTED MILITARY MEMBERS. The enlisted military members at Williams reported significantly more strain than did Williams officers (rated and support) and more than the control base contractors. In terms of coping, Williams enlisted personnel reported significantly higher levels of self-care than did their control base counterparts and higher levels (although not significantly so) than all other groups measured. Although coping skills appeared adequate, interpersonal strain was relatively high, higher than all other groups except for Williams contractors (slightly higher than OSI 50th percentile scores). Referring again to the time line of events, the measurement occurred (June) just after decisions were required for voluntary separation (April) and just prior to enlisted assignments (October). Enlisted members were involved in making significant decisions in their career during this period that may have been impeded by their colleagues who were competing for the same promotion opportunities needed for position retention and for the limited assignments available.

SUPPORT OFFICERS. Interestingly, job stressors for the support officers at the control base were higher than for their counterparts at Williams although the difference only approached significance ($p = .0541$). Looking at stressor subscales, control base support officers experienced higher role overload than did control base civil servants, enlisted personnel, or contractors. The role overload of control base support officers was higher than that of Williams civil servants, enlisted personnel, and officers. These differences were unexpected given that the support officers' level of responsibility at the closure base had increased as higher ranking officers left and responsibilities fell to the lower ranking members remaining.

PILOTS. Pilots tend to be a remarkably homogeneous population in terms of personality and behavior (Fine & Hartman, 1968). This finding held true for the OSI results as well. Pilot mean scores on all scales were fairly consistent across bases and were comparable to the raw scores reported for the 50th percentile on the normative OSI sample. The only difference was for control base pilots who experienced higher role overload than did control base civil servants and contractors and Williams civil servants and enlisted personnel.

Looking Toward the Future: Lessons Learned

Barriers to Successful Transition

Leadership. All forms of organizational transformation, including decline, require consistent, strong, and effective leadership. To be successful, leaders must fully envision and effectively communicate the new mission and catalyze people to move toward that vision. Once the leader in a change process is trusted by the general base population, progress can begin toward releasing the past and accomplishing new mission objectives associated with closure. Changing leaders disrupts the process and re-energizes feelings of loss and betrayal. Unfortunately, at Williams, the Wing Commander was changed during the last year prior to closure. The general base population responded with increased verbalizations of distress, decreased morale and cooperativeness, and lack of acceptance of the new leadership style displayed by the incoming commander. Fortunately, squadron-level supervision and support agency personnel remained fairly consistent and provided an element of continuity, familiarity, and support.

Predictability of events. Predictable timetables of projected events increase a sense of control for individuals making significant life decisions. Extensive planning and preparation are required to develop a projected sequence of events that is realistic and sufficiently detailed. Early development and effective and repeated communication to employees and community members can help calm fears and provide an opportunity for planning of personal and community events (Mundy & Gilcreast, 1994). At Williams, a realistic timetable was produced early in the closure process and was communicated through various formats to all interested parties. However, new leadership directives accelerated the timetable several months without adequate justification of the change to the base population, precipitating panic-based behaviors among employees who had little time to accomplish remaining personal and occupational tasks. A large portion of base personnel had departed prior to this change, minimizing its impact.

Monitoring and process adjustment. Critical processes require assessment to ensure on-target planning. The CMT attempted assessment through the OSI, HRAs and needs assessments. The OSI was readministered within the last few months of closure; however, because of time and personnel constraints, the data were unavailable for timely use in monitoring and adjusting intervention processes based on the changes in leadership. Baseline data prior to the closing announcement along with periodic readministration could have provided a more complete database on which to base effective action throughout the closure process.

Effective Intervention Strategies

Transactional–ecological focus. According to the current public health model, stress-related research and practice have emphasized too strongly the aspect of individual responsibility for stress management. Advocates of this line of thought argue for a shift toward increasing attention to stress reduction or environmental change to remove stress hazards from the environment (e.g., Hurrell, 1987). Lazarus (1995) presented a third strategy that suggests taking the person or group within the work environment as a single analytic unit, attempting to change stressful relationships within the work context for individuals and/or groups. Complementing these ideas, the transactional–ecological approach argues that all points of intervention are valid in that each change affects the system and the relationships within that system. The objective is to develop a balanced approach incorporating multiple sites of intervention (Halverson & Bliese, 1995; Ivancevich et al., 1990), any and all of which can change the process and guide further intervention and change as the process continues to evolve.

The transactional–ecological model successfully guided intervention efforts during the closure process at Williams Air Force Base. Tailored interventions, focusing on needs and perceptions of individuals and groups within the work context and across time, increased effectiveness and efficiency in allocating scarce and diminishing resources. Providing organizational assessments of and increasing support to high-stress and high-risk work groups further allowed targeting of services and effective prevention of problem escalation.

Change management team. Taking a multidisciplinary team approach to change facilitation effected a fully integrated method which improved consistency, eliminated redundancies, and provided monitoring of all aspects of the process by a single team of stakeholders. Change does not fall into the domain of any single discipline, only through cross-functional, comprehensive planning and action will the full spectrum of issues receive attention. Furthermore, effectiveness would have been decreased without the presence of senior leadership which allowed direct and timely action. As others have found (Fisher & Pratt, 1995), this single aspect of change facilitation was invaluable.

Social support. Social support for all groups ranging from leadership to support personnel reduced the negative impact of the stress transaction that could not be eliminated or removed from the system.

Wellness initiatives. Comprehensive wellness strategies proved effective not only in promoting individual health and safety, but in providing effective avenues for social support and team identity. Reports of high levels of self-care behaviors among personnel at Williams appear to validate the effectiveness of the wellness initiatives.

Education and training. Education and training including job training, transition skills, and personal change and stress management strategies, were in high demand. Broad-ranging transition assistance programs were well received and reportedly effective in assisting personnel in finding new jobs and in calming fears associated with job security.

Information and communication. The extensive use of all forms of communication and information distribution available assisted in carrying consistent messages to all constituents. Planning communication strategies early and maximizing opportunities for timely distribution of information are essential to an effective base closure process.

Healthy preexisting culture. Williams was fortunate to begin the closure process with a relatively healthy organizational culture and climate. Bases that begin the process with unresolved corporate problems escalate quickly into crisis situations, reducing the time for effective planning and communication. The most effective strategy for successful organizational decline is to build and maintain strong organizational health during times of growth or stability.

Strategies for effective change facilitation during drawndown are not unique to the base closure process. In many ways, they represent concepts that are easily transferred to the naturally occurring cycles of change, growth, and decline that occur in every organization. The success of the change management process at Williams spurred further development of a comprehensive, systems-oriented Organizational Health Center program (Adkins, 1996b) designed to facilitate organizational intervention, management innovation, and change management at other military installations and to increase preparedness for continued organizational change.

References

Adkins, J. A. (1995, February). *Occupational stress: A leadership challenge.* Paper presented at Horizons: Air Force Material Command Leadership Conference, Albuquerque, NM.

Adkins, J. A. (1996a, April). *Continuum of occupational violence prevention*. Paper presented at the Eleventh Annual Conference of the Society for Organizational and Industrial Psychology, San Diego, CA.

Adkins, J. A. (1996b, June). Organizational health: An organizational systems perspective. *Proceedings of the Third Biennial International Conference on Advances in Management, Boston, MA, 3*, 100.

Allen, G., Gutmanis, I., & Rockey, M. A. (1996, Winter). Better national defense at half the cost: Actions to desegregate the U.S. industrial base. *National Security Studies Quarterly, II*(I), 69–77.

Bales, J. D. (1993). Preparing for the downsizing and closure of Letterman Army Medical Center: A case study. *Military Medicine, 158*(2), 84–90.

Barone, D. F. (1995). Work stress conceived and researched transactionally. In R. Crandall & P. L. Perrewe (Eds.), *Occupational stress* (pp. 29–38). Washington, DC: Taylor & Francis.

Beer, M., & Walton, E. (1990). Developing the competitive organization: Intervention and strategies. *American Psychologist, 45*, 154–161.

Bray, R. M., Kroutil, L. A., Wheeless, S. C., Marsden, M. E., Bailey, S. L., Fairbank, J. A., & Hartford, T. C. (1995). *1995 Department of Defense survey of health-related behaviors among military personnel* (RTI/601/06-FR). Research Triangle Park, NC: Research Triangle Institute.

Brief, A. P., & George, J. M. (1995). Psychological stress and the workplace: A brief comment on Lazarus' outlook. In R. Crandall & P. L. Perrewe (Eds.), *Occupational stress* (pp. 15–19). Washington, DC: Taylor & Francis.

Carey, R. (1996). *Facing the future: A practical guide to career transitions*. Huntsville, AL: FMPI Communications.

Carnes, R. B. (1991, May). Productivity in industry and government. *Monthly Labor Review*, pp. 23–33.

Cliatt, S. R., & Stanley, G. A. (1994). *A case study of the base-closure community initial redevelopment process* (AFIT/GLM/LAL/94S-7). Unpublished master's thesis, Air Force Institute of Technology, Wright Patterson Air Force Base, Ohio.

Cummings, L. L., & Schwab, D. P. (1973). *Performance in organizations: Determinants and appraisal*. Glenview, IL: Scott Foresman.

Day, D. V., & Vance, R. J. (1996, April). *Challenges in defense conversion and downsizing: Understanding the role of I/O psychologists*. Paper presented at the Eleventh Annual Conference of the Society for Industrial and Organizational Psychology, San Diego, CA.

Defense Conversion Commission. (1992, December 31). *Adjusting to the drawdown*. Washington, DC: Author.

Deits, B. (1988). *Life after loss: A personal guide*. Tucson: Fisher Books.

Department of Defense, Office of the Assistant Secretary of Defense for Economic Security. (1995, August). *Closing bases right: A commander's handbook*. Washington, DC: Author.

Dewey, J., & Bentley, A. (1949). *The knowing and the known*. Boston: Beacon Press.

Fine, M., & Hartman, B. O. (1968). *Psychiatric strengths and weaknesses of typical Air Force pilots* (TR-68-121). San Antonio, TX: USAF School of Aerospace Medicine.

Fisher, K. M., & Pratt, D. S. (1995, September). *Supporting the wounded workforce: A team approach to coping with downsizing*. Paper presented at Work, Stress and Health 95: Creating Healthier Workplaces, Washington, DC.

Flach, F. C. (1988). *Resilience: Discovering a new strength at times of stress*. New York: Fawcett Columbine.

Flint, J. (1988, October 12). Comes the RIF. *Forbes*, 58–62.

Gebhardt, D. L., & Crump, C. E. (1990). Employee fitness and wellness programs in the workplace. *American Psychologist, 45*, 262–272.

Geller, E. S. (1995, September). *Psychology of occupational health and safety*. Paper presented at Work, Stress and Health 95: Creating Healthier Workplaces, Washington, DC.

General Accounting Office. (1993, May). *Defense civilian downsizing: Challenges remain even with availability of financial separation incentives*. (GAO/NSIAD-93-194). Washington, DC: Author.

General Accounting Office. (1993, September). *Military downsizing: Balancing accessions and losses is key to shaping the future force* (GAO/NSIAD-93-241). Washington, DC: Author.

General Accounting Office. (1995, February). *Military bases: Environmental impact at closing installations* (GAO/NSIAD-95-70). Washington, DC: Author.

General Accounting Office. (1995, March). *Workforce reductions: Downsizing strategies used in selected organizations* (GAO/GGD-95-54). Washington, DC: Author.

General Accounting Office. (1995, April). *Analysis of DOD's 1995 process and recommendations for closure and realignment* (GAO/NSIAD-95-133). Washington, DC: Author.

Gleick, J. (1987). *Chaos: Making a new science.* New York: Viking Books.

Gore, A. (1993, September 7). *Creating a government that works better and costs less: Report of the National Performance Review.* Washington, DC: Government Printing Office.

Grayson, J. P. (1985). The closure of a factory and its impact on health. *International Journal of Health Services, 15,* 69–93.

Harrison, V. R. (1978). Person–environment fit and job stress. In C. L. Cooper & R. Payne (Eds.), *Stress at work* (pp. 175–208). New York: Wiley.

Halverson, R. R., & Bliese, P. D. (1995, September). *Using multi-level investigations to assess stressors and strains in the workplace.* Paper presented at Work, Stress and Health 95: Creating Healthier Workplaces, Washington, DC.

Helgerson, S. D. (1988). Review of unemployment and health: A disaster and challenge. *Journal of the American Medical Association, 10,* 21–29.

Hinman, A. R. (1996, May). *The directions of preventive medicine.* Assistant Surgeon General Keynote Lecture at the 67th Annual Scientific Meeting of the Aerospace Medical Association, Atlanta, GA.

Holliman, S. D. (1993, February). Civilian personnel: Employment levels, separations, transition programs and downsizing strategy. In Defense Conversion Commission, *Adjusting to Drawdown* (Annex K, pp. 1–33). Washington, DC: Defense Conversion Commission.

Hurrell, J. J. (1987). An overview of organizational stress and health. In L. M. Murphy & T. F. Schoenborn (Eds.), *Stress management in work settings* (pp. 31–39). Cincinnati, OH: National Institute of Occupational Safety and Health.

Hurrell, J. J., & Murphy, L. R. (1993). Psychological job stress. In W. N. Rom (Ed.), *Environmental and occupational medicine* (2nd Ed., pp. 675–684). Boston: Little, Brown.

Ivancevich, J. M., Matteson, M. T., Freedman, S. M., & Phillips, J. S. (1990). Worksite stress management interventions. *American Psychologist, 45*(2), 252–261.

Jeffreys, J. S. (1995). *Coping with workplace loss: Dealing with grief and loss.* Columbia, MD: Crisp Publications.

Jones, J. W., & Boye, M. W. (1992). Job stress and employee counterproductivity. In J. C. Quick, L. R. Murphy, & J. J. Hurrell, Jr. (Eds.), *Stress and well-being at work* (pp. 239–251). Washington, DC: American Psychological Association.

Kasl, S. V., & Cobb, S. (1982). Variability of stress effects among men experiencing job loss. In L. Goldberger & S. Breznitz, *Handbook of stress* (pp. 445–465). New York: The Free Press.

Katz, D., & Kahn, R. (1966). *The social psychology of organizations.* New York: Wiley.

Kobasa, S. (1979). Stressful events, personality and health: An inquiry into hardiness. *Journal of Personality and Social Psychology, 37,* 1–11.

Krantz, J. (1985). Group process under conditions of organizational decline. *Journal of Applied Behavioral Science, 21*(1), 1–17.

Kuhn, T. S. (1962). *The structure of scientific revolution.* Chicago: University of Chicago Press.

Lazarus, R. S. (1995). Psychological stress in the workplace. In R. Crandall & P. L. Perrewe (Eds.), *Occupational stress* (pp. 3–14). Washington, DC: Taylor & Francis.

Lazarus, R., & Folkman, S. (1984). *Stress, appraisal and coping.* New York: Springer.

Leonard, G. (1978). *The silent pulse.* New York: Elsevier-Dutton Publishing Co.

Levi, L. (1992). Psychosocial, occupational, environment, and health concepts; research results; and applications. In G. P. Keita & S. L. Sauter (Eds.), *Work and well-being: An agenda for the 1990s* (pp. 199–210). Washington, DC: American Psychological Association.

Lewin, K. (1951). *Field theory in social science.* New York: Harper.

Lieberman, M. A. (1982). The effects of social support on responses to stress. In L. Goldberger & S. Breznitz, *Handbook of Stress* (pp. 764–784). New York: The Free Press.

LoRocco, J., House, J., & French, J. (1980). Social support, occupational stress and health. *Journal of Health and Social Behavior, 21*, 202–218.

Madique, M. A., & Hayes, R. H. (1989). The art of high-technology management. In A. D. Timpe (Ed.), *Productivity* (pp. 11–20). New York: Kend Publishing.

Mangelsdorff, A. D., Osipow, S., Alexander, D. E., & Spokane, A. R. (1995, September). *Work stress assessment, prevention and intervention using the Occupational Stress Inventory.* Symposium presented at Work, Stress and Health 95: Creating Healthier Workplaces, Washington, DC.

Meichenbaum, D. (1985). *Stress inoculation training*. New York: Pergamon Press.

Miller, E. M., & Rice, A. K. (1967). *Systems of organization*. London: Travistock.

Miner, J. B. (1985). *People problems: The executive answer book*. New York: Random House Business Division.

Mink, O. G., Esterhuysen, P. W., Mink, B. P., & Owen, K. Q. (1993). *Change at work*. San Francisco, CA: Jossey-Bass.

Morris, J. K., & Cook, D. G. (1991). A critical review of the effect of factory closure on health. *British Journal of Industrial Medicine, 48*, 1–8.

Mundy, C. M., & Gilcreast, D. M. (1994). Organizational downsizing and closure in two U.S. Army hospitals. *Military Medicine, 159*, 224–226.

Murphy, L. R., & Hurrell, J. J., Jr. (1987). Stress management in the process of occupational stress reduction. *Journal of Managerial Psychology, 2*, 18–23.

Noer, D. M. (1993). *Healing the wounds: Overcoming the trauma of layoffs and revitalizing downsized organizations*. San Francisco: Jossey-Bass.

Office for Prevention and Health Services Assessment (OPHSA). (1996). *Health of the USAF: The Morbidity, Mortality, and Disability Study (MMD)*. Brooks AFB, TX: Author.

O'Hare, D. A., & Vilardi, C. F. (1994). *A meta-analytic study of downsizing, behaviors and attitudes prevalent among survivors* (AFIT/GLM/LAR/94S-29). Unpublished master's thesis, Air Force Institute of Technology, Wright Patterson Air Force Base, Ohio.

Olson, V. A. (1992). *Closure stress: A study to determine the effect of military base closure on affiliated personnel*. Unpublished master's thesis. Embry-Riddle Aeronautical University, Phoenix, AZ.

Osipow, S. H., & Spokane, A. R. (1992). *Occupational Stress Inventory: Manual, Research Version*. Odessa, FL: Psychological Assessment Resources.

Quick, J. D., Quick, J. C., & Horn, R. S. (1986). Health consequences of stress. *Journal of Organizational Behavior Management, 8*, 19–36.

Reischl, D., & Koca, G. (1995). Life after government. *Government Executive, 27*, 14–17.

Sargeant, S. (1996, Winter). Force shaping: The key to cost effective cooperative security. *National Security Studies Quarterly, II*(I), 37–57.

Sauter, S. L., Murphy, L. R., & Hurrell, J. J., Jr. (1992). Prevention of work-related psychological disorders. A national strategy proposed by the National Institute for Occupational Safety and Health (NIOSH). In G. P. Keita & S. L. Sauter (Eds.), *Work and well-being: An agenda for the 1990s* (pp. 17–40). Washington, DC: American Psychological Association.

Schlossberg, N. (1984). *Counseling adults in transition*. New York: Springer.

Schore, L., & Atkin, J. (1993). *The role of social support in dislocated worker programs in the United States*. Paper presented at Sixth Annual Occupational Safety and Health Institute, Berkeley, CA.

Schroetel, A. H. (1993, February). Military personnel: End strength, separations, transition programs and downsizing strategies. In Defense Conversion Commission, *Adjusting to Drawdown* (Annex J, pp. 1–25). Washington, DC: Defense Conversion Commission.

Seligman, M. (1992). *Helplessness*. New York: W. H. Freeman.

Spokane, A. (1995, September). *The OSI and OSI-R: Current findings and future possibilities*. Presented at Work, Stress and Health 95: Creating Healthier Workplaces, Washington, DC.

Theorell, T., & Karasek, R. A. (1996). Current issues relating to psychosocial job strain and cardiovascular disease research. *Journal of Occupational Health Psychology, 1*(1), 9–26.

Wanberg, C. R., & Hough, L. M. (1996, February). *Unemployment and outplacement*: *Evidence and insights from an organizational psychology perspective*. Paper presented at the Dept. of Defense/National Academy of Sciences Workshop on Civilian Outplacement Strategies, Washington, DC.

Wickens, C. D., & Flach, J. M. (1988). Information processing. In E. L. Weiner & D. C. Nagel (Eds.), *Human Factors in Aviation* (pp. 111–149). San Diego: Academic Press.

Williams Air Force Base. (1991). *Williams Air Force Base*. San Diego, CA: MARCOA Publishing, Inc.

Wright, W. L. (1989). Overcoming barriers to productivity. In A. D. Timpe (Ed.), *Productivity* (pp. 343–357). New York: Kend Publishing.

Yaverbaum, G. J., & Culpan, O. (1989). Human resource planning. In A. D. Timpe (Ed.), *Productivity* (pp. 57–68). New York: Kend Publishing.

7

Results-Based Career Transition and Revitalization at the U.S. Office of Personnel Management

Michael Grant and John D. Kraft

At a meeting we attended in the Rose Garden of the White House on September 7, 1993, President Bill Clinton and Vice President Al Gore stood in front of two forklifts holding huge stacks of government documents. "Mr. President," the vice president said, "if you want to know why government doesn't work, look behind you. The answer is at least partly on those forklifts." The forklifts, the vice president explained, bore copies of budget rules, procurement rules, and the personnel code. "The personnel code alone weighs in at over 1,000 pounds," Vice President Gore said. "That code and the regulations stacked up there no longer help government work: they hurt it; they hurt it badly. And we recommend getting rid of it." The vice president then presented to President Clinton the results of a 6-month review of the federal government known as the *National Performance Review* (NPR). The NPR report, *From Red Tape to Results: Creating a Government That Works Better and Costs Less* (Gore, 1993), called for major changes throughout government.

Conducted by a team of experienced federal employees under the direction of Vice President Gore, the NPR began on March 3, 1993. The review focused primarily on how government should work, not on what it should do. Four key objectives guided the review: (a) cutting red tape; (b) putting customers first; (c) empowering employees to get results; and (d) cutting back to basics—producing better government for less. What the reviewers found was a government that does not work as well as it should, but *not* because the government has bad workers. "The problem is not lazy or incompetent people," the report stated. "It is red tape and regulation so suffocating that they stifle everyone of creativity." Federal employees are "good people trapped in bad systems." The "bad systems" named in the report were procurement, financial management, information, and personnel.

Simplifying and decentralizing personnel policy were the keys to cutting red tape. The report stated that "managers should be given the tools they need to manage effectively—the authority to hire, promote, reward, and fire." This meant reforming "virtually the entire personnel system: recruitment, hiring, classification, promotion, pay, and reward systems" (i.e., the core functions of the U.S. Office of Personnel Management [OPM]). OPM was in for major change, change that would affect how the agency would operate from that point on.

This chapter describes the planned and unplanned changes that took place in OPM from January 1993 through July 1996. Some of OPM's role as the central personnel agency for the federal government was changed by policy and statute. The agency's mission, vision, and values also underwent major change. The overall agency staff was reduced by nearly 50%, with some entire programs being eliminated. About 50% of the total loss of employees was voluntary, with the other 50% the result of termination. The agency also went through two major staff reorganizations.

The OPM revolving fund, which funded a large number of OPM staff positions in the investigations and training programs, faced mounting deficits. The result of these losses was a major downsizing that took place in three waves of "reductions in force" during 1994 and 1995. *Reduction in force* (RIF) is a phrase used by the federal government to cover a structural process for downsizing that considers employee seniority, performance appraisal, and veteran's preference. A fourth wave of downsizing was required by losses in the OPM's budget for 1996, but an employee stock ownership program (ESOP) was created for the remaining employees in the investigations program. RIF procedures were used to terminate and place those few employees who did not choose to transfer to the ESOP.

OPM was created as a result of the Civil Service Reform Act of 1978. In 1883, the United States Civil Service Commission (CSC) was established by federal statute. That organization continued until the Civil Service Reform Act of 1978 separated the CSC into three agencies (OPM, the Merit Systems Protection Board, and the Federal Labor Relations Authority) and moved enforcement of equal employment opportunity to the U.S. Equal Employment Opportunity Commission. The director of OPM serves 4-year terms and must be recertified by Congress every 4 years; the director and deputy director are of the same political party as the president.

OPM has responsibility for overseeing the operation of the federal civil service in federal agencies and maintaining the merit system principles. These principles call for fair pay and treatment of employees and the selection and promotion of the best qualified. OPM has a responsibility to carry out research and demonstration projects to determine whether there are better ways to conduct business. It also provides guidance to the president on federal employee pay and many services to other federal agencies on a reimbursable basis through a capitalized revolving fund and through reimbursement of staff and other costs.

National Performance Review and Revisions to Labor–Management Relations

National Performance Review

The NPR represented the first major change in federal personnel organization and practices since 1978, when OPM was established from the U.S.

Civil Service Commission. To make the government more efficient, Vice President Al Gore set up the NPR and issued guidance to all federal agencies.

For the federal personnel system, this guidance included the decentralization of policy and practice decisions to federal agencies, with OPM having an oversight role. It called for a reduction in the size of the personnel overhead burden for federal agencies (by approximately 20%), the elimination ("sunset") of the voluminous set of personnel documents (of more than 10,000 pages) in the *Federal Personnel Manual*, and the elimination of the tediously detailed standard application form for federal employment (Standard Form 171). NPR called for (a) a new partnership with federal employee unions, (b) a supervisor–employee ratio of 1 to 15, (c) the establishment in each agency of a Reinvention Committee to look at all of the activities of the agency and make recommendations for change, and (d) privatization of those functions that could be done better by the private sector.

Reinvention Initiatives Task Force and Reinvention Themes

One of the OPM's first actions was to establish the Reinvention Initiatives Task Force as part of its revitalization. In a letter to employees on April 29, 1993, OPM director James King asked all OPM workers for "ideas on how to improve our agency's effectiveness" (King, 1993). His letter was followed by an "all-hands" meeting on May 18, 1993, in which he underscored his request and urged employees to consider how a future OPM should be viewed by its constituents and its workers. He established the Reinvention Initiatives Task Force to review these suggestions, prioritize them, and make recommendations on how they could be implemented.

The task force consisted of 22 employees, representing the OPM's Senior Executive Service, professional staff, clerical staff, and support staff. Various employee groups, and especially the local union, also were represented. The task force operated as a consensus-based team. Suggestion boxes were placed throughout the agency for employees to make proposals for change, and within a few months, a total of 430 written proposals, prepared by 300 people, had flowed into the office of the Reinvention Initiatives Task Force. As recommended by the NPR, employees were empowered to suggest changes in all areas of personnel operations. One key area in which the union assisted OPM management was in helping to implement many of the approved proposals of the Reinvention Initiatives Task Force.

When Director King set up the Reinvention Initiatives Task Force, he also established a high-level OPM Steering Committee made up of the associate directors (heads) of the various OPM major organizations. This Steering Committee dealt with organizational conflict issues where they occurred and jurisdiction conflicts between OPM divisions. It was informally disbanded in May 1994, when the Agency Redesign Task Force was established (to be discussed later). Also, the Steering Committee evolved into the Director's Business Council, which was composed of associate directors, other office heads, and members of key employee groups, including the local union.

Elimination of the Federal Personnel Manual

In August 1993, eliminating the *Federal Personnel Manual (FPM)* was discussed with the Interagency Group (IAG) of federal personnel directors, who decided that it could be accomplished by December 31, 1993. As recommended by the NPR, interagency and OPM task forces were established to review every word in the *FPM*, federal personnel statutes (*United States Code*, Vol. 5), and federal personnel regulations. The OPM task force included representatives from every office in the agency that had responsibility for maintaining the *FPM*.

These task forces identified where *FPM* guidance was required for the efficient operation of the government because such guidance was not found in the law or regulations. For those few topics for which the information to be omitted was considered vital, an omnibus set of regulations was issued in January 1994. A few short sections of the *FPM* that discussed personnel operations that needed to be standard across the government, primarily because of computer-based, standardized data systems, were put in the form of handbooks. These handbooks were developed for retirement and insurance programs and for the maintenance of the data files in the governmentwide Central Personnel Data File.

The *FPM* was eliminated in January 1994, with few complaints, but the change did affect one area: labor–management relations. Federal law requires agencies to negotiate conditions of work that are not listed in statute, regulation, or the *FPM*. Therefore, agencies found themselves with a larger role in union–management negotiations than they had in the past.

Elimination of Standard Forms 171, 171-A, and 172

In October 1993, Mr. James King, director of OPM, discussed eliminating the very lengthy and bureaucratic standard application forms with the IAG (federal personnel directors), who decided that it could be accomplished by December 31, 1993. As recommended by the NPR, interagency and OPM task forces were established to review the forms to decide which questions were required by law of applicants and which were required at time of appointment. Agencies were encouraged by the NPR to accept resumes from applicants. Also, agencies were given authority by OPM to develop their own forms. A new brochure was developed that provided instructions to applicants on how to prepare a resume that would include the information required by federal law, such as veterans' preference status, history of criminal activity, and history of receiving retirement benefits from the federal government. Also, a one-page form that included these critical questions was developed for agencies to use if they considered it helpful.

Changes in Labor–Management Relations

The Administrative Dispute Resolution Act of 1990; the NPR; Executive Order 12871, *Labor–Management Partnerships*, signed by President Clinton on October 1, 1993; and the elimination of the *FPM* changed the way labor–management relations took place in all federal agencies, including OPM. The director of OPM and the presidents of key governmentwide federal unions formed a National Partnership Council to make these changes as smoothly as possible within the federal government. A key element in achieving the objectives of Executive Order 12871 was the formation of Partnership Councils at all appropriate levels in federal agencies. The Partnership Councils involved union and management officials as full partners to identify problems and develop solutions to them that would improve the way agencies carry out their missions and serve the American people. To have effective union–management teams, it was considered essential to train both union and management staffs; where the union mainly represented personnel of lower grades, extensive additional training was considered necessary to help union officials become more secure in their new roles.

OPM established its own Partnership Council in January 1994, which was envisioned to consider guidance to the operating divisions of OPM on such issues as who does the work, how the work gets done, and how technology affects the work. OPM anticipated that this partnership would result in less formal bargaining and more informal cooperation between union and management.

OPM paid to send union officers and stewards and management officials to training to help them implement the new partnership. For example, three union officials and four management officials (including Director King) attended a course on labor–management negotiations at Harvard University. OPM also provided in-house training. For example, at Howard University, a 2-day facilitated retreat was conducted for management and union representatives. The facilitator was an outside contractor specializing in team building. The first author of this chapter planned and directed this retreat, while the second author actively participated in it. The retreat formed a well-received kickoff to the partnership efforts.

Because of their true interest in the partnership, Director King, many associate directors, and many other key management staff joined the American Federation of Government Employees (AFGE) Local 32 as dues-paying members (ourselves included). Although supervisory and management officials could not receive any personal benefit from their membership, it did go a long way in showing support for the union.

OPM officials decided that with the elimination of the *FPM*, a set of guides would be developed to aid agencies and unions in their negotiations. One key guide developed was *Alternative Dispute Resolution: A Resource Guide* (OPM, 1994a). This guide, issued in May 1995, summarizes case studies, court precedents, and management theory concerning dispute resolution and arbitration. OPM also continued to provide agencies and national unions, without charge, a publication entitled, *New Developments in Employee and Labor Relations* (OPM, 1995b). This periodic publication was designed to identify important new case law, policies, and initiatives in federal employee and labor relations. Along with this publication, OPM has for many years maintained a comprehensive database of court and administrative decisions on labor–management relations issues. This database can be searched by topic and is available on OPM's computer-based Mainstreet Bulletin Board and on its Internet connection (OPM, 1996).

The Model Agency: Mission, Vision, and Values

As noted earlier, the NPR had as one of its goals the empowerment of federal employees to lead and change the way work is done. In implementing the NPR, in the fall of 1993, Director King placed large banners around the agency that said "OPM, The Model Agency." He began a series of letters to employees that asked for ideas concerning the agency's mission, vision, and values for the future. OPM had not previously had official statements on the agency's mission, vision, and values. He also encouraged each OPM organization to develop its own mission, vision, and values statements to mesh with the overall agency statements.

After some work with focus groups, a set of statements was developed, which was then provided to all employees for further comment. The director received more than 70 written responses. These responses were incorporated into the final set of statements issued by him in a letter to employees on January 31, 1994, in which he asked each employee to consider how these statements relate to his or her own work. Director King said that these were "living" statements that would change over time as OPM changed. He stated, "The future will bring a smaller, flatter and more competitive OPM. Change is a necessity not an option, and the mission, vision, and values statements provide us with a blueprint. Each OPM employee can be part of the solution."

A key topic in this letter was "how we measure our success." Mr. King stated, "Offering high-quality products and services that are desired by our customers is first and foremost at OPM. We measure our success by: our public customers' satisfaction and our Government customers' willingness to seek our advice and purchase our services." The mission statement was "OPM serves the public by providing human resource management leadership and high-quality services based on merit principles, in partnership with federal agencies and employees." OPM's vision statement was separated into three sections: "Our Purpose," "Our Resources," and "How We Measure Success." OPM's values statement was somewhat detailed; its opening statement was "Our core values are constant and they embody: respect for institutions of democracy, a civil service based on merit principles, the dignity of the individual employee and customer, and the ability to change and adapt."

The Diversity Council

In January 1994, the OPM Diversity Council was established. Composed of the associate directors (heads) of each of the major organizations, representatives of each of the recognized professional groups, the union, and members of women's and minority groups, its purpose, in accordance with the NPR, was to encourage the career development of all employees; to give recognition to various identifiable population groups of employees, such as veterans, African Americans, Asian Americans, Hispanic Americans, Native Americans, people with disabilities, and lesbians and gay men; and to investigate any complaints of systemic bias or discrimination as opposed to individual cases of discrimination. The Diversity Council was set up as a proactive advisory group reporting to the OPM director, and it prepared recognition employee letters, policy statements, displays in buildings, and an employee Organizational Assessment Survey that will be discussed later in terms of revitalization.

Agency Redesign Task Force

In May 1994, Director King established the Agency Redesign Task Force to advise him on how the agency should be organized for the future. This task force used in its deliberations themes developed by the Reinvention Initiatives Task Force from all of the proposals it had received and input from employees. The Agency Redesign Task Force was composed of key officials and representatives from the union and employee professional groups, and its recommendations were disseminated in letters to employees. On the basis of this task force's recommendations, Director King reorganized OPM in the fall of 1994 and again in the fall of 1995. The central office was restructured in 1994.

President Clinton's Decision to Reduce Federal Employment by 272,000

In late 1993, federal hiring had clearly dropped significantly as a result of President Clinton's decision to reduce the federal workforce by 252,000 at first and by 272,000 later. The number of new hires in 1993 was significantly less than in 1992, which suggested that the number of employees in the staffing area of OPM should be decreased. Also, with the drop in new employment, there was less need for as many personnel background investigations by the investigations group. This is the topic of the next section of this chapter: the sudden loss of revolving-fund revenue that required a large number of staff positions to be eliminated.

Downsizing Required by Major Losses in Revolving Funds

OPM's finances for reimbursable services to other federal agencies in personnel background investigations and in training declined significantly in the fall of 1993 and through the summer of 1996. As a result, it became necessary to eliminate more than one third of the staff positions in OPM. OPM management was aware from the beginning of this administration that funds throughout government would be very scarce and recognized from the recommendations of the NPR and other sources that for most agencies, positions in overhead activities such as personnel, contracting, and buildings and grounds would be cut by at least 20%. The impact on OPM's revolving funds, however, was not anticipated. OPM has had for many years a large program of reimbursable services to other agencies in personnel background investigations and training.

On February 9, 1994, the chief financial officer reported to the director and associate directors that OPM would be in violation of the Antideficiency Act in regard to the revolving fund by mid-June 1994, unless major corrective actions were taken immediately. (The Antideficiency Act provides that an agency may not spend more funds than are approved by Congress.) The chief financial officer pointed out that this revolving-fund program, capitalized at the cost of $6.8 million to the U.S. Treasury and which had a total of $216 million in expenditures in 1993, had faced a deficit of $34 million on September 31, 1993. This deficit was projected to be more than $47 million by the end of June 1994. The problem can be simply stated: Prior to 1993, OPM had hired and maintained a permanent career staff to conduct the same number of investigations and training courses that it had carried out for many years. With a drop in new governmentwide hires of approximately 50% in 1993, however, OPM did not need the number of employees it had in the investigations program. Also, the Department of Defense, because of its anticipated budget cuts, had stopped sending its employees to OPM's training courses. Therefore, OPM did not need its large training staff. An additional complication was the fact that prior to 1993, proper accounting for all costs had not been included in the price charged to other agencies for the services rendered. OPM had not used a true cost accounting model for its reimbursable business.

On February 11, 1994, Director King announced that a RIF would be required. On May 3, 1994, 501 employees in investigations, training, and positions related to these two functions were notified that they would be terminated in 60 days. This RIF was discussed with the union, which agreed to help in the outplacement effort. (This outplacement effort is discussed later in this chapter.)

The two major revolving-fund activities, investigations and training, continued to lose money even with this RIF. A second wave of RIFs, caused by the loss of overhead funds from the investigations and training programs, eliminated administrative positions in the summer of 1994. In this round, the OPM General Counsel, the Office of Communications, the Office of Personnel, the Library, the Administration Group, and other offices were affected.

In 1995, a third wave of RIFs was required because of losses in the revolving fund. This time, the training program was terminated. Most of the OPM training staff were hired by the Department of Agriculture Graduate School, and most of the training materials developed by OPM were transferred to that program. The graduate school is a separate, not-for-profit, corporation established by the federal government. A fourth wave of RIFs was required because of the budget problems caused by the lack of a congressionally approved budget for the agency. When it became apparent that OPM would have its congressionally approved budget cut substantially for FY 1996, the director ordered a RIF to handle this funding shortfall. His quick action saved 196 positions that would have been lost if he had waited until the budget was actually completed. It also meant that 196 employees and their families were spared an abrupt disruption in their lives. This fourth wave also brought a reorganization of OPM's regional structure.

In 1995, the field offices were restructured. The reduction in the number of field staff was the result of two considerations. First, it was decided that with the extensive development and use of automated voice and data networks between OPM area offices, the central office, and key agency headquarters and field offices, regional offices were no longer needed. Second, with the budget shortfall in 1995, it was decided that only those field offices that were essential to meet frontline service to OPM's customers would remain. The service centers were reduced from 26 to 17.

To complete the process of downsizing, the remainder of the investigations program was privatized in July 1996. The employees were polled, and the majority recommended that a separate ESOP be established. Forming an ESOP was recommended by the NPR as one way to assist the government in its downsizing efforts. OPM's ESOP is the first to operate from the federal government. The reader will quickly recognize that this is a common practice in the private sector; when an organization looks like it may go bankrupt, employees will occasionally buy the firm or its buildings and equipment and continue the operation. However, unlike in the private sector, the new ESOP has contracts with OPM guaranteeing business for 2 years. All employees in the investigations group were offered positions in the new ESOP. RIF procedures were used in this process, although most employees chose to move over to the new organization.

In early 1995, when the extent of the RIFs finally was realized, the union became alarmed. Some union members claimed in their campaign literature that they had been "taken-for-a-ride" when RIFs began in May 1994. This was unfortunate because OPM management had mounted a massive communication effort about the downsizing to keep all employees, supervisors, and managers informed of the reasons for the RIFs and the progress that was being made to restructure and revitalize the organization. For this purpose, newsletters, town meetings, and group seminars had been held. In 1995, it was time for a new election of officers, and three separate slates of officers were proposed. Candidates on one of the new slates claimed that the union officers were too eager to please management, to the possible detriment of union members. That new slate of officers was elected.

The new officers immediately filed charges of unfair labor practices against OPM's management for not allowing it to negotiate the "competitive areas" for the RIFs and on other issues. The term *competitive area* refers to the smallest organizational unit in which employees in the same occupation and grade levels compete with each other in terms of performance appraisal, seniority, and veterans' preference for retention during a RIF. Federal law states that the area of consideration for a RIF is a management function. The union lost in its appeals. Many employees also appealed their terminations, but OPM management won in each case. Although there were differences between the new union management and the OPM management, the latter group made every effort to support the union and maintain rapport with the union management.

Early in 1994 Director King asked the independent inspector general (IG) to investigate all aspects of the financial state of the agency's revolving fund and to make reports on it available to employees. The IG did comprehensive investigations and reported that by early 1994 programs were severely overstaffed and workloads were rapidly decreasing. The IG investigated the history of the revolving funds and pointed out that every year in its appropriation bills before the Office of Management and Budget and Congress, the nature and extent of revolving-fund activities were thoroughly explored, publicly known, and approved by Congress. Unfortunately, the major impact of the decrease in hiring activities in other agencies had simply not been anticipated by anyone, and drastic action was required. The IG also investigated the many rumors that were rampant, which suggested either that (a) political decisions rather than financial necessity were the cause of staff reductions or (b) that the reductions were the result of incompetence in long-range planning by management. These rumors were thoroughly studied and shown to be false, but costs for services were shown to be a problem and were corrected.

OPM's Results-Based Program for Internal Career Transition

OPM established an effective, results-based program for internal career transition to help employees who were to be terminated find other employment or to otherwise complete a transition out of OPM's employment that was satisfactory to them. OPM management could not have known in early 1993 that it would need to reduce its staff by nearly 50% within 3 years; however, when it became necessary to begin this process at the beginning of 1994, the agency was ready. More than 90% of the employees to be terminated were placed in a new job or otherwise completed a successful career transition, as defined by the employee, within 6 months of receiving their RIF notices. This section describes the program in detail.

A senior executive at OPM had previously started and run his own outplacement firm for several years. When he sold it, he came back to work for the government. When Director King realized that RIFs would be required, he asked this executive to take over running the program. The executive directed the first two waves of RIFs during 1994 and continually made himself available during the next waves. His handbook, *Counselor Training Manual*, formed the framework for the program. The executive and his colleagues conducted a search for the best practices in career transition before setting up OPM's internal program. This background search proved to be invaluable to the program's success. The executive represented the best of all worlds to OPM. He knew the agency, he knew government, and he had previously run results-based career transition programs. He had experience in running results-oriented programs, programs that represent a dramatic departure from the passive, process-oriented programs normally found in downsizing operations. OPM's transition staff was very successful in its efforts to assist RIFed staff in becoming managers of their own transitions and in successfully moving from a tenure based to a market based approach to their careers.

The union was involved in the downsizing efforts. Their officers, stewards, and other members were involved or consulted in carrying out the RIFs in a humane manner. Management kept the union informed on all matters. For example, throughout this time frame (1993–1996) the union always had a representative at the senior executive staff meetings in the agency. The new union officers have been provided the same role and opportunities that the previous union officers had.

Downsizing does not mean simply terminating employees. Instead, it is a strategy that emphasizes voluntary personnel reductions through early retirement, separation incentives, attrition, and outplacement, with involuntary RIFs being the last and least-preferred resort. (A formal RIF allows severance pay and unemployment insurance benefits to employees that will encourage many to leave and thereby reduce the staff.) The goal is to meet personnel reduction targets in a fair and humane manner and leave the federal government with an effective and, to the extent possible, representative workforce.

Because of legal requirements, planning for a first RIF can be complex in terms of putting personnel records (e.g., job descriptions, performance appraisals, actual location of official duties, etc.) in order. One problem in some RIFs is the fact that a large number of employees are on the same official position description (PD) even though individual employees may have developed extensive expertise in one or more areas on their jobs that is not reflected in their position descriptions. Such specialized employees should be on separate PDs so that they would not be included in a competitive area to be RIFed unless management wanted to do so. OPM's top management conducted a needs analysis and looked at every feasible way to reduce its staff before going to a RIF, providing options for early retirements and buyouts and instituting a freeze on hiring and promotions. For new hiring since the first RIF, OPM has filled critical positions only, and most of those have been filled with long-term temporary appointments, called *term appointments*.

Establishing OPM's Program for Results-Based Career Transition

OPM's program is based on the proactive use of trained peer facilitators, who encourage and guide employees who receive RIF notices to take charge of their lives and complete the transition out of OPM employment. It assumes the use of in-house employee assistance program specialists (EAP), personnel specialists, and trainers, supplemented by outside experts where needed. OPM's transition program was modeled on the best in the business and then tailored to OPM's specific requirements.

OPM used the career transition policy shown in Exhibit 1 to guide it through each of the RIFs. This policy was provided in writing to both the people who were RIFed and to the facilitators and was emphasized to all management officials in OPM on a consistent basis.

Exhibit 1. OPM's Career Transition Policy

The Principles

— If an employee is subject to separation, that person's primary job is to effect a successful career transition (see discussion). The job ends when the transition has been made or when the employee voluntarily withdraws from the program.

— We have the responsibility, shared with the employee, to make the transition happen successfully in the shortest time possible.

— The career transition program will be staffed and funded within OPM.

The Model Program

— We will install a career transition program in every location where employees are subject to separation.

— The program will consist of these elements:
  + *Career focus.* Deciding on the next step for the employee; providing a bottom-up definition of career options to explore, guided by a trained career facilitator.
  + *Career tools.* Developing resumes, preparing applications, developing interviewing skills, building networks, dealing with placement agencies and search firms, marketing, and mounting an effective career search.
  + *Lead development.* Finding published and unpublished sources of leads, using strategies for uncovering leads, and using OPM-provided tools.
  + *Follow through and conclusion.* Tailoring the search, ensuring activity, debriefings, closing the deal, and counseling about the first days on a new job.

— The program will be
  + *Results-based.* This is true for both the employee and the agency.
  + *Accountability based.* For both the employee and the agency, this includes
    • Costs
    • Savings
    • Trend toward more private sector employment

The implied social contract the federal government has had with its career service workforce has led to an employee outlook of working in a "tenured" culture. In 1993 and 1994, a series of circumstances put OPM in much more of a "market-based" situation. The result was an evolution of the implied social contract. This change, though predictable, came as a shock to civil service managers and workers alike.

The key benefits that OPM saw in conducting an effective career transition program were as follows. First, and most important, OPM had a humanitarian concern for those workers facing RIF and an organizational management challenge with employees who were staying. OPM leadership believed it was essential to be accountable for a highly successful career transition effort. Second, with the major loss in staff, the agency had to be healed quickly enough in order to move on with its mission. Failure to recover quickly as an organization ran the risk of further difficulty in delivering services to the federal community, potentially leading to further need for cuts at OPM. Third, OPM was concerned about downsizing costs. Severance pay and unemployment insurance employer costs can be very expensive and, if not controlled, could result in the need for another RIF. The more successful the career transition program is, the lower the downsizing costs are.

Employees were strongly encouraged to take responsibility for their own job security in the future. The assurance of a lifetime career in the federal government was no longer a given. The employee now had to plan for his or her future and find ways to ensure that those plans were consummated. A system of career transition facilitators, workshops, and seminars was established to encourage employees to take charge of their careers and make successful transitions out of OPM's employment and into a new phase of life.

OPM's in-house career transition program relied on a strong management component to achieve results. The management structure consisted of a key OPM executive, lead transition facilitators, and other facilitators who reported to the lead facilitators. Each career transition facilitator was given a 2-day training course and a comprehensive handbook. They were assigned an average of 10 employees who had received RIF notices. These facilitators guided their employees through the process of identifying new opportunities and completing their transitions. The lead facilitators met on at least a weekly basis with top OPM management and on a weekly basis with the other facilitators in their subgroup. All facilitators reported on a weekly basis the status of each of their assigned employees.

During the first two waves of RIFs, employees who received the RIF notices were informed that their primary job would be to find other employment or otherwise complete a transition out of OPM's employment. During the last two waves, because OPM's staff had learned earlier that many employees did not need the entire allotted time to carry out their transition program and because of the loss of staff and resources, the time allocated for transition planning was negotiated with the employee's supervisor. Employees were given in each case at least a 60-day notice of their planned termination. They were provided access to computers, computer programs, and telephones to assess their skills and interests, explore job vacancies, and prepare resumes, job applications, and cover letters to apply to job vacancies. They were also asked to attend various workshops and seminars relating to change management, time management, career exploration, and networking. The facilitators and employees were also given a biweekly newsletter, *Tips and Resources*, which kept them informed of the progress of other employees searching for new employment and gave them tips on job leads and other issues related to career transition.

The facilitators helped each other as well as their clients. Throughout the process, top-level management showed interest in the progress of outplacement, and associate directors and regional directors were required to report on it weekly to the OPM director. In one OPM region, placements were made at a much lower rate than for other parts of the agency for the first three RIFs. As a result, the director of that region was required to report weekly what he was doing personally to correct this situation. This regional director also was periodically required to come to Washington, DC, to articulate what he was doing to increase placements.

Director King personally contacted the heads of other federal agencies and the Metropolitan DC Council of Governments to help place RIFed OPM employees. A resume book was also prepared that contained the resumes of all employees slated for separation. This resume book was given to each federal agency director of personnel.

OPM's career transition was an aggressive program managed from the top of the agency, and it has continued to be successful for two reasons. First, the program asks the affected employee to become the manager of his or her career transition, whereas the agency takes responsibility for the program's results. The primary goal of the program is to provide employment and income. The second reason, and what separates this program from others, is the results-based aggressiveness in which it is carried out. The facilitator training, the training manual, and the transition program management offer hands-on involvement and accountability-oriented procedures. See Exhibit 2 for the content of this training.

Selection of Facilitators

The program began with the selection of outplacement transition facilitators. In the usual case, facilitators were recruited by profile; these employees were known to be compassionate and capable. The individuals chosen could refuse the assignment, but most of them accepted. Also, a few people self-selected themselves to be facilitators, and management agreed to it. The facilitators were selected on the basis of the following criteria: a personal sense of responsibility with a focus on end results; performance at the optimal level, even when roles were ambiguous; a feeling for and understanding of the real world; and high-level interpersonal skills.

Exhibit 2. Content of OPM's Facilitator Training Program

The facilitator training and training manual covered the following topics:

— An overview of the separation process
  A. Preseparation
  B. Separation: Meeting with the separated employee. Handling the reaction to loss.
— Establishing the focus of the employee
  A. Work experience history
  B. Goal setting
— Psychological testing
  A. Filling out interest and personality indicators: just an indicator; the goal is not to change, just evaluate.
  B. Demystify the psychological interview that may be used by organizations.
— Developing the resume: Functional and chronological, and when to use each.
  A. Step-by-step process
  B. Model resumes for comparison and critique
— Interview training—comprehensive guides
  A. What to ask.
  B. What they will ask, how to respond.
  C. What they are looking for.
— Lead generation: Job search techniques: Where to start. What to do. Getting the opportunities. Setting up the interview.
— Information resources: Who's hiring. What jobs are out there.
— Getting the best start on the next job.
— Negotiating an offer: What to do. When to do it. Setting up win–win situations.

Transition facilitators became career transition specialists; they did not play the role of "psychological therapist." (Originally, the term *career counselor* was used when referring to the facilitators; however, the staff quickly realized that this term was confusing because of the role of the facilitator in OPM.) They received general sensitivity training on personal problems, but were told to use resources within the agency; they could and should refer the employee to the EAP specialist.

Program Assistance

OPM recognized that the facilitator would need to help the client evaluate his or her own experience and skills, which takes time and should not be hurried. Based on the client's self-evaluation, a plan of action for the client would be mutually developed and agreed upon, and the facilitator was expected to see that this plan was followed by regularly contacting his or her client on, at a minimum, a weekly basis. Review and encouragement were essential parts of the transition program. For the few terminated employees who had disabilities, other trained staff in OPM came forward with extensive and very personalized assistance. Michael Grant, for example, worked with deaf employees to place them in other federal jobs. The employees with disabilities successfully completed their career transitions.

Protection of the Organization

OPM's top management recognized from the beginning the importance of planning for how the organization would operate after the loss of employees. It carefully encouraged managers to be sure to protect historical and project files and pointed out that the managers were responsible for ensuring that the project files were up-to-date and that transitions were planned for programs. The top management also stated that program responsibilities probably would not be diminished after downsizing and that staff may have additional responsibilities given to them by other OPM departments. It emphasized that downsizing can be very disruptive for the employees who remain and that it was important for managers to support their staff during this time.

Program Evaluation

OPM's transition staff recognized from the beginning the absolute necessity of program evaluation. On a weekly basis, each facilitator reported on the status of each of his or her clients. A biweekly statistical report was prepared for the director, the management staff, and the union on the status of the employees in each RIF. These reports were given to the press when questions arose about the status of the employees in each RIF.

The evaluation was based on how successful OPM was in placing people in a career transition, as defined by the employee. The program evaluation also called for a careful monitoring of costs, which were kept under control. The OPM Career Center, established in Washington, DC, served the central office and the field installations. In the field, OPM provided computer programs that were licensed for the entire agency for skills and interest evaluation, job-lead exploration, resume writing, and other transition tasks. Hard-copy materials, such as videotapes and books, could be borrowed from the central office for use rather than purchasing copies for each small office.

Summary of OPM's Career Transition Program

The OPM program is results-based and designed to empower the employee to make his or her own transition decisions and to find ways to make those decisions happen, not only at this juncture, but for the rest of their careers. It is based on the proactive use of trained peer facilitators who encourage and guide RIFed employees to take charge of their situations and complete the transition out of OPM. The program assumes the use of in-house EAP specialists, personnel specialists, and trainers, supplemented by outside experts where needed. The OPM program also is based on a humane interest in the welfare of both those employees who were terminated and those who remain. Furthermore, it reflects the view that money will be required in any downsizing to pay for either severance pay and unemployment insurance or the costs of running an effective program. OPM found that it costs less to fund an effective career transition program. OPM's transition program was modeled on the best in the business and then tailored to OPM's specific requirements.

OPM's and Other Federal Agencies' Collaborative Program for Career Transition Services

As is evident in the discussion so far, the federal government, like parts of the private sector, is in a period of downsizing. Congress and the president have ordered extensive cuts in many federal programs. In March 1995, the Interagency Advisory Group (IAG) of Personnel Directors established a Career Transition Committee. In addition to the members of the IAG, the committee included members of governmentwide employee unions, OPM staff (including the second author of this chapter), and officials from the Dislocated Worker Program of the Department of Labor.[1] The IAG is a permanent group that advises the director of OPM.

This effort of the director of OPM and the IAG was further expanded by a presidential memorandum issued to all executive branch agencies on September 12, 1995, that required all agencies to develop career transition assistance programs to help their employees affected by the RIF to find other employment or otherwise complete their career transition. Specifically, the president required agencies to establish

- programs to provide career transition services to the agency's surplus and displaced employees;
- policies for retraining displaced employees for new career opportunities; and
- policies that require the selection of a well-qualified surplus or displaced internal agency employee who applies for a vacant position in the local commuting area, before selecting any other candidate from either within or outside the agency.

---

[1]Any public or private organization that is undergoing a downsizing program should contact the Dislocated Worker Unit of their local Employment Service. This unit is funded by the Department of Labor under the provisions of the Economic Dislocation and Worker Adjustment Assistance Act (EDWAA). Training funds and technical assistance can be provided to the organization. Likewise, the Dislocated Worker Unit can assist in the use of America's Job Bank on the Internet. America's Job Bank is an automated service that is updated regularly with job openings in the public and private sectors. Another resource used by the IAG and OPM is the Small Business Administration (SBA) of the Department of Commerce, which helps individuals start up businesses and gives them advice on how to manage their businesses. This service is located in communities across the nation. Extensive assistance is also available on the SBA bulletin boards and the Internet.

In January 1996, OPM issued new regulations to implement these instructions. A much more humane system to help displaced federal workers receive priority consideration for employment in other agencies was established, and other changes were made.

Besides this presidential memorandum and these regulations, the IAG and OPM have prepared a comprehensive program to help other federal agencies. Both authors prepared a handbook entitled *Career Transition: A Resource Guide* (OPM, 1995a) to help agencies plan for restructuring and deliver career transition services. Governmentwide automated and telephonic job information systems are available for use by employees in any location. Other delivery methods are also being explored, including assistance units and assistance modules for use on computers. The written materials are available on the OPM Mainstreet Bulletin Board and on its Internet connection, without charge. An interagency transition center was established in Washington, DC, to assist federal employees who are being RIFed or who have been told in writing of an expected separation. OPM also developed an automated career counseling system, called *USACAREERS* (OPM, 1997), that is connected to the OPM governmentwide job bank through the Internet. It enables employees to take an interest inventory, explore different employment areas tied to education and experience levels, and to write resumes and apply for jobs on-line. It also lists all of the major government training courses related to the employee's competencies.

OPM has developed an outplacement service to help these agencies. OPM management, with the IAG, sees a responsibility to give agency staff assistance in preparing for and finding jobs when an agency is undergoing a RIF and is doing this to help agencies prepare for a strong future. Where detailed, hands-on technical assistance, planning, and program monitoring are required, OPM works with agencies on a reimbursable basis. This reimbursable work is tailored to combine the needs of the agency's unique culture with OPM's methodology of results-based career transition and organizational revitalization.

Organizational Revitalization at OPM

As OPM went through its many changes, brought on by changes in administration policy, executive orders, and statutes and by the severe shortfall in the revolving funds, the top agency management tried to keep morale high and to ensure that employees received the message that the agency had an important, ongoing mission and function to render as the central personnel agency. Director King held periodic "town meetings" in which all employees in the central office were invited, and these were taped and sent to the field installations. He and his other top staff also traveled to the various field installations to hold employee forums.

In late 1994, OPM decided that a climate and culture inventory (*Organizational Assessment Survey* [OPM, 1993]) should be administered to all employees to assess strengths and weaknesses in different OPM organizations and across the agency. The Diversity Council and the Partnership Council each had a section devoted to those topics. The inventory was administered in an anonymous fashion in February and March 1995.

Reports were prepared for each staff office and for the Diversity Council and the Partnership Council on the results of the survey in June 1995. Feedback sessions were provided to each of these groups by psychologists from the OPM Personnel Resources and Development Center (PRDC). For those organizations that felt a need, PRDC also provided intervention programs. Supervisors in these organizations were administered the *Leadership Opinion Questionnaire* (Fleishman, 1960), and individual supervisors were given private sessions on their leadership style (Consideration vs. Structure). Action plans were developed by focus groups in these organizations. Other interventions included focus groups of employees, studies of communication systems, and assistance with strategic planning and business process reengineering. The survey and interventions had the full support of top management in OPM.

A new emphasis was placed on the assessment of customer needs to help ensure that OPM would be viable in the future. Each organization is now required to survey their internal and external customers periodically and report on the findings. This practice helps ensure that good customer relations are maintained. Likewise, each organization has established one or more communications (i.e., marketing) outreach programs to its customers. The result of this new emphasis is a customer-focused agency, even though it continues to maintain its legal and regulatory oversight of the merit system principles in federal agencies.

Lessons Learned

OPM was very successful in its downsizing and revitalization efforts. The results-based career transition program was effective, and the transition staff learned the following lessons.

Location of the Program in the Organization

The program must be housed so that it can use direction and continuous support from the top of the organization. Either the head of the organization or his or her principal deputy should be in charge of the program if it is to respond quickly to needed changes in direction and to use available resources. At OPM, the Counselor to the Director was the responsible executive.

Currency of Records

Personnel records and organizational files must be kept up-to-date in times of massive change. The RIF list uses the three variables of veterans' preference, longevity, and performance appraisal to determine who will be terminated.

Culture Change

In an organization's restructuring, its culture will change. Employees will be expected to do more because the organization's mission usually has not changed but there are fewer people. They will have less direct supervision because of delayering of supervisory levels. And they may lose their ability to work as independent employees, but rather often work in cross-skilled, functional teams. Furthermore, employees will feel that their social contract for lifetime employment has been broken, and through no fault of their own. Survivors suffer as much as those who leave. Effective intervention is required in individual subunits of the organization and in employee organizations.

Post-RIF Assistance to the Organization

Post-RIF assistance is needed for many organizations undergoing massive change. OPM had the staff to provide some of this work. In doing so, absolute confidentiality was assured to the program managers and staff. We found that an organizational assessment survey taken during or after the RIF or delayering can provide useful information. It is important to work with focus groups of employees to determine what additional changes are required in the agency to make it a well-functioning organization. These changes may include (a) employee and organizational interventions, (b) a need for communication to the survivors and survivor recommitment, and (c) revamping the climate to meet customer needs with reduced staff resources (i.e., restructuring and reengineering the organization for the future). Top management also must provide a transitional healing process for those who remain.

Strategic Communication Planning Is a Must

Open communication is essential to increase successful transitions. The top managers must keep all employees informed of all developments relating to budget, staffing, and mission. Honesty is absolutely necessary. Top management must tell what they know and what they do not know. They must assure each employee who is let go that he or she is not leaving because of unsatisfactory job performance. Talking about what is happening is important. The grieving process is real and must be recognized. If it is not carried out effectively, the organization will have problems for many years.

Evaluation

Concerning downsizing itself, we learned that we could not do an effective follow-up survey of people after they are gone because the response rates were too low. We realize now that we should have arranged for targeted structured interviews with a stratified random sample at the times of "placement" or successful career transition or dropout from the program. We learned that personnel files must be in order. We also learned that management cannot wait to conduct a RIF; it must do it immediately or the cost of salary and benefits will end up costing so much that additional people will need to be terminated. Strategic planning by the human resources staff also is required to ensure that the staff with critical skills needed to accomplish the mission remain in the organization.

References

Fleishman, E. A. (1960). *Leadership opinion questionnaire*. Rosemont, IL: McGraw-Hill/London House Publishers.

Gore, A. (1993). *From red tape to results: Creating a government that works better and costs less*. Washington, DC: The White House.

King, J. B. (1993). *Reinventing government* [Letter to employees]. Washington, DC: US Office of Personnel Management.

Schroeder, Flynn, & Company. (1992). *Counselor training manual*. Atlanta: Author.

U.S. Office of Personnel Management. (1993). *Organizational assessment survey*. Washington, DC: Author, Personnel Resources and Development Center.

U.S. Office of Personnel Management. (1994a). *Alternative dispute resolution: A resource guide*. Washington, DC: Office of Labor Relations and Workforce Performance.

U.S. Office of Personnel Management. (1994b). *Federal personnel manual*. Washington, DC: Author.

U.S. Office of Personnel Management. (1994–1996). *Tips and resources*. Washington, DC: Author.

U.S. Office of Personnel Management. (1995a). *Career transition: A resource guide*. Washington, DC: Author, Interagency Advisory Committee of Federal Personnel Directors.

U.S. Office of Personnel Management. (1995b). *New developments in employee and labor relations*. Washington, DC: Author, Office of Labor Relations and Workforce Performance.

U.S. Office of Personnel Management. (1996). *Mainstreet Bulletin Board: 202-606-4800 and http://www.opm.gov*. [Agency-wide computer-based bulletin board and Internet connection for on-line forums and downloading various OPM publications]. Washington, DC: Author.

U.S. Office of Personnel Management. (1997). *USACAREERS* [Computer software]. Washington, DC: Author, Personnel Resources and Development Center.

8

Reorganizing a Government Human Resources Office: Lessons in Planning

Clarence Hardy and Eduardo S. Rodela

The purpose of this chapter is to share an experience in planning major organizational change at the U.S. Environmental Protection Agency's (EPA's) Office of Human Resources and Organizational Services (OHROS), in Washington, DC.[1] One of our objectives is to demonstrate how the use of conceptual and theoretical frameworks can aid in building a reality-based strategy for change in a public organization. The outcome of the plan was the reorganization of an agency-level human resources office. Several concepts will be used to demonstrate how the planning deliberations occurred. These concepts do not represent the change process itself, but rather provide a guide in formulating the change effort.

We will briefly discuss the context behind the continuing effort to bring the Office of Human Resources Management (OHRM), the former name of OHROS, into congruence with the current needs of EPA programs. We also will describe the process that was used to bring customers, human resources managers, and employees together to conduct an assessment of the current human resource (HR) organization and lay out the macrolevel model prescribing what the organization should look like after the reorganization. We summarize highlights and results of Future Search and design conferences as main forums of deliberation on the change strategy, and we conclude with a commentary reflecting some of the lessons learned. The Future Search Conference is a total systems approach to strategic planning. The Future Search Conference allows for flexibility and versa-

---

The ideas presented in the chapter are those of the authors and do not necessarily represent the views of the U.S. Environmental Protection Agency.

[1]OHROS is responsible for policies, procedures, program development, and implementation of the full spectrum of the HR functional areas. Those HR functional areas include but are not limited to, HR customer services, staffing and employment, classification and pay administration, employee services (including benefits and counseling), training and learning services, employee relations, labor management partnerships, recruitment and academic relations, organizational development, workplace issues, strategic and workforce planning, executive HR administration, incentives and awards, performance management, and automated HR systems.

tility in facilitating a variety of change situations including policies, organizations, systems, processes, or new ways of doing business. The future search conference is designed to involve the largest possible number of people with vested interest in a particular subject.

Context for Organizational Change

The National Performance Review (NPR) and its reinvention and organizational renewal efforts were among the first initiatives of President Clinton and Vice President Gore on entering office. As already discussed in the previous chapter (Grant and Kraft), these initiatives have been a big part of the "new reality" in the U.S. federal government (Gore, 1993). The EPA, as an independent federal agency, has closely followed the NPR script and has built the EPA reinvention plan around a theme of "empowering EPA employees" (Browner, 1994), but its emphasis on empowering its employees did not just start with the NPR. This emphasis can be traced back to at least as early as the second administration of William D. Ruckelshaus in the 1980s (National Academy of Public Administration [NAPA], 1984). On his return, one of the first things that Ruckelshaus did was to establish 23 different task forces of EPA employees to address a variety of management and programmatic issues.

The NAPA report (1984), which was based on a comprehensive review of human resources programs and practices at EPA, brought about expanded career development programs, greater emphasis on leadership development, and a host of initiatives on quality of work life for EPA employees. Empowerment forums, such as the EPA Learning Institute, the EPA National Human Resources Council, local human resources councils at all EPA field locations, and career management advisory committees reflective of EPA mainstream occupations, are some examples of the earlier empowerment movement at EPA (NAPA, 1985). Furthermore, in the late 1980s, one of Ruckelshaus' successors, William Riley, launched an agencywide total quality management (TQM) initiative that focused on customers, process improvement, and teamwork. In many ways these events charted the course for the current wave of experimentation and innovation at EPA, and although the current HR systems changes were triggered by the NPR and reinvention agendas, the Future Search change process responded in a very real way to the need for greater "integration and strengthening" of key employee services and management support to the agency. This is a need that was identified in the agency's guidance on reorganization. Beyond providing the traditional HR policy and operational support to EPA programs, EPA's assistant administrator in charge of human resources and other management functions, Jonathan Z. Cannon, made it clear that he expected the new OHROS to test innovative customer service approaches, develop ways to apply team-based work processes, and assist EPA program offices in becoming high-performing organizations (Cannon, 1994b).

Beyond viewing the change process as an important learning opportunity, it was essential to settle on criteria for success, and three basic concepts emerged and prevailed throughout all deliberations. The formula for success requires

1. viewing the HR function as an open system,
2. focusing on improving customer service, and
3. empowering OHROS employees.

In the conclusion, we discuss these three concepts individually. The bringing together of the interests and perspectives of customers, managers, employees, and other important stakeholders underscores the reality of the interrelationship of the three concepts and the many benefits of the Future Search Conference (Weisbord, 1992). As we discuss the change process in terms of the preplanning efforts, the OHROS redesign steering committee, and the results of the future search and design conferences, the advantages of using an open-systems approach, focusing on customers and empowering employees, should become even more evident. The story begins with a description of the various stages of planning and preparation that shaped the change process.

Preplanning for the OHROS Change Process

Meeting the expectations set forth in the Cannon reorganization directive called for a comprehensive conceptual but reality-based approach to creating and building the new organization. This approach was driven by and responsive to a defined need. A special preplanning team was created to conceptualize the process. The preplanning began in late August 1994, and the preplanning team submitted its report approximately 2 weeks later, September 16, 1994.

The product of the preplanning team was a concept paper entitled *Creating a New Human Resources and Organizational Services Office: Process Design* (OHRM, 1994b). To oversee and guide the change process, the early planners recommended establishing a steering committee with broad-based membership composed of employees from all components of the interim organization, customers from throughout EPA, and various stakeholders from both inside and outside EPA. The other key recommendation from the preplanning team called for convening one or more future search conferences as a way of gaining maximum empowerment of OHROS employees and assuring strong commitment to the extensive changes needed to implement the OHROS reorganization successfully (Cannon, 1994a, 1994b).

The concept paper outlined a very ambitious schedule for the change, projecting that the process would require approximately 200 work days (a little more than 6 months) to reach full implementation. The paper also estimated that the structures and functions of the new organization and the basic staffing at the senior level could possibly be done in approximately 110 days (OHRM, 1994b). In the end, the effective date of reorganization was September 30, 1995, approximately 14 months after Mr. Cannon's decision to restructure (Cannon, 1994b). This length of time illustrates the difficulty of undertaking and successfully completing broad-based organizational change as much as the difficulty of reliable change-management planning. Achieving the September 1995 milestone was a highly commendable feat when one considers all the collaborations and extensive involvement mandated by agency guidance (EPA, 1994), Cannon's reorganization directive, and even the script outlined by the pre-planning team itself. The preplanning team and its concept paper forcefully emphasized that the process should be as inclusive as possible, involving many stakeholders, customers, and employees of all levels from within OHROS and throughout EPA. The prevailing assumption was that the broader the input from the beginning, the better the chance for success for the new organization, because maximum involvement would gain greater commitment to the plan, the process, and the results of the change effort.

The preplanning team also recommended that because of the complexity, scope, and difficulty of the changes needed to "reinvent" the HR function, the new office director should appoint an outside organizational change "expert" to advise and assist him and the steering committee on leading and directing the change. The OHROS director accepted virtually all of the early planners' recommendations but showed a special personal commitment to the suggestions on the Future Search Conference and the steering committee and the recommendation on using an organizational change expert to facilitate the process.

Creation of the OHROS Redesign Steering Committee

Relying extensively on the preplanning concept paper, the new director officially launched the "voyage into the future" with a special public announcement on September 19, 1994. That communication set up the steering committee and asked for volunteers (O'Connor & Lowe, 1994). The announcement on the steering committee was cosigned by the OHROS director and the president of the EPA headquarters' local union, even though only a small number of OHROS employees are members of a collective bargaining unit. This communication from the new director and union president also included a copy of the preplanning concept paper for OHROS employees and an announcement on the appointment of an outside organizational change consultant to advise and assist the process (O'Connor & Lowe, 1994). This same message stated that the main purpose and role of the steering committee were to guide the efforts and the decisions in this redesign process. The announcement also spelled out expectations for the steering committee volunteer members, with a special direct appeal for their commitment to seeking fundamental change, bold pursuit of innovative ideas, and willingness to dedicate the time required for the steering committee schedule and activities (O'Connor & Lowe, 1994). A second important communication (O'Connor, 1994b) was sent to

newly appointed steering committee members, congratulating and wel-
coming them to the steering committee and providing them with background information for the first meetings on October 3 and 4, 1994.

A third communication (O'Connor, 1994a) was sent to OHROS employees notifying them about the steering committee appointments, the
first steering committee meeting, and the appointment of the outside consultant. In addition, OHROS employees were urged to get involved in the
steering committee activities. The OHROS director encouraged OHROS
employees to write, fax, telephone, or send electronic mail with comments
and suggestions on the process (O'Connor, 1994a). With these important
messages, the steering committee was launched officially and the change
process was formally initiated.

The Role of the Redesign Steering Committee

From the time of its opening meeting in October 1994 until the date of
the design selection meeting of April 1995, the steering committee wielded
considerable presence, authority, and influence over the change process.
On the basis of the ambitious charter it had adopted for itself, the steering
committee presided over an extensive list of actions and decisions that
affected the scope, substance, and success of the change process.

Some of the highlights in the eventful life of the steering committee
are briefly captured in the following chronicle of several key steering committee meetings. These events illustrate that the leaders of the change
process were preoccupied with openness, empowerment, and customers as
preeminent guideposts for the change process. The stage was set with the
preplanning efforts and the three just-mentioned important, ground-
breaking communications.

Day 1 of the steering committee meeting featured a team-building
exercise for committee members to get them off to a good start in working
together. This exercise produced a lot of energy that fueled a thorough
discussion of a charter for the steering committee and began establishing
norms and expectations for the group. A portion of the afternoon session
was spent reviewing the report from the preplanning team, and most of
the recommendations were adopted. This first day of exploration gave the
steering committee a direction and a foundation for setting priorities and
determining its overall schedule.

Day 2 of the inaugural meeting focused on using the Future Search
Conference as the "strategic planning" approach to the change process.
The group heard a formal presentation by a Future Search expert, and
that module consumed the morning session. The afternoon session was
used for extensive discussions and deliberations on how to apply *Future
Search methodology* to meet the needs of OHROS, its employees, customers, and stakeholders. The Future Search methodology is a conference format that uses plenary and small group sessions to identify common
ground, to agree on shared visions of the future, and to develop an action
plan to accomplish desired changes. This first meeting was considered by

all in attendance to be very successful and extremely productive because the steering committee (a) resolved most of the questions and issues related to its charter and decided to "finalize" the charter at its next meeting; (b) decided on its subcommittee structure and chose work teams to handle communications, plan Future Search Conferences, and collect and analyze data on OHROS services; (c) established operating procedures, facilitation support, and a general schedule for steering committee meetings; and (d) scheduled follow-up meetings for October and November 1994.

The steering committee also authorized its subcommittees and work teams to recruit additional OHROS employees and customers to be involved in the steering committee's work, and, in between the steering committee's regular meetings, these groups were empowered to make decisions to enhance the process and to keep the work on track.

These work groups contributed substantially to the steering committee's capacity to keep things moving smoothly. Later steering committee meetings were more productive as a result. These meetings served as effective decision-making forums on the schedule, content, and protocols for the Future Search and design conferences. By unanimous consent, the steering committee decided that all its members would attend one of the conferences scheduled for December and that a steering committee meeting scheduled for January would be devoted entirely to reviewing the results of the Future Search Conferences and deciding on the script for the design conference.

The January meeting proved to be a critical milestone for the steering committee. There the steering committee became preoccupied with analysis and synthesis of what had gone on up to that point, and it began to narrow its focus to expected products and results. This was one of the steering committee's most productive sessions, with the accomplishment of the following outcomes: (a) Future Search Conference reports were discussed and endorsed; (b) eight themes as focus areas to guide the design conference were considered and adopted; (c) the design conference dates, content, structure, processes, and success criteria were established; (d) an agencywide communication on the OHROS change process was agreed on; and (e) a general consensus was reached on what the steering committee's role and continued involvement would be after its decision on a new organizational design for OHROS.

These actions and decisions helped to focus the change process more sharply on its main purpose of creating a more effective OHROS organization. To accomplish this goal, the "OHROS change planners" well understood the importance of viewing the HR function as an open system, focusing on improving customer service, and empowering OHROS employees. The Future Search approach was the "glue" that held it all together.

The Future Search Approach

As the change process began to show steady progress, the steering committee became more and more comfortable with the decision it had made to use the Future Search approach. Experts and consultants on the Future Search Conference describe it as a "total systems approach" to strategic planning (Weisbord, 1992), and this was one of its selling points that impressed the steering committee and conference participants as well. The versatility of the search conference allows it to be used in a variety of change situations, including policy and program changes, reorganizations, and redesigns of major systems and work processes. The search conference methodology is designed to involve the largest possible number of people with a vested interest in a particular subject and to do so making the most efficient use of a predetermined block of time. OHROS change planners considered this to be a definite advantage. In Future Search jargon, people with a vested interest are referred to collectively as "stakeholders."

The basic goals that energize and drive the Future Search Conference are the searching for common ground, reaching consensus, and confirming a shared vision of the future. Brainstorming, collaboration, and consensus building are some of the basic tools used in working through a search conference agenda. A typical Future Search Conference format alternates plenary sessions and specifically designated small-group sessions to perform specific tasks related to the conference agenda. The OHROS Future Search Conferences were typical in this regard; however, the steering committee and conference planners found several compelling needs to alter the Future Search model to fit the EPA way of doing things. A brief description of those variations is included in the later discussion of highlights from Future Search Conferences.

The decision to sponsor multiple conferences was made largely to create opportunity for maximum involvement and participation of employees and customers. The two identical conferences were set up to stimulate innovative ideas, set new directions, and help sort out priorities and options for providing HR and organizational services to OHROS's customers. In a very real sense, these conferences were exploratory, developmental, and fact finding in nature. They generated many valuable insights and a large amount of useful data and information that energized and focused later stages of the change process.

Highlights of the Future Search Conference

As mentioned earlier, the steering committee decided to hold two identical Future Search Conferences, with 72 participants for each conference. This decision was made to allow a large number of OHROS stakeholders (a total of 144) to participate directly in the OHROS change process. In developing the list of conference attendees, the steering committee gave priority to making sure that the attendees would represent a broad cross-section of OHROS customers and a variety of experiences in dealing with OHROS. The 144 stakeholders represented a variety of interests, and mutual convenience usually determined which of the two conferences they would attend. Conference attendees were grouped into 16 different work teams that reflected all categories of stakeholders. The categories of stakeholders included (a) line managers from EPA program offices, (b) nonmanagerial employees from EPA at large, (c) nonmanagerial employees from OHROS, (d) OHROS managerial staff, (e) EPA HR officers, (f) representatives from central agencies of the federal government (e.g., U.S. Office of Personnel Management and Office of Management and Budget), (g) members of EPA's Senior Leadership Council (senior political appointees and their deputies), and (h) EPA assistant regional administrators and laboratory directors. The sizes of the stakeholder groups ranged from the smallest, 2 to 4 representatives, to the largest, 12 to 15 representatives.

The role of the conference work teams was to generate information about the past, present, and future in both general and specific terms relative to OHROS. This information provided a foundation for later identifying opportunities and options for improving the way OHROS does business.

We tailored the process to fit our needs by structuring a special customer service module that we called the "fish bowl." This was approved by the steering committee on the basis of suggestions and recommendations from the conference planning team on ways to make the Future Search process more "compatible with the EPA culture." The fish bowl was an honest and constructive give-and-take about service quality and the expectations of OHROS.

Mixed stakeholder groups were formed to discuss OHROS's services specifically in terms of "the way they are" and the way they "should be," to help analyze and synthesize key messages and important revelations contained in the fish bowl information. Some groups made lists of the top three important messages about current or future service needs from OHROS. Other groups concentrated on making lists of three to five new things they learned from listening to the fish bowl exchange. Many of the messages and lessons learned from the fish bowl exercise found their way into the eight common themes that emerged from the two future search conferences.

All stakeholder groups had the opportunity to contribute to the eight themes that resulted from the future search conferences that became the guideposts for the design conference:

1. *Strategic workforce planning and development.* OHROS must anticipate EPA's need for employees with certain combinations of skills to achieve its mission, and it must integrate this effort into an overall planning process.
2. *Automation.* OHROS needs immediate, on-line access to an array of automated services, information, and learning.
3. *Consulting services.* OHROS should provide leadership and assistance in handling change throughout the agency.
4. *Valuing diversity.* OHROS has a diverse workforce and a diverse customer base and needs to take advantage of its diversity to make the organization more effective.

5. *Flexible policy and guidance.* OHROS must anticipate and provide this support in a timely and consistent manner.
6. *Customer partnership.* OHROS's goals should be to improve customer service and to provide core services, the basic functions OHROS was set up to perform.
7. *Working in teams.* OHROS needs to provide support, nurturing, and guidance so that EPA can evolve into an organization of self-directed teams.
8. *Stewardship.* OHROS must balance its customer service roles and its duty to ensure oversight with integrity in applying relevant laws.

The Design Conference Results

The design conference, which was a variation on the basic Future Search model, became the primary vehicle for sorting, synthesizing, and elaborating on the results of two Future Search conferences. The main challenge and expectation for the 2-day design conference that was held in January 1995 was to come up with a definitive and workable product, a design for a streamlined, team-based, customer-focused, and innovative organization plan for OHROS. The design conference process and deliberations were structured so that the 64 conference participants, who were all alumni of the two Future Search Conferences, had meaningful parts to play in planning, designing, and developing the new organization. The 144 Future Search participants were the source list for participants for the design conference. The steering committee decided that the design conference needed to be broad to make sure that all stakeholder interests were represented, but that it need not be as large as the Future Search Conference. Building on the Future Search Conference model, the design conference work was done in alternating plenary and small-group sessions. The design conference started with a review of the results of the Future Search Conference reports. The first major small-group task was to use the eight themes produced by the search conferences to develop alternative organizational designs for OHROS (OHRM, 1994a). An iterative and consensus process was used to develop the OHROS design options.

Eight mixed-stakeholder work groups developed preliminary designs for OHROS. The "straw proposals" went through much deliberation, analysis, synthesis, and refinement as the 2-day conference progressed to a final decision point. The design conference is a good example of the iterative and cumulative nature of the empowerment process: It built on blocks of progress laid by the preplanning team, the steering committee, the Future Search Conferences, and its earlier small-group exercises to come up with its recommendation for the steering committee. The openness and the collaborative style of the design process mirrored the Future Search Conferences that had preceded it. The deliberations were not without struggle and tensions, but creativity and the desire for real improvement of OHROS propelled the conference to a consensus on two similar design options that were forwarded to the steering committee. Alternating between plenary sessions and small-group sessions, the eight options that had been developed were repeatedly analyzed, discussed, and screened by rounds of multi-voting until consensus was reached. ("Multi-voting" is a total quality management tool that allows weighted votes to determine priorities.) The organizational options that prevailed from the rigorous design conference debate were affectionately referred to as "the wheel of fortune" and "the spider web."

Finally, in April 1995 the steering committee held its decision meeting to select an organizational design for OHROS. After a thorough review and examination of the design conference recommendations, the steering committee picked the best features of the two design options. The final design that was preferred by the steering committee and later approved by the OHROS director resembled a "molecular" structure but clearly was a hybrid of the two options forwarded from the design conference (see Figure 1). Within this design the core functions and services form the "nucleus" of the structure and the dedicated service teams revolving in the outer shell appear as "electrons." Focusing energy, sustaining effective relationships for serving OHROS's customers, and maintaining flexibility and adaptability to changing needs are the essential philosophical and

Figure 1.   Final design for EPA's Office of Human Resources and Organizational Services.

operational tenets of the new OHROS organization. The final organizational design, what it stands for and how it will operate, has the advantage of broad-based support from OHROS employees, customers, and stakeholders. It is the product of the Future Search approach to change, characterized by openness, empowerment, and customer focus.

Appreciating the Lessons Learned

Viewing the HR Function as an Open System

Like any human resources office, the EPA human resource organization is an adaptive structure. Because it is an open system, it is in constant touch with external social and organizational elements (Katz & Kahn, 1978). Viewing OHROS as an open system helps change advocates to better articulate the need for change and to do so in an objective and persuasive manner. Change does not occur in a vacuum, and it is difficult to sell others on the need for change if persons or groups directly involved are not able to articulate the why, what, where, and how of change. This is particularly true for a large-scale change effort such as the one involving OHROS. Customer needs will vary from time to time, and OHROS needs to be in a position to adapt to new demands and its changing environment if it is to remain a viable organization. Thus, the need for communication between the customers and those who provide service is critical to the success of the change process. It is important for the customer to know and be involved so that the change can work better. The Future Search Conferences more than adequately met these needs.

Customer Service

Stressing customer service is a way to get both management and employees to think in terms of the customers and not primarily in terms of administrative rules and regulations. This shift in emphasis requires an organization that (a) acts as a team in fulfilling customer needs; (b) defines itself on the basis of what it achieves for its customers; (c) prepares to change its services and products to meet changing customer demands; (d) modifies its operating systems to adapt to changing demands for its services; (e) obtains feedback from customers to assess and revise working strategies and processes; and (f) assumes responsibility, when given the appropriate level of discretion, to make judgments about how to help customers (Barzelay, 1992).

Instead of defining itself in terms of what resources it controls and what tasks it performs, or in terms of narrow niches, the new OHROS organization now defines itself on the basis of what it does for its customers. This definition challenges people to think in terms of organizing themselves on the basis of service and products, processes, and contacts with the customers and not by using the functional speciality approach that is typical of the traditional personnel office. The steering committee, and later the Future Search Conferences, had many spirited discussions on these points.

The HR business is complex and complicated, and it has its own unique set of requirements. "One size fits all" has not worked well in the past, and there is no indication that it has any prospects for success in a reinvented OHROS. Building teams, for example, will require that each is assessed and designed to its particular purpose; any off-the-shelf team pattern will not be an acceptable design. The new OHROS must think of the real implications of its new strategic and consultative roles. This consideration must be done in terms of time, utility, and adaptability and with a sophisticated understanding of human diversity and the ever-changing environmental and business situations.

Concentration on customer requirements prompts major changes across bureaucratic organizations (Barzelay, 1992), but nowhere is such concentration more important than in those service units that have front-line and primary responsibility for dealing with the customers. The new OHROS organization design that emerged from the Future Search process features customer service staffs as the main "portals" of access to OHROS services. All service units that deal directly with customers need to feel empowered in relationship to the customer and to each other. Empowering OHROS employees to deal effectively with changing customer needs was emphasized persistently in every phase of the change process, and it continues to be a major focus of actions being taken to implement the OHROS reorganization.

Empowerment

In this discussion we are defining *empowerment* in a work organization to mean the ability to get done what needs to be done. In the way that we are using it, there are two major components: direction and capability (Mohrman, Cohen, & Mohrman, 1995). *Direction* consists of clear organizational purpose, goals, and objectives. *Capability* results from an employee having skills and access to information, resources, and authority. Both are crucial if empowerment is to be a viable management approach. When one is not available, then the power that employees need to have in an effective organization is reduced, if not eliminated altogether. The OHROS preplanning group, the OHROS director, and the steering committee were very mindful of this concept of empowerment.

A Work in Progress

The OHROS change process has come a long way since the preplanners convened to develop a framework for the change. The new organization became official on October 1, 1995, but because of budget uncertainties and eventual government shutdowns, full-scale implementation was delayed. Momentum has been regained and real progress is being made, as suggested by the following list of postimplementation activities:

1. A reorganization celebration and employee recognition program was held to focus on the work that was accomplished through the Future Search Conference and to reinforce the new vision, goals, and priorities for the reinvented OHROS. Employee groups were recognized for their contributions to the change process and its outcome, the new organization. This was the leadership's way of acknowledging the new role of employee participation. Much more was being said at the ceremony, however. Flexibility, as a component of change, was now recognized by management and employees as a crucial way of conducting their business.

    One very prominent feature at the ceremony was a bridge at the entrance to the auditorium, which was built with the used flipchart sheets collected from the Future Search and design conferences. To employees, it symbolized their role in the reorganization. In addition, we witnessed a high degree of spontaneity among the ceremony participants as they discussed their own experiences and feelings at either the Future Search Conference, design conference, or other reorganization activity. These interactions took place in small groups that had gathered to share food and their experiences with the recent changes. We were witnessing the birth of new norms as they were taking root in the new organization, participation as manifested in sharing and open dialogue.

2. Extensive efforts are under way to integrate structures and to solidify internal and external relationships critical to OHROS's success in working within the new paradigm. An important example is that OHROS's HR staff directors have formed a council to deal with ongoing service delivery issues. Although discussions of communications, responsibilities, and coordination are taking place in formal settings such as the council, one can also observe these same types of discussions taking place in more informal places, such as employee offices. The objective, however, appears to be the same: the continued clarifying and sorting of the new managerial and employee roles. In addition, managers and employees are discussing ways in which to coordinate the work processes so customers can be better served with a minimum of difficulty. In many cases these interactions are taking place among managers and employees who have no formal reporting requirements among themselves, people from different parts of OHROS engaging in fruitful discussions about work processes, service, and performance. What we are observing is a greater degree of lateral communication and coordination.

3. All OHROS employees who have been assigned to work teams have had basic training on working in teams and providing customer service. Some have had advanced customer service training.

One OHROS employee has been certified as a master trainer by an external consulting firm, and he is training OHROS employees to conduct the team training curriculum. The training modules include, but are not limited to, (a) basic principles of team work, (b) team leadership, (c) consensus building, and (d) managing the individual's role in the change process. Although most of the training has been voluntary, the training schedule has been full throughout the summer months. In addition, the workshop evaluations have been very supportive, and the written feedback has helped the training staff modify the modules to suit OHROS's employee and manager needs.

4. Several leadership training sessions have been conducted for the OHROS leadership cadre, with an emphasis on how to lead a team-based organization and how to foster innovations in providing high-quality customer service. Managing in a lateral type of organization presents many challenges, and the management is participating to the fullest extent. One of the authors has participated in a number of management forums and acknowledges the managers' efforts to recognize, understand, and apply the principles of customer service and employee empowerment. The topics of their discussions have focused on issues pertaining to customers' participation in modifying work processes, obtaining customer feedback through surveys and interviews, and coordination through cross-functional work groups, to name a few.

5. A follow-up system to fine-tune or adjust earlier staffing alignment decisions has been initiated. This process will assure continuous progress in matching organizational needs with employees' strengths and preferences. OHROS leadership has been very candid about its vision for the future, given the federal government's changing environment. It has discussed the changing nature of government work and has conveyed its knowledge about how government is changing in general and that all employees should be prepared to change roles at some point in their government career. As a result of these discussions, employees are in a good position to make well-informed decisions about their careers in OHROS and the government in general. Although at this time we do not know how many employees will ask to be shifted from their current assignment to a new one, we think it will be a very small percentage of OHROS's workforce.

The reorganization has generated a keen sense of awareness of and interest in customer service, and appreciation for empowerment has been raised to a new level of consciousness. OHROS employees must be more agile and creative to adapt continuously to changing customer needs. How will we keep the momentum going and maintain interest, commitment, and ownership among OHROS employees? This is a story of a bright beginning on a long journey. We have defined our work, and we are eager to get on with it.

References

Barzelay, M. (1992). *Breaking through bureaucracy: A new vision for managing in government*. Los Angeles: University of California Press.

Browner, C. M. (1994, November 1). *Improving environmental protection through empowered employees: Streamlining the U.S. Environmental Protection Agency*. Washington, DC: U.S. Environmental Protection Agency.

Cannon, J. Z. (1994a, June 17). *Reinventing OARM*. Washington, DC: U.S. Environmental Protection Agency.

Cannon, J. Z. (1994b, July 27). *Reinventing OARM—Decisions and future steps*. Washington, DC: U.S. Environmental Protection Agency.

Gore, A. (1993). *Creating a government that works better and costs less: The report of the National Performance Review*. New York: Penguin Books.

Katz, D., & Kahn, R. L. (1978). *The social psychology of organizations* (2nd ed.). New York: Wiley.

Mohrman, S. A., Cohen, S. G., & Mohrman, A. M. (1995). *Designing team-based organizations: New forms of knowledge work*. San Francisco: Jossey-Bass.

National Academy of Public Administration. (1984). *Steps towards a stable future: Assessing budget and personnel processes at the Environmental Protection Agency*. Washington, DC: Author.

National Academy of Public Administration. (1985). *Steps towards a stable future: A progress report on human resources at the Environmental Protection Agency* [Draft]. Washington, DC: Author.

O'Connor, D. J. (1994a, September 29). *Redesign steering committee members*. Washington, DC: U.S. Environmental Protection Agency, Office of Human Resources Management.

O'Connor, D. J. (1994b, September 29). *Welcome to the redesign steering committee*. Washington, DC: U.S. Environmental Protection Agency, Office of Human Resources Management.

O'Connor, D. J., & Lowe, C. (1994, September 19). *Volunteers for redesign steering committee*. Washington, DC: U.S. Environmental Protection Agency, Office of Human Resources Management.

Office of Human Resources Management. (1994a December). Changing the future for organizational and human resources services. *Data book: OHROS future search conferences*. Washington, DC: U.S. Environmental Protection Agency.

Office of Human Resources Management. (1994b, September 16). *Creating a new human resources and organizational services office: Process design*. Washington, DC: U.S. Environmental Protection Agency.

U.S. Environmental Protection Agency. (1994, June). *Reinventing EPA—Stronger environmental protection through empowered employees*. Washington, DC: Office of Administration and Resources Management.

Weisbord, M. (1992). *Discovering common ground*. San Francisco: Berrett-Koehler.

Part III

Strategies for Revitalizing the New Organization

Introduction

This section presents some advice and answers from seasoned practitioners who have been monitoring and participating in the major organizational transformations underway in corporate America. They provide valuable perspectives regarding the keys to the revitalization of our workforce. Revitalization is clearly essential if we are to retain our competitive advantage in the global economy. These chapters stress the importance of focusing on individual, team, and organizational strategies to regain the commitment of our workers and the health and productivity of our organizations.

In Chapter 9, Jaffe and Scott draw upon their extensive consulting experience to report "from the trenches" on how best to get people to reconnect to the organization. The authors view the rekindling of organizational commitment after a massive change and the development of an empowered workplace as the greatest organizational challenges of our time. "Empowerment" is the mobilization of an individual's inner capacity for the benefit of the organization. Empowerment is the core of the organizational energy of the 90s. If organizations take the needs of their workers into account as they experience organizational change and the establishment of a new work contract, then they can recover more quickly and sustain the commitment and capability of the people who remain with them. Jaffe and Scott suggest that employers must overcome both the "crisis of will" (lack of worker motivation) and the "crisis of skill" (shortage of workers with the necessary competencies for the new organization). Several case studies are presented as examples of transformational change.

Chapter 10, by Noer, outlines a fundamental shift in the paradigm defining the working relationship between individuals and organizations. The end result of this shifting paradigm is a new psychological contract which, if not dealt with positively, can result in devastating effects on employees who remain in downsized organizations. The author defines this condition as "layoff survivor sickness." The chapter offers a four-level model for intervention. Level 1 focuses on proper management of the layoff process itself. Level 2 emphasizes the acceptance of pain and the facilitation of grieving. Level 3 aims to break the chains of codependency without destroying trusting and honest relationships. Level 4 works to develop systems that are compatible with the new organizational reality, and to foster a new employment contract of responsibility.

In Chapter 11, Rosen describes the eight principles of good leadership collected from interviews with leaders in huge multinational corporations and small family businesses. He provides a convincing case that healthy, high-performance enterprises are the models of organizations that will succeed in the 21st century. A healthy organization is one that nurtures and taps the talents, ideas, and energy of its employees. The only way to alter an organization in the deep, long-term ways that inspire people to perform well is to transform the organization's leadership. The leader's job is maximizing the organization's most valuable asset, the employees, while overcoming the "crisis of commitment" resulting from major organizational change. The bottom line is ultimately the result of human endeavor. Dr. Rosen provides an impressive summary of research demonstrating the effect of good leadership practices and healthy organizational environments on organizational outcomes such as increased profits and customer satisfaction.

In Chapter 12, Monroy, Jonas, Mathey, and Murphy discuss important revitalization strategies at Corning, Inc. Corning has not downsized; instead the company remained stable in terms of overall employment while undergoing reengineering. The authors describe a research partnership between a federal safety and health agency and a U.S. manufacturing company. The partnership worked to develop a better understanding of occupational stress, to identify the relationship between stress and organizational practices and effectiveness, to evaluate interventions to reduce stress and worker medical costs, and to improve worker health and productivity. Corning is an example of a proactive organization working to prevent employee problems rather than waiting to correct those problems after they occur. Although their initial work concentrated on individual interventions (stress management training for employees), their future work will explore team and organizational interventions to reduce workplace stress.

9

Rekindling Work Commitment and Effectiveness Through a New Work Contract

Dennis T. Jaffe and Cynthia D. Scott

This chapter, a "report from the trenches," is about using psychological skills to change, revitalize, and renew organizations and work units. We describe activities and processes that derive from common psychological principles and from our understanding of not only today's stressful work environment but also the conditions that lead to high-performance work.

Today, the nature of work and the "glue" that connects the person to the organization are changing profoundly. Employee expectations from work have shifted from dependency, entitlement, stability, and security to a more conditional relationship based on mutual maturity. Workers are confused and upset about how and why their company has both changed and demanded that they change. Changing workplaces need policies, actions, and processes that increase employees' willingness to reconnect to the organization and that help overcome the pressures that disconnect them.

The central challenge is to produce high-performance, high-commitment work relationships in workplaces that have abruptly but necessarily changed the basic expectations between employee and employer. The new workplace that many successful companies are creating is one where employees and leaders work together to implement a new form of organization and forge a new agreement between employees and the organization. We will present several "snapshots" of initiatives taking place in large companies that are attempting to overcome the disastrous effects of insensitive downsizing with processes that take people into account.

These evolving new work relationships have been called a *new work contract*. It is not a legal document but the implicit, understood, and often unarticulated set of expectations and understandings that lie beyond the specific task responsibilities and work role. This work contract has been shifting to correspond to a new set of expectations and style of work. The challenge is to deal effectively with people who feel deprived and threatened by the changes and will not accept, understand, or agree to the changes, no matter how necessary they may be or how much they reflect the new realities of work.

Not everyone is able or willing to enter into these new agreements. The organization must make sure that those who stay on are the best people, but often this is not the case. Frequently the people who stay are not ready or willing to make the new commitment and just go through the motions of doing their work. Afraid to leave and afraid to admit that things have changed, they live in denial or perpetual resistance.

The shift toward empowerment of employees represents work relationships in which employees operate within the new work relationship. From our consulting experience in organizations, we see empowerment as an initiative that strives to balance individual freedom and organizational constraint. The ongoing recalibration of this balance to release the most energy and creativity is the challenge of building an empowered workplace. For the past two decades, we have observed and participated in various methods for creating empowered organizations. We used the tools of the human potential movement when we initially approached this challenge of how to support people in making the required changes: self-awareness, self-regulation, stress management, and health promotion training and workshops. After rigorous application of individual techniques did not produce the expected degree of organizational change, we began to look at resistance to change from both the psychological and structural–organizational viewpoints. At the same time, our clients were struggling with these challenges in the face of increased global competition, which increased the pressure to produce higher quality goods and services while mobilizing human capital by encouraging employee involvement and commitment to the organization's success.

In this chapter, we discuss how organizations are changing the nature of the work expectations for employees, the effects these changes have on employees, and how these changes are linked to greater organizational effectiveness and the ability to continue to work. Specifically, we discuss (a) the historical roots of change in the organizational work environment; (b) the new organizational focus on empowerment—the creation of new, empowered workers in the changed environment that holds new challenges for employees; (c) the new work contract; (d) the development of new organizational processes with a particular focus on organizational leaders and middle managers; (e) the initiation of real change by focusing on the needs of employees; (f) the four stages of individual, group, and organizational transitions; and (g) case studies that illustrate some of these points.

Historical Roots of Organizational Change.

This has been an era of the most massive changes in the nature and behavior of organizations ever experienced. Over a decade, millions of jobs have been eliminated, and the nature of work has shifted from the industrial model of production to an information-based model. This is not theory, but a living transformation experienced in varying degrees by every workplace. Many people have left organizations that have "gone on diets," and those who remain tend to work in teams, have instantaneous access to information, are forced to make their own decisions, must continually justify the value of their work, and struggle to overcome the vestiges of the old control-oriented and bureaucratic culture that once was the foundation of all organizations.

The transition has been painful for almost everyone. Some people are casualties, losing their jobs and their identities. Others have been winners, taking up new work styles and working in new ways. Others have sought shelter where they could find it, by downward mobility, by hanging on to old jobs, or by doing new work in the old way. They hope they can hang on long enough to retire.

The current changes deeply affect the people inside organizations. Employees have been through a turbulent decade. As organizations downsized, flattened, and restructured, they left a wake of people who felt the trust in their workplace shattered, their sense of security severely called into question, their personal sense of identity and competency shaken, and their overall morale plummeting.

Even companies that have "successfully" negotiated the reengineering process have faced the challenge of restoring their human capital. National Semiconductor, Inc., was 8 months into a major transformation project when we received a call from Gil Amelio, the company's chief executive officer (CEO), who said, "The thing that is keeping me up at night is the loss of our sense of unity. How do I bring people back emotionally?" (This and other cases are discussed in more detail in Jaffe, Scott, & Tobe, 1995.)

To understand the historical background for this challenge to change, we begin by noting that the traditional large bureaucracies have had their day. Over one third of the Fortune 500 companies of a decade ago no longer exist. Giants that previously were synonymous with good management and stability, such as IBM, GM, AT&T, Chrysler, and Macy's, now find that their difficulty with change endangers their existence. These large companies want to renew themselves, and each one has a strategy to accomplish that. The thesis of this chapter is that along with strategic redefinition, new technology, new products aligned to customer needs, and intercompany alliances, the challenge of the future is for a company to redefine fundamentally the way people work together and to build and support this new kind of work environment.

Change today happens so fast that organizations cannot respond to it as slowly as they have in the past. The following are some of the challenges facing organizations today:

- doing more with less,
- remaining competitive in a fast-changing work environment,
- motivating employees to do more difficult and complex work,
- overcoming workers' difficulties in completing major changes,
- recognizing that traditional ways do not work any more,
- helping workers to overcome feeling upset and betrayed by the organization for changing, and

- developing higher levels of skills and initiative from every employee.

In summary, the vast changes in the work environment and the acceleration of the pace and degree of change have produced the need for a new style of organization. We see five recurring themes in the way that the new empowered, network organization is defined:

1. *Information focus: From closed to open.* Everyone in the organization has nearly complete information about it and the key markers that lead to business success.
2. *Customer focus: From inside to outside.* Workers try to please the customer rather than looking up the hierarchy to please the boss.
3. *Systems focus: From parts to wholes.* Employees look at the needs of the organization as a whole, not on the particular demands of their own functional area or group.
4. *Learning focus: From status quo to emerging possibility.* The organization seeks new possibilities and new ways rather than resting on established wisdom.
5. *Empowerment focus: From organization to person.* Individuals are empowered to act rather than waiting for instructions and procedures from the organization.

We will focus here on the empowerment aspect of the new workplace, but emphasize that the other elements of the shift are all frequent in workplaces moving toward greater employee empowerment.

Creating Empowered Workers in the Changed Environment

Employees experience the global shift in the nature of the organization as a shift in the way they are expected to do their jobs and get work done. Particularly, the ground rules constituting what sort of employee expectations and behavior will be seen as successful have changed in some of the following ways: The shift in work paradigms represents a shift away from compliance to commitment; entitlement to empowerment; conformity to alignment around values; specialization to generalist, within a broad band; clearly defined jobs to competencies, projects, and outcomes; manager to leader–coach; functional autonomy to cross-functional teamwork; functions to competencies; career ladders to flat organizations and project focus; and one career to many.

To actually produce the desired new workplace, every expectation and assumption about good work and how to do it must be turned around. Although not every workplace embodies every one of these emphases, the current wave of new management models, initiatives, and learning processes are all aimed at helping people make the shifts just defined. Let us look more closely at how this can come about.

When change is successful, the organization begins to make a major transformation, a change in the way it does everything. Such transformational change has been compared with the usual form of gradual, incremental change. (See Argyris & Schon, 1995, who use the terms *Learning I* and *Learning II*, taken from Gregory Bateson.) The new organization both needs and desires to enhance the capacity of individuals, teams, and larger organizations to be more creative and agile and to produce higher quality, customer-focused services. All organizations aim to produce a workplace where employees truly care about the results the organization produces and feel ownership of results such that they continually strive to make them better. This attitude and style of organizational activity has been called the *empowered workplace*. Although some executives are put off by this word, because it has a connotation of either unbridled freedom, loss of control, or pushing accountability and work on fewer people, we find that when properly defined and implemented, it best expresses the spirit of the new workplace.

Empowerment, the mobilization of inner capacity within and for the benefit of the organization, has become the core of organizational energy of the 1990s. As an organization downsizes and changes, several consequences occur: (a) With fewer workers, each person has to be more efficient; (b) with fewer middle managers to watch them work and tell them what to do, employees have to be responsible for their own behavior; (c) with change happening continuously, workers need to adapt and redesign how they do things and at the same time produce continually improving results; and (d) employees have to listen to their customers and people outside their work group and respond to their needs rather than being oriented to pleasing their boss. With more complex, ambiguous tasks, requiring more individual judgment and responsibility, every employee must collaborate with many other people, with different skills and in many different configurations of work groups.

The shift to empowerment entails two types of change in individuals: what we call overcoming the crisis of will and the crisis of skill. Overcoming the *crisis of will*, or motivation, relates to workers' overcoming their painful and negative feelings about the process of change, especially downsizing and drastic redesign, and deciding to recommit to their workplace. Many managers think that will, or motivation, is enough. But workers can have will and not know what to do or how to do things.

The *crisis of skill*, or capability, refers to the need to develop the new competencies, the new capabilities and attitudes that will make that person successful in the new workplace. Employees cannot be ordered to change, give up control, or take more responsibility if they have never learned how to do it. That is the dilemma in the Eastern bloc countries today. Workers need to see and practice new models of behavior and have time to learn and space to experiment and even to make mistakes.

Reengineering, rightsizing, and *total quality management* are today's buzzwords that represent a range of initiatives, such as training programs, motivational speeches, and structural shifts, to achieve the desired fast and radical change. At the same time as they strive for empowerment, the initiatives that cut costs and staff have had exactly the opposite effect: Employees have become dispirited, demoralized, embittered, detached, and apathetic about their workplaces. Yet, to succeed in the future, these lean organizations need more, not less, from the people who remain. The rekindling of organizational commitment after a massive change and the development of an empowered workplace are the greatest organizational challenges of our time.

In a workshop for store associates at a large retail company that wanted to reduce turnover and get them to take more responsibility for sales, one person expressed a concern that empowerment would just lead to people not doing their jobs, showing up late, not looking businesslike, and using bad judgment with customers. The store associates themselves were uncertain about empowerment, about whether they really would be allowed to make the decisions they wanted to make about merchandise placement, offering refunds, and pricing. The result was a standoff until the two groups were able to air their concerns together and create what we called a *license for success*: a clear, specific agreement about the rights and responsibilities of managers and store associates.

We found ourselves returning to our roots as behavioral scientists and looking at the interconnection between individual competency and organizational structure. Empowerment is not merely an individual process. One cannot lead a workshop in empowerment skills unless simultaneously the organization or context in which the person works is prepared to make structural changes that will support the new behaviors. Many organizations invested heavily in training interventions that gave individuals new skills and ideas only to send those same employees back to work environments and relationships that had not changed. This kind of "workshop high" tended to produce momentary resolve to change and then bitter disappointment and cynicism.

Team relationships have to change as well. In a division at Chevron, 14 work teams have met and come up with "empowerment charters." Each charter has two statements. The team members come up with a list of empowered behaviors, and then the managers meet and come up with a corresponding list of how they as managers will support these new behaviors. The managers and the employees work together to change their behaviors. The managers have to learn to allow empowerment and support initiative and employee development by letting go of control. Employees have to develop their business skills and learn to take actions and be responsible for results, not for just doing their jobs. These are major changes that do not take root overnight but need some fine-tuning and adjustment as each group practices new behaviors.

In transformational efforts, the task is to move from first- to second-order change. Most organizations see change as changing the way things are done. They do some things differently, but their basic structures are unchanged. This is first-order change. The argument here is that the type of change that organizations need is so basic and far-reaching that it changes everything about the way things are done. There must be transformational, second-order change. New skills, new languages, and new maps are needed to guide teams and organizations as they reinvent themselves.

In summary, empowerment is not just built into individuals but has to be built into team relationships and the organizational structure. Real change has to include changes in individual mindsets, attitudes and roles, team relationships, and organizational structures.

One of the ongoing challenges is to reinforce constantly that an employee's success and career advancement should be dependent on his or her ability to be successful in the new, empowered work setting. The ability of top managers to shift from one set of behavior reinforcers to another set is one of the measures of the degree to which the new model will be sustained. As the numbers of top and middle managers thin rapidly, the remaining managers increasingly will be only those who can work as coaches, collaborators, and facilitators rather than as traditional, directive leaders.

Role Shift: Building the New Work Contract

Getting through this deep and fundamental organizational change entails employees' building a new type of relationship with the organization. The new work contract means a corresponding shift in both the employees' role and the company's assurances to them. One cannot change without the other. Some of the qualities of this new relationship include (a) new expectations of what they need to give to the organization; (b) new expectations of what they can get from the organization in return; (c) a new understanding of the nature and scope of work, including responsibility, role, and accountability; and (d) a new willingness of everyone to do what it takes to achieve success.

The employee, no matter what his or her function, must shift to a new role in which he or she takes more responsibility for business outcomes and for improving the organization. This greater role encompasses the following:

- exercising more personal judgment within;
- utilizing broad guidelines and values rather than just following established policies;
- having broader job descriptions that demand multiple competencies;
- having more responsibility for strategy for developing the organization;
- looking for ways to improve how things are done;
- demonstrating team and interpersonal skills;
- dealing with less certainty and more ambiguity and knowing that change is part of the reality; and
- having greater latitude to make decisions and the ability to act and be successful.

The employee cannot be expected to make this tremendous shift on a dime. In the traditional workplace, the just-mentioned behaviors would be met by retaliation of managers and pressures to do what the boss says, play it safe, keep one's mouth shut, and not take initiative or go beyond narrow job expectations. Therefore, the employee needs powerful and continual reinforcement that the organization recognizes the implications of the change.

In response to this new employee commitment, empowerment, and responsibility, the organization must offer something in return, such as

- credibility and fairness in making changes, especially layoffs;
- support for the emotional upheaval of the transition;
- respect for employees as people;
- information about what is happening;
- participation in how to overcome challenges and discover new ways to improve;
- learning opportunities for self-development; and
- the challenge to use oneself meaningfully.

A successful shift to the new work structure, the empowered, network workplace, will only occur if these shifts in roles and expectations occur as well. Underlying the one-time shifts of reengineering, downsizing, mergers, and various reorganizations must be changes in the mutual expectations between employees, managers, and the organization.

Developing New Organizational Processes: Focus on Leaders and Managers

Leadership

As an organization tries to change, several challenges arise. First, the people at the top, who have benefited and succeeded within the traditional structures, are in many ways the least willing or able to change. The informal values, rewards, and promotions all support the old ways, leaving the employees who have more progressive ideas feeling frustrated. We see the leaders of large companies falling into several pitfalls when they try to achieve transformation:

Not supporting people's needs in change. We call this *emotional illiteracy*, which is not understanding the complex dynamics of people faced with drastic and total shifts in the nature of their work. Leaders often fail to understand that people need psychological security before they can change. Change is terrifying, and the company needs to provide some form of psychological security. That does not mean job security, which does not exist, but to at least offer clear information on what is happening, options, and possibilities and then allow employees time to move through the phases of transition.

Not including themselves in the process. Sometimes leaders see incongruence between their stated goals and what they do (e.g., they act directive and controlling while asking workers to act empowered). Leaders often feel they do not have to change, just the people below them. They act as if they have already changed or are too smart to change. This attitude leaves them less open to listening and learning from the people below them.

Not giving up control. Empowerment needs to be accompanied by trust, rooted in an understanding that the leader alone cannot solve the problems. Employees need to be allowed to come up with innovations and trust in leaders' good will. Although this can be difficult for managers who have held onto power for most of their lives, some learn to do it, with spectacular results.

Isolation. Sometimes leaders do not come out of their offices and do not really seek out and listen to distressing information from employees. One of the easiest ways leaders maintain illusions is by staying on the phone with the central office, traveling a lot, and relying on subordinates to tell them what is going on. The essence of this behavior is fear of listening and inability to manage people in distress.

Impatience. Often a promising program is discontinued just as it is on the verge of accomplishing its goal because the management feels it is not working, or worse, the leaders find a new fad or program and move on to that. The key factors in successful change seem to be persistence in a path, with prudent feedback and course correction along the way.

Most of these mistakes are made almost unconsciously; yet, as we have noted, their effect on the organization is to undermine its goals of change. We believe it is imperative for leaders to develop the self-awareness to understand that unless they see these pitfalls, they themselves become the problem and the reason why change is not going well. Of course, those who fall into these traps have elaborate theories about who is to blame: unmotivated employees, lack of resources, corporate policies, bad competitors, or the economic climate. But the truth, which they deny and avoid, is that the major obstacle to change in many large companies is the lack of self-awareness in the top management, their lack of capacity to see that they themselves need to change in ways they at first do not fully comprehend, and that they need to let go of control and allow the power of the employees below them to grow.

Middle Managers

In the new workplace, middle managers are an endangered species, and in many change efforts they are the most threatened. Because the pyramid is flattening, there is less need for people who supervise people. The role of the middle manager must shift to coordinating the work of more people and to becoming a point person for the necessary role shift. Many middle managers leave the organization, and the few who are left are under tremendous pressure. As the organization changes, they are expected to produce results from above, and they feel the pressure of newly empowered, newly competent people from below. Under threat, they dig in. They need support, security, and help in learning new ways.

One large pharmaceutical company, seeing that the top management was the least able to see how quickly the environment was changing, initiated a development program for the new generation of leaders who were in middle management. The top leaders were only a few years from retirement, and the question of succession was wide open. Top leadership decided that there needed to be a concerted effort to develop a new style of leadership and management.

In in-depth interviews we asked a cross-section of the most successful managers (as defined by their performance evaluations) about the skills and learning experiences that were most important to them in developing their leadership and the skills they felt were most necessary to be effective leaders in the future. These managers realized that the keys to success in the future were the abilities to develop people, manage change collaboratively, understand the whole organization and not just their own division, and understand and respond to customers. They also realized that the traditional culture that kept people allied with their individual business unit, stressed caution and tradition, did not seek innovation, and depended on customers' always buying what they offered did not represent the values needed for the future. Another theme was that their recent history of layoffs had caused the remaining employees to be confused about what was expected of them and how they could succeed in the changing company.

The company had in effect a clash between the traditional hierarchical culture and the new work values. The human resources leadership decided that the best way to resolve this conflict progressively was to encourage the development of new leadership skills and capabilities. Several activities were initiated to facilitate change. First, new leadership values and competencies were proposed that consisted of three areas: leading oneself, developing people, and achieving business results. These areas were clearly defined, and learning programs based on each of them were created. Feedback processes that measured the presence of these competencies were initiated, and managers who represented them were visibly rewarded. The focus in the organization shifted with the emphasis on the new role of the manager. The manager was now charged not just with delivering business results, "the numbers," but also with developing individual employees, supporting their career and leadership development, and managing by the new values. The focus on manager behavior was a good leverage point for changing the attitudes and actual behavior of thousands of employees, in contrast with an approach that would try to train thousands of employees in new work practices without making sure that the new behaviors would actually be supported by the people in authority.

Initiating Real Change: Focusing on the Employees

In asking people to commit to a redesigned organization, we are really asking them to sign up for an entirely new way of working. A common belief is that employees will welcome this change, but managers resist giving up their power, and employees are often afraid of their new responsibilities. As people leave the organization, more responsibility falls on the shoulders of those who remain. These employees are often concerned about their new level of responsibility, and we have seen resistance to it at all levels. For some employees, strong needs for structure, identity, defined roles, and limited risk taking were met by the pyramid structure. These employees had also become comfortable in blaming management as a means of managing anxiety. As one such employee stated, "I'd rather be dead than empowered."

From the study of trauma and of people's responses to disastrous change, we discovered several principles: (a) change is deeply disruptive and upsetting; (b) people will get worse before they get better; (c) some people are never going to change; (d) when forced into a crisis or trauma, people frequently regress and tilt toward stereotyped, rigid, and unproductive behavior. With all of these consequences, we cannot expect that change in organizations will produce a work family of high performers without a lot of help and patience. Yet, that is precisely what companies expect and try to make happen.

Organizations today must decide how they will handle change. There are four possible responses to change:

- avoid it;
- lurch randomly from side to side, and initiative to initiative, without planning or integration;
- change when one absolutely has to, in response to others; and
- anticipate and plan change, designing a process to shift from the traditional to newer styles of working.

The first two ways will ultimately endanger the ability of the organization to survive.

Increasingly often we hear that loyalty to the organization is frayed, especially among the employees who survive these major changes. Creating change demands activities that challenge these feelings and attitudes. In this context, the restoration and rebuilding of loyalty and commitment is difficult to imagine. The people who remain are often shell-shocked, hurt, and angry, although they are so afraid of the future that they do their best to hide this. Their leaders are often willing to go along with the charade, because they, too, fear the feelings they are having about change.

Four Stages of Individual, Group, and Organizational Transition

Even if the new roles are attractive, individuals need to travel through a process toward accepting change. We have observed four distinct stages:

1. denial,
2. resistance,
3. exploration, and
4. commitment.

Everyone in the organization will go through these four stages, but the speed of the process may vary according to the individual's personality and position within the organization. Although management may be able to influence the rate at which some employees move through the stages, and can act to provide resources at the stage at which employees can best use them, attempting to force employees to skip or move too quickly through a stage will only send issues "underground."

Denial

Denial, refusing to believe that something is happening or feeling frustrated when it does not happen instantly, is a psychological defense against change that takes the form of either ignoring or not responding to information that shows a demand for change. Denial is an attempt to hold onto the safety and comfort of the past by ignoring signs that something is over.

At this stage, employees may seem unaffected, or at least undisturbed, by the proposed change. They see the change as an "it," not something happening to them. In fact, sometimes performance improves because of employees' belief that if they just perform better now, nothing really will need to change. It is tempting for managers to let this stage go on as long as possible, because pain and conflict are minimized. In reality, however, anger and resistance are just simmering, waiting to emerge at that point at which the individuals' work lives change so much that it can no longer be denied. Leaders are especially prone to one form of denial: the assumption that change can be painless, easy, and instant. Leaders in denial execute a "Tarzan swing" into commitment, by isolating themselves from the people who have to change and just assuming it will happen. By the time they recognize that change is not painless, easy, and instant, it is too late, and the change is more costly and difficult.

Resistance

Awakening from denial is traumatic. Workers are still not ready to change when they emerge from denial into the stage of *resistance*, where they feel anger and depression at the unfairness of having a change thrust on them and justifiable fear of what the future holds. This stage is about loss, and people in it need to mourn. We found this out when we were engaged in 1983 to develop a team renewal process for AT&T just after they had announced their first layoffs in history, cutting 24,000 jobs and initiating the breakup into several smaller "Baby Bells." As we traveled from branch to branch through the country, we found that it was inconceivable for the people we met to simply come together in new teams. They were sad, feeling that the cornerstone of their identity, Ma Bell, had suddenly died. They were terrified and feeling that they did not know what would happen to them. They were angry, feeling that the company had let them down and changed the rules without warning. This was the first time we had seen such responses, but even after more than a decade, we still see the same phases of emotional response to downsizing in other companies pursuing this course.

Managers have their own resistance to change as well, which must be diminished. What happens to the managers is that suddenly the clarity of their "plan, control, and schedule" role, all the things they learned at school, does not work any more. They are asked to coach, inspire, and negotiate. If you are an engineer, you have focused on becoming a technical expert, and now you are supposed to focus on people development and self-management—this is very upsetting. Managers can be upset because they suddenly have to give up blaming their own manager, their employees, or the system. Employees do not readily want to be accountable. They want someone to keep open the old career path, and they will be mad at the organization for not keeping to their agreement. Nobody—employees or their managers—wants to be responsible for their own career development.

There is no simple answer as to what must be done to respond to employee resistance, but there are three basic principles.

- The organization needs to give workers a chance to express their feelings and understand where they will stand in the new order of things.
- It needs to supply timely and full information, candidly explaining the new expectations, the reasons for them, and what options and choices employees have.
- Then employees need training and a chance to practice new skills and ways of working together.

At this point employees will begin to experience acceptance of the change, even if they do not particularly like it.

Not everyone emerges from his or her resistance, and not everyone is able or willing to learn new ways. Some people hold on to the sense of being a victim, and some organizations give them ample reasons to feel this way. The organization needs to understand that the way it approaches the change sows the seeds for the way that people will reconnect to the organization. If people are treated rudely, insensitively, and unfairly as they leave, how can it convince those who stay that the organization is worthy of their commitment? As we put it, saying good good-byes is essential to saying hello.

Exploration

Resistance is followed by exploration as people shift from holding onto the past to looking ahead at how they will fit into the future. An organization that allows people to go through resistance is rewarded by a group of people who are ready to find ways to meet the new challenge. At this phase, employees are finally open to learning new ways.

Commitment

The final stage of managed change is a new commitment. It is important to note that a manager experiences this transition process from two points of view. Managers as individuals go through the transition process themselves, but they also need to lead others as they go through it.

The organizations that emerge from downsizings and drastic change by respecting their employees, offering those who remain reasonable opportunities to make a difference, helping them develop their skills so that they remain competitive and employable, and showing willingness to learn and question the old ways will be the ones that are able to regain the commitment of their workers.

Representative Approaches to Organizational Renewal: Some Case Studies

Organizations are implementing the new work contract and changing work relationships through a variety of initiatives and processes. We have arranged them along a continuum, from those that focus more on individuals to those that focus on the organization. They are not mutually exclusive, although we have seen a progression whereby organizations usually begin with a more individually oriented approach and then shift to a more organizational focus in order to achieve real change. Our view is that only an approach that combines the individual and organizational perspectives will be successful and complete. The organization can help their employees sustain productivity and commitment by pursuing four paths.

1. Support Employees Through the Emotional Phases of Transition

Change is a great upheaval, and change initiatives need to deal with the struggle of every person to deal with change. People need to develop new change skills, and organizations need to offer emotional support to people through change. Change strategies at this level include individual support processes such as employee assistance programs and outplacement workshops, as well as workshops and team meetings that recognize the deep struggle of change. We have used the four-phase transition model to help people understand and leaders and employees adjust to the trauma of continuing change.

2. Teach New Skills and Roles for Managers, Employees, and Teams

To succeed in the new workplace, people need to work by new rules and learn new roles, new competencies, and a new set of work responsibilities. Managers need to become facilitative leaders, and employees need to become empowered. Together, managers and employees need to build new teams that operate with new roles under a new set of work understandings. Workshops and learning activities can help people learn and practice these new skills. However, to get people to adopt new roles in the workplace, they need more than just a training workshop. The new behaviors need to be reinforced and supported by actions, policies, and values of the organization. The first case study, of Washington Natural Gas, exemplifies these first two approaches to change.

3. Cultivate New Human Resource Partnerships

The infrastructure of work values, compensation, incentives, training, employee and career development, and supervision must shift from the traditional perspective to the expanded work roles. Managers need to become change leaders, coaches who develop and motivate their people. Everyone must develop new work roles and skills. Interventions on this level focus on supporting new organizational roles and values through organizational policies on recruitment, training and development, performance evaluation, supervision, career development, promotion, and succession planning. If a change is not reinforced and supported by changes in these policies and cultural elements, then the initial positive changes will tend to decay over time. The process mentioned earlier in the pharmaceutical company, in which managers learned new capabilities and were encouraged to take on new roles, is an example of this sort of change.

4. Whole-Systems Change

One way to rebuild commitment and manage change is to conduct large group-learning and community-building events. These gatherings produce a deep understanding of various stakeholders' perspectives, produce a common view, develop cross-boundary relationships, and create a greater sense of participation and commitment in participants. They also resolve problems and produce real-time change. The second case study, of the IBM software laboratory experiencing change, will exemplify the whole-systems approach to change.

Case Study 1: Helping Employees to Begin a New Work Partnership

The top leaders of Washington Natural Gas believed that their 1,200 employees needed to change because they were part of an underperforming utility facing competition for the first time. They were in the midst of a major reengineering effort that began with a major reorganization, with new technologies. They were in the middle of a merger and wanted a new culture, with higher levels of employee involvement and satisfaction. We decided to involve all 1,200 people in this process. Now, by the time we got to it, it was a little too late for them to involve all 1,200 people, as the decision had already been made and people could only decide how to implement it. With groups of 70 people at a time (it could have been more, but the leaders of the change process were uncomfortable with larger groups), representing a cross-section of levels and areas of the company, we convened a 3-day workshop on creating the new workplace. The groups were composed of workers from different sites to avoid the possibility of people from one site just retelling their own group's story to each other.

The first morning focused on helping the workers to see the big picture to understand why all these changes had to happen. Having a coherent understanding of the problem is very important to an employee's ability to grieve for the old organization and make the transition to the new one with a sense of commitment. Humans have a deep need to understand events and to be able to tell the larger story about them. The company wanted its 1,200 people telling the same story, especially when they went home and tried to explain it to their families. So the first morning was spent explaining the rationale behind the changes. Then we worked on understanding what the leadership was seeing and some of the issues behind their decisions. At first, the leaders were very hesitant and dismayed. Having hired a consulting firm that had said, "We will do this for you, therefore you don't have to mess with this," they were taken aback and resistant when they were told they had to attend all 23 sessions. We explained to them that it was about showing up and being in dialogue without a script. To the leaders it was very scary to go live, without a prepared presentation, but this was the time to talk openly and freely to the employees about what was happening.

In the first session, a senior manager stood up and reported the feedback from an employee attitude survey of what the workers were feeling about the organization: betrayed, let down, angry, and shocked. This manager burst into tears because he felt so bad about having to present such negative information about his organization. He said, "I don't know how it got this bad." Such openness and truth telling are a part of taking responsibility for change. It is not that the leader who is there takes all the responsibility but just that there needs to be a time when leaders tell the truth, because that moves employees more than all the statements, financial reports, and employee newsletters.

The 3-day program, repeated 23 times, was more than a dialogue with top leaders; it was also a time to share responses to change and time to learn and practice the new skills and practices that made up the new employee role. The phases of transition were presented, and workers explored their own and the organization's responses to the changes. They also looked at where they were in relation to the four phases of transition and their work group and top leadership. Many employees believed that the top leaders were behind them, ironically, in their ability to accept the transition and often in denial of the reality of the changes. This perception in itself provoked dialogue.

Such workshops are like a tonic to an organization. The quality of the environment of this company shifted dramatically in the months that the program was under way. Employees believed that they had been brought into the change, and the process became less mysterious and more real to them. They would say that although they still did not like it, they at least felt treated like adults and understood the changes. The top leaders felt free of some of their burdens and were able to focus on managing the more difficult transitions and strategic changes at the company. Both the leaders and the workers learned some new ways to work together and developed a new openness to sharing information, feelings, and planning.

Case Study 2: Renewal Through Large Systems Change

This case study examines a large-scale renewal process within one division of IBM that has been ongoing since the mid-1980s. To accomplish this renewal, a number of top-down corporate initiatives have been launched successively to achieve business excellence, market-driven quality, and massive culture change. Because of the magnitude of these initiatives and the scope of their applications, we will focus this discussion on our direct experience as consultants in the task of applying the philosophy and structure of new work relationships in one organizational setting within IBM, a work unit of 2,000 employees that is responsible for software development for a large network of products and applications. The unit has developed its own cultural style, influenced by the Silicon Valley, and its business is profitable.

The overall pressures to change came from larger initiatives in the worldwide business climate: a general shift from hardware to software and a more dramatic shift in the "psychological contract" of employee's expectations about their jobs. But a change of this magnitude could not be accomplished by first-order change (i.e., change that is incremental and stepwise). What was called for in this setting was second-order change, change that changes the change. To work at this transformational level, we looked interactively at four areas of effort: (a) *structure*—such as the roles, functions, information systems, and reporting relationships; (b) *team relationships*, such as group accountability, self-management, and responsibility for task accomplishment; (c) *intergroup relationships*, such as how groups collaborate, cooperate, and teach each other within a learning community; and (d) *culture*, the symbolic events that indicate direction, vision, and meaning about the work. Any one of these areas could have been the beginning point, but all had to be considered and engaged in making the change work. The phases of the transformation process included the following.

1. New leadership: New direction. New leadership arrived with a mandate to renew the unit. The new leader had credibility due to previous success and was well thought of by the higher levels of the company. Thus, he was able to call for change and negotiate among other units to have time to allow the change to take place. This time is especially important because basic change usually takes longer than optimistic projections assume, and productivity, morale, and effectiveness go down drastically before they go up.

The arrival of a new plant manager initiated a structural realignment of 20 individual product focuses into two major clusters. This structural change was initiated to also accomplish a cultural shift from focus on external customers to include internal customers. A sense of complacency had developed in this laboratory regarding continuous improvement and cross-product linkages. To bring creativity and innovation to focus on new challenges, a Center for Software Excellence was established to act as a built-in information-gathering and sharing group that would surface innovation from inside and outside the organization. A cross-departmental planning function was organized to focus on customer needs. To further shift the structure, a total quality management initiative was instituted with ambitious goals for defect reduction.

The lab manager was convinced that these structural changes would push the lab into transformational change. Of interest is the gap between what the leader of a change perceives the change process to be and the actual implementation process.

2. Councils: Practice in collaborative process. Because employees of this company have, by and large, never worked for any other company, their knowledge and ability to work in new ways is severely constrained. How can one act empowered if one has never experienced it, either in school or at work? So the first set of innovations was designed to create "parallel structures," to have people learn and practice cross-group collaboration in which fundamental problems are addressed.

"Councils" were set up with a mandate to address basic issues of change: excellence, management, development, planning, support, and innovation. Membership included representatives of various levels of the organization, crossing all groups. People served for a limited time, and connectors were appointed with membership in two councils. These councils were designed to break down the barriers that had existed between professional groups. Each council was asked to formulate action plans to improve the targeted area.

3. Crisis. Having a clear organizational challenge is a great impetus to change. Often, without a clear crisis, change is faced with a mixture of denial and resistance that tends to slow real change efforts. The lab manager was faced with immense complacency brought on by past success and the semi-isolation of a research and development environment. Both anxiety and vision seem to be fuel for change, and both can be used to motivate and engage an organization to change direction. There was time to ask questions, seek information, and present feelings and facts about the new directions.

4. Building community: The leadership institute. To mark the initiation of these new changes, a 5-day leadership institute was convened. Its purpose was to support and reinforce a combination of skills and mindsets that would move the 400 managers and technical leaders to implement the structural shifts, but it was also a community-building event. All the managers were strongly encouraged to be there, especially because the lab manager would attend for the full time. Never before had the top management been together for a sustained period to exchange issues of shared frustration and build new agreements for action. The most powerful part of the institute came in the open dialogue with the lab manager.

In the presentation of components on leadership of change and empowerment, a number of surprises emerged:

- Many managers did not see the need for change.
- Managers believed that this need was the perception of the lab manager only and not an overall corporate strategy.
- Managers did not think change was their responsibility.
- Empowerment was not supported in the organizational structure.

The lab manager participated fully in each of these sessions and was surprised by many of the themes. He kept saying, "I've told them the mission, why don't they believe it?"

5. New tools: Maps for navigation. Our work in organizations is to address the cultural, team, and individual-mindset shifts that are needed to support structural changes. To this end, we provided a 2-day program that focused on a series of what we call "learning maps" that engage participants in experiential learning experiences about change and empowerment. We designed these learning maps to replace traditional group learning tools, workbooks, overheads, and feed-forward presentations. Instead, the participants were grouped in random discussion table groups and involved in discussions catalyzed by a facilitator. Participants were encouraged to write questions, paradoxes, and areas for future discussion on their maps.

Predictably, conflict and resistance emerged during the institute. The maps presented a framework for discussions and understanding as well as connection to their own experience. For example, people responded to our model of the four stages of transition, noting where they, their team, and their organization were on the change curve. The themes of the other maps were understanding resistance to change, change leadership, personal and organizational empowerment, organizational transformation, and creating empowered mindsets.

6. Creating change partnerships: The organization learns. After the initial institute experience, the managers pushed to have all 1,500 employees of the lab exposed to the maps program. These sessions were held again in large groups of 150 at a time. The goal was to sow the same concepts and skills presented to the managers and prepare them for partnership with their management in creating the transformation. The employees were quite vocal in their denial and resistance to the changes. One of the symbolic focuses of these sessions was to provide a "safe" sounding board with an outside facilitator to surface resistance and engage in dialogue with others from the same setting about change and empowerment. The lab manager was still amazed at the lack of understanding in the organization about the need for and the direction of the change. He said, "I keep sounding the alarm, and they keep pushing the snooze button." One of the core learnings of this phase is that the leader cannot make the lab successful; it will only come with the involvement of everybody.

7. Organization redesign. Many attempts at empowerment end with just concepts and slogans. The lab is currently moving into the next phase, where the organization structurally realigns itself with the new philosophy of empowerment. Organizational redesign is one of the necessary outcomes of empowerment. During this phase the structure, the relationships, and the strategy of the organization are questioned. A high-quality initiative can be a prime impetus for this redesign. Thus, quality, empowerment, and organizational redesign are three elements of one process.

Next Steps

We approach the transformation of an organization as a journey, with no quick fixes, and we believe that with activation, organizations, like people, have an immense capacity for self-regulation. Much of our approach is to engage an organization as a learning community where feedback, linked to continuous improvement, can move an organization toward outstanding performance.

The maps were intended to be used by the managers to go back to their work groups and engage in a dialogue with their team. Some of the questions generated in these sessions were

- Where does empowerment end and management begin?
- How can employees get forgiveness guaranteed up front so that as they risk mistakes through empowered actions, they will not be punished?
- On what will employees' performance ratings be based—individual, team, or overall lab performance?
- How do employees get their peers to cooperate with them when they do not have the same manager?

The previous phases were aimed at individual change, building new skills and mindsets to support more responsibility. Now those changes need to be institutionalized and reinforced on a work-group level. Each work team needs to become a democratic unit, like the council, and meet with its manager, who assumes a new role as facilitator, coach, and people developer, to look at what it is doing and how it can operate in a more empowered way. The team, with the manager and coach, examines what it is doing and then questions each of its activities.

This phase begins with the management team for each part of the unit meeting together and asking themselves, How would we act differently if we were an empowered group? They need to look at the new roles of teacher, coach, and facilitator and ask themselves what specific behaviors they need to adopt to become empowered. Most likely, there are no simple answers, only much conflict and heated discussion ahead.

Conclusion

Creating a new work contract that empowers people involves a profound transformation. Every element of the organization has to shift. The top leaders have to shift their attention from other people and start with themselves. It takes time, conscious and careful planning, and a series of steps to teach people new ways and move toward new structures. Employees have to be deeply and fully involved in every element of the change, and the culture and organizational policies and procedures have to shift to reflect the new expectations and realities.

References

Argyris, C., & Schon, D. (1995). *Organizational learning II.* New York: Addison-Wesley.
Jaffe, D., Scott, C., & Tobe, G. (1995). *Rekindling commitment.* San Francisco: Jossey-Bass.

10

Layoff Survivor Sickness: What It Is and What to Do About It

David Noer

Some years ago, I visited an old friend whom I had not seen in almost a year. It was a crisp, clear autumn afternoon, the kind of day that makes one walk a little faster and smile a little quicker. I was looking forward both to seeing my friend and to renewing my acquaintance with the organization in which he was vice president of marketing, a small but exciting high-technology spin-off from a large multinational corporation. The last time I had visited, this vibrant company was just 3 years old. Its 500 employees were turned on, bureaucracy was turned off, and one could feel the energy; the organization was brimming with spirit and creativity.

But things had changed. The open, cheerful smiling faces had been replaced by tense, rigid masks. One can gather useful data just by walking through organizational corridors, and I had picked up some distressing nonverbal messages on my way to my friend's office. The delightful, almost playful, tone of the organization that I remembered had turned somber, almost sullen.

The first thing my friend did was to hand me his resume; next he told me about the past 9 months. The venture capitalists who had bankrolled the spin-off were unhappy with the financial results and had brought in a new president. He was a "turnaround" expert, which meant that his first step was to institute significant across-the-board layoffs. In the ensuing 6 months, several more waves of reductions took place. Now there were too few people, too much work, and the organization was in steep decline. I was amazed at the drastic change in organizational culture.

After a brief tour, I had had enough. The people who had survived the reductions were fearful, angry, and depressed. Yet this was the same workforce that was expected to turn the organization around to meet global competition!

"I hope you sold your charter stock," I told my friend as I walked out the door. The sun was setting behind some dark clouds, and the chill I felt was due as much to my organizational encounter as to the weather.

Some of the ideas in this chapter have been discussed by the author in *Healing the Wounds: Overcoming the Trauma of Layoffs and Revitalizing Downsized Organizations* (Jossey-Bass, 1993) and "Leadership in an Age of Layoffs" (*Issues and Observations, 13*[3], 1993).

As I walked to my car, I reflected on the rapidity with which an organization that had once brimmed over with joy in work had been reduced to a place filled with sullen and angry survivors. I did not know it at the time, but I had had my first face-to-face encounter with what I was later to name *layoff survivor sickness*.

For the past 15 years, I have been working to understand and help organizations deal with layoff survivor sickness. My conclusions are partially a reflection of my initial research (Noer, 1993a) and more recently have been influenced by personal interaction with a large number of managers and employees struggling with postlayoff revitalization, both for themselves and their organizations. This chapter will both describe the nature of the problem and present a model for personal and organizational intervention.

The Basic Bind: Lean and Mean Leads to Sad and Angry

Layoffs are intended to reduce costs and promote an efficient, lean, and mean organization. However, what tends to result is a sad and angry organization, populated by depressed survivors. The *basic bind* is that the process of reducing staff to achieve increased efficiency and productivity often creates conditions that lead to the opposite result: an organization that is risk averse and less productive. The key variable is the survivors' sense of personal violation. The greater their perception of violation, the greater their susceptibility to survivor sickness. The perception of violation appears directly related to the degree of trust employees have had that the organization will take care of them. Because nearly all organizations of the past had strategies for taking care of their employees, this basic bind (see Figure 1) is alive and well.

Another way of conceptualizing the problem is as a basic and per-

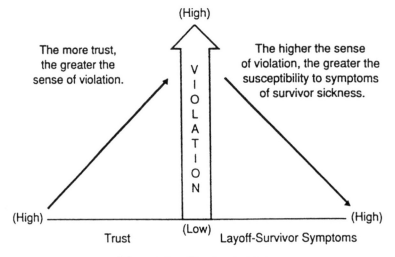

Figure 1. The basic bind.

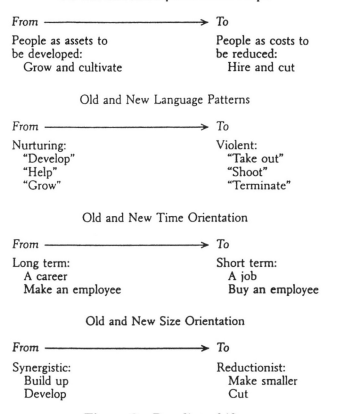

Figure 2. Paradigm shifts.

manent change in the relationship between employee and employer. The profound and basic change in the typical relationship between employee and organization, and between organization and society, is nothing less than the fundamental change in worldview envisioned by Thomas Kuhn (1970) when he rescued the word *paradigm* from obscurity. We *are* in the midst of a fundamental paradigm shift. Although it is difficult to see change when we are in the middle of it, there are four yardsticks that we can use to assess its validity. These yardsticks have an old worldview at one end and a new worldview at the other (see Figure 2). The changes occur in the assumptions organizations make about the purpose of employees, language patterns, long-term versus short-term time orientation, and values in regard to organizational size.

From Assets To Costs: The New View of Employees

Perhaps the clearest evidence of the paradigm shift is that organizations that used to perceive people as long-term assets to be nurtured and developed now see people as short-term costs to be reduced. This basic change has a radical impact on the staffing and development cycle (hiring, training, career planning, and succession planning). Even more important, it represents a fundamental shift in the psychological covenant between the organization and the individual. Under the values of the old contract, employees in most large business, military, government, and religious hierarchies were perceived as assets to be nurtured and grown (often through organizational training and developmental programs) over the long term. Even Frederick Taylor's (1911) scientific management, mechanistic though it was, never envisioned a throwaway employee. Employees, like machines, were intended to be properly fit into the system, tuned, lubricated, and maintained over the long haul. Today, many organizations view people as "things" that are but one variable in the production equation, "things" that can be discarded when the profit and loss numbers do not come out as desired. However, unlike machines, people who are discarded have a significant effect on those who remain within the system.

Old to New Language

Clinical behavioral practitioners have always carefully examined and given credence to the symbolism of communication patterns. Leaders struggling to revitalize organizations should do the same. Robert Marshak and Judith Katz (1992) provide a good guideline for leaders when they say, "Explore literal messages symbolically, and symbolic messages literally," because "when symbolic communications are looked at, or listened to, for their literal as well as symbolic meaning a wider range of diagnostic speculation and/or inquiry is revealed" (p. 2). If leaders follow this guideline and understand the language of violence literally, they can see that managers who are "taking out" or "terminating" their fellow employees see themselves, at some level, as doing severe harm to others. Consequently, these managers experience anger and survivor guilt. It is neither a coincidence nor a matter to be lightly dismissed that the language of layoffs is the language of assassination.

From Long-Term to Short-Term: The Shrinking Planning Horizon

Another harbinger of the new paradigm is the shrinking time frame that organizations apply to almost everything. Organizations are reducing cycle time, planning time, budgeting time, travel time, development time, and, significantly, employee tenure time.

Stimulated by the current fenzy and driven primarily by security analysts to make short-term (sometimes less than quarterly) incremental profit gains, many organizations find that their strategic horizon has been drastically shortened. In one organization, the so-called long-range strategic plan is now an 18-month document, and even that time period seems contrived and artificial to those who are involved in leading and managing the organization. Employees, too, are affected by the short-term frenzy. Their long-term careers have become short-term jobs. In the new reality, people are becoming task-specific, disposable components of a system that is already short term and getting shorter. We are approaching the era of the *just-in-time employee.*

From Synergistic to Reductionistic: Taking Apart Is Better Than Putting Together

Synergy is an old-paradigm word. Once, organizations added components, built themselves up, developed people for the long term, and a form of magic happened: Two and two came out to more than four. No longer. The new paradigm is reductionistic. The shift in preference is from large to small. In human resource terms, the shift is from long-term employee development to short-term employee fit.

Under the Rocks

Beneath the sterile and analytical reports of organizational downsizings, mergers, and restructurings lurks something that is decidedly not as antiseptic as the sanitized reports would lead one to believe. Turn over the layoff rock in most organizations and you will find some ugly and toxic creatures. The few of us who have both turned the rock over and written about what we have seen have seen the same creatures. Like the blind people exploring the elephant, each of us has had a different view of these phenomena and labeled this view accordingly. It is the "dirty dozen": a combination of scapegoating, decreasing morale, increased conflict, and other "dysfunctional effects" (Cameron, Kim, & Whetten, 1987). It is the acting out of survivor guilt (Brockner et al., 1986). It is a combination of guilt, depression, loss of control, increased substance abuse, sleeplessness, and tension (Marks, 1991). It is a form of depression that leads to wasting away (Harvey, 1981). Despite the varying labels, what is becoming increasingly clear to everyone is the magnitude of damage done by these phenomena.

Layoffs are often seen as a subset of overall downsizing strategies. However, the symptoms of layoff survivor sickness are a major barrier to productivity gains. In an extensive best-practice survey of automotive industry downsizing, Kim Cameron, Sarah Freeman, and April Mishra (1991) found evidence of survivor guilt. They also found that one characteristic of firms with the best practices was paying special attention to survivors, which they implied was successful in alleviating survivor guilt. The way most of the downsizings were implemented, however, had caused quality and productivity to deteriorate rather than increase. Consulting companies, long in the front lines of the downsizing movement, have made similar reports. A study of more than 1,000 downsized organizations by the Wyatt Company (1991) indicated that most of these organizations did not meet their initial goals. Mitchell and Company (Dorfman, 1991) followed 16 large restructurings from 1982 to 1988. At the end of this period, the organizations' stock performance trailed that of their competition by an average of 26%. In a survey of 909 managers, Right Associates (1992) found that 70% reported that survivors felt insecure about their future and had reduced confidence in their ability to manage their own careers. Seventy-two percent of the managers indicated that the survivors believed that the restructured organization was not a better place to work.

Layoff Survivor Feeling Clusters and Coping Strategies

Whether layoff survivor sickness is perceived as the result of ineffective downsizings (Cameron et al., 1991) or as a moral issue caused by collusion and a lack of courage (Harvey, 1988), the outcome is the same. Layoffs have drained the work spirit, creativity, and productivity from many of our organizations. The stories of survivors of more traumatic events, my own experience with downsized organizations, and layoff survivor research all show that layoff survivors experience the following feelings.

Feeling Clusters

- *Fear, insecurity, and uncertainty.* These feelings clustered together are among the easier ones to identify, and are found in every layoff survivor situation.
- *Frustration, resentment, and anger.* Layoff survivors are often unable to express these emotions openly within their organization. The suppression of these emotions creates further problems.
- *Sadness, depression, and guilt.* Layoff survivors often mask depression and sadness in order to fit in with group norms that reinforce an artificial sense of bravado and denial.
- *Unfairness, betrayal, and distrust.* These feelings are often acted out through coping mechanisms, such as blaming others, and a seemingly insatiable need for information.

Coping Methods

Layoff survivors cope with their feelings in ways that are neither personally healthy nor organizationally productive.

- *Reduced risk taking.* Layoff survivors tend to hunker down in the trenches. They report risk-averse behavior, reluctance to take on new projects, and fear of finishing existing ones. They are seen as becoming more rigid and conservative.
- *Lowered productivity.* Layoff survivors are initially consumed with seeking information and understanding their new environment. The relationship between survivor stress and productivity is com-

plex, and some evidence exists that moderate job insecurity will increase productivity (Brockner, 1992). As time progresses and layoff symptoms solidify, however, it appears that survivors lose their work spirit and creativity.

- *Unquenchable thirst for information.* Layoff survivors soak up and demand information. They seek information not only from formal channels and newspapers but also from rumors and nonverbal messages from management.
- *Survivor blaming.* Layoff survivors cope by blaming others, usually those above them. Top managers tend to blame the chief executive officer (CEO), each other, or those below them. CEOs with whom I have worked tend to blame the economy, competition, other executives, the work ethic, or, in one case, the labor union.
- *Denial.* Many organizations exhibit a hierarchical pattern of denial. The higher a person is in the organization, the greater his or her denial. This denial chain must be broken before any meaningful intervention strategy can be implemented.

Persistence of Symptoms Over Time

The symptoms of surviving all forms of human trauma require powerful interventions. They do not go away on their own. Layoff survivor symptoms are no different. Not only do they persist over time, but certain of them seem to intensify.

- *Increase in resignation, fatigue, and depression.* In organizations undergoing continuing reductions and change, survivors seem to lose their spark, become flat and tired, and simply go through the motions of their job, without hope.
- *Deepening sense of loss of control.* Long-term layoff survivors tend to give the organization control of their work life and often their self-esteem. Instead of taking control of their own destiny, they hang on and wait for external events to direct them.
- *Heightened and more focused anger.* Long-term layoff survivors are very angry. Compared with the anger of others, their anger seems sharpened and more personally focused (Noer, 1993a). In one large organization study, this anger was directed at top executive compensation and severance payments. In other organizations, the anger is focused more on individuals and is a clear extension of the survivor-blaming phenomenon.

A Model for Intervention

Although there is a recent trend toward focusing on the survivors and describing successful interventions, most research and practice continues to focus more on describing the problem, or on how to "do" layoffs, than

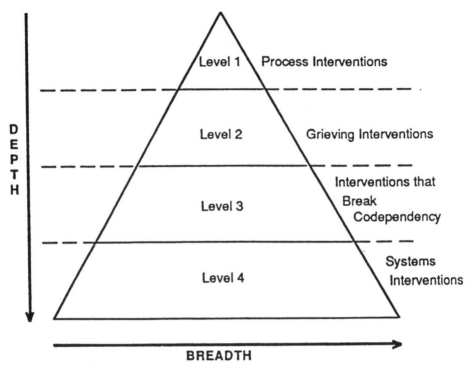

Figure 3.   Layoff survivor intentions.

on helping the survivors. My four-level intervention model deals with those who remain (see Figure 3).

Level 1: Manage the Layoff Processes

Although Level 1 interventions occur at the tip of the layoff "iceberg," they are tactically important. They keep survivors from sinking too deeply into depression and guilt, helping them stay afloat until other, more permanent interventions can be applied to pull them out. Most layoff planners work out the processes of severance pay, communications sequencing, benefits, outplacement services, and often how desks get cleaned out and the victims are escorted to the door, with little or no thought of the impact on those who stay. Line managers and staff groups commonly spend days obsessing over the most intricate details of notification and implementation, with no consideration of the survivors. However, studies (Brockner, 1992; Davy & Tansik, 1986) point out that layoff processes have major effects on survivors, too. Survivors' involvement in the decision-making process, their level of attachment to the victims, and their perceptions as to the fairness and equity of layoffs have all been documented as important process factors that planners should consider.

A key Level 1 intervention is facilitating communication. Field research has shown that layoff survivors have an unquenchable need for information before, during, and after reductions. They become "information junkies." If they do not get information, they go through withdrawal. Eventually, they will manufacture information themselves. It is impossible for managers to overcommunicate during layoffs. The system should be flooded with information—verbal, nonverbal, oral, written, formal, informal, up, down, and laterally—over and over again. Even when a manager has repeatedly said the same thing to the same audience in the same way, he or she should redouble the effort. I have yet to find an organization that has satisfied the need of layoff survivors for information.

It is important for managers to communicate everything that is going on. During layoffs, employees are not concerned only with the obvious questions of who is going, when, and how they are chosen. They are desperately striving for control over a frightening environment. They want to know that the cafeteria will be operational, that paychecks will not bounce, that the softball league will continue, that the dental plan will stay in effect, that the Monday morning staff meeting will still take place.

And written communication alone is not enough. Sad though it is, a surprising number of employees have difficulty reading, and others simply prefer oral information. Hearing or reading information is not enough, either. Employees want to see it, and not just on video. Nonverbal messages are stronger than words. Bosses must be visible.

Despite the evidence that information is essential during layoffs, it is often difficult for managers to stimulate and maintain the free flow of information. Instead, they often begin to manage it, to control it. Announcements are carefully crafted and scripted. Comments made when walking around are rehearsed.

Managers also are under some pressure not to tell the truth. People want them to say, and they themselves want to say, "It is over. Your job is safe." It is never over. This is as close to a law as anything I have found in the study of layoffs. The forces of the economy, the dynamics of technology, and the emergence of a new relationship between employer and employee make any kind of long-range employment promise an illusion.

The Level 1 interventions of letting the information flow and telling the truth take courage. They will not cure the sickness, but they will help prepare people for Level 2 interventions.

Level 2: Facilitate Grieving

Level 2 interventions help unblock repressed feelings. Even in the best-handled layoffs, survivors feel violated. Because organizations often have strong norms against employees even admitting the presence of survivor emotions, let alone sharing and dealing with them, interventions must tease out repressed emotions. Although some survivors have support systems that allow them to sort out their feelings, the majority of layoff survivors have no personal or organizationally sanctioned outlet for anger and fear.

The bad news is that repressed anger and other emotions are widespread. The good news is that an intervention process is not difficult to start, and once it is started, the feelings do come out. Although individual counseling is useful, I have found group work to be the most effective and efficient method of bringing survivor emotions to the surface.

The nature of the group chosen for intervention can, of course, vary. I have done and observed interventions with, among others, "family" groups (i.e., existing work teams) and with systemwide, "stranger" groups (i.e., people who do not work with each other directly). I have found that family groups can make a great deal of progress in a relatively short time but that the "head" of the family, the boss, must take part. The group should be prepared to meet several times; one-shot meetings will not work.

Systemwide interventions are difficult to sustain within organizations experiencing significant flux and change. Something is better than nothing, however, and even a limited success can make a difference. Line managers must be involved in implementing a systemwide intervention; even though some of them are not gifted at teasing out survivor symptoms, others are, and even awkward management intervention can have a positive effect.

Ultimately, organizations need to develop a cadre of trained internal interveners. It is important not to create a dependence on outsiders, who eventually will not be there. Many of these internal consultants will come from the organizational development or human resources functions. Although these staff groups can be very helpful in solving survivor problems, another group must take an active part if the job is to be completed: line managers. The most effective Level 2 work takes place at the interface between employee and boss.

Ask any veteran manager, and instructors at many of today's business schools, to define the manager's role, and the description will usually involve some combination of well-known "-ings": planning, organizing, directing, coordinating, and evaluating. It is unlikely that "helping" will be mentioned, but managers with basic helping skills are powerful tools in a survivor workforce. Managers should be trained in such skills and given recognition, in appraisal and compensation systems, for demonstrating them.

Dealing with repressed survivor feelings and facilitating grieving are not the end of the intervention process. But the catharsis that occurs during Level 2 interventions is a milestone along the road that will lead to breaking organizational codependency.

Level 3: Break the Codependency Chain

Level 3 interventions both are more complex and inspire more hope than Levels 1 and 2. They are complex because, in the final analysis, they are played out within each person's human spirit. They create optimism because they have the potential to help people move from being victims to being adventurers in control of their own identity, happiness, and creative powers. The field of codependency research and treatment offers both a language and a frame of reference that can help managers and employees understand how to bring about this transformation.

Codependent behavior is ancient. One could say that it started in the Garden of Eden, but the label and the formal concept date only from 1979 (Beattie, 1987). The initial, relatively simple idea was that people who deny their feelings, alter their identity, and invest a great amount of energy in the attempt to control an alcoholic share the alcoholic's addiction; they are codependent with the alcoholic. The idea has now been expanded to cover many other forms of addiction, and codependency is considered by some to be an underlying, primary disease in itself (Schaef, 1986). Just as a person can exist in a codependent state with another person in relation to an addiction, a person can also be codependent with an organizational system.

People are the "carriers" of organizational codependency. The network of organizational codependency can be visualized as a series of chain links, from bottom to top and across all levels, as though a chain-mesh net covered the organizational pyramid, with each link a reciprocal codependent relationship. The people in these relationships are all conspiring to be collectively something that they do not want to be individually.

A primary characteristic of this situation is that the codependent's sense of value and identity is based on pleasing, and often controlling, not himself or herself, but someone or something else. Codependents make themselves into permanent victims. People suffering from layoff survivor sickness are similar full-time victims. Survivor symptoms are caused by survivors surrendering to organizationally imposed values and an organizationally imposed identity. The Level 3 intervention aims to break this codependent relationship.

To do this, individuals must maintain internal control, keep their personal power, and love themselves without making this love conditional on organizational approval. They must maintain their authenticity without attempting to both please and control the system. The organizational goal is empowered employees working with minimal control. They work because they are invested in the task and interested in producing a high-quality product, not because they need to control or please others to maintain their self-esteem. Like the efforts of individuals, the efforts of organizations to maintain a culture that allows empowerment and shuns codependency must be unending.

Several common codependency treatment strategies can be effectively translated into Level 3 survivor interventions, including detachment, letting go, and connecting with a core purpose. *Detachment* is a facilitating strategy. Without it the codependent cannot take actions that promote personal autonomy and healing. *Letting go* deals with the codependent's compulsion to control others. The folly of trying to control the uncontrollable must be admitted. *Connecting with a core purpose* is the culminating strategy. Whereas the first two involve removal, this one involves putting back. And once it has been accomplished, it is the basis of the self-empowerment that prevents layoff survivor sickness.

Breaking organizational codependency is essentially an individual effort. The individual detaches from the organizational system as a culture. Organizations, too, need to detach, let go, and discover their core purposes. Searching for a new purpose and vision in the face of global competition and world economic parity involves the pain of creating a new identity. However, for both individuals and organizations, the gain is well worth the pain. The payoff is survival.

Level 4: Develop Systems That Are Compatible With the New Reality

Level 4 interventions create systems and processes that structurally mitigate layoff survivor sickness. These interventions involve the relationship between the employer and employee.

In the years after World War II, when the United States enjoyed a clear competitive advantage over other countries—one that seemed unlikely to be threatened for years to come—and when big was better, a distinct relationship was forged. It was built on several implicit assumptions that were shared by employer and employee. Among these were that the employment relationship should be long term, good performance should be rewarded with promotion, and management should take care of employees.

In recent years, however, business realities have changed, calling these assumptions and the strategies derived from them into question. The employment relationship now has to be restructured to reflect the new realities, for example, increased international competition and the need for organizations to be quickly adaptive.

Level 4 interventions thus attempt to help individuals and organizations move from the old set of assumptions to a new set, from the old employment contract to a new employment contract.

What is required today is a just-in-time workforce, one that is situational and available when good work is needed. To get such a workforce, we must make our systems compatible with the new reality. For instance, there is a need for adequate and affordable health insurance that is not tied to the place where people work. This, even though it requires a change in national policy, is essential, both for the health of U.S. citizens and for the efficiency and competitiveness of U.S. organizations. Similarly, pension plans must be made portable for everyone (they already are in some professions, such as education). Government and private sectors must cooperate if we are to develop benefit plans that facilitate work for organizations and individuals alike.

Revamping recognition programs is something that organizations can accomplish without government assistance. It makes no sense to celebrate employees' tenure in an organization that attempts to be situational and flexible in the way it employs people. This change is a hard-sell in companies where top management has risen up through the ranks and has a great deal of cultural identity invested in honoring tenure. Nonetheless, looking for events to celebrate that are more consistent with a new employment contract is a very important intervention. Organizations could stop awarding trinkets (such as tie bars, cuff links, bracelets, and wall plaques) that celebrate merely tenure and start celebrating achievement. There is nothing wrong with using trinkets, dinners, theater tickets, or simply public pats on the back as rewards, as long as they highlight the desired behavior.

Another approach is to blur the distinction between full-time, part-time, and temporary employees. To develop a truly flexible just-in-time workforce, organizations must remove artificial pay, benefits, and status distinctions among employee classifications. Given what has been happening in many organizations for the past 10 years, full-time permanent employees are an endangered species. All employees are now in a sense temporary. Organizations that continue to maintain sharp differentiations between employment categories not only cut themselves off from a growing (witnessed by the increase in contract employment firms) and fresh source of new people and ideas, they also put unnecessary barriers in the way of the crucial flexibility they need for future survival.

Organizations typically do not like to think of themselves as paternalistic, but the reality is that most take pride in "taking care" of their employees. Employee caretaking was an integral part of the old employment contract. It is difficult to reverse, but it is no longer beneficial to either party. On the one hand, it creates dependent employees who do not develop the skills necessary to be mobile in the marketplace; on the other hand, employers are finding it impossible to hold up their end of the bargain. Organizations must facilitate the new employment contract through measures such as letting employees plan their own careers.

Organizationally specific, long-term career paths are artifacts of the old contract. Job planning, not career planning, is the order of the day. In the past, employees wanted to know the experiences and education that would, over a career lifetime, get them to the top of a particular organization. Organizations responded with detailed, often elaborately prepared, graphically illustrated, and professionally packaged prescriptions for the "tickets" employees needed to have punched to rise to the top. Today, a new paradigm is developing in which organizations are flat, growth is not hierarchical, systems are temporary, and careers are short-term and situational. If organizations persist in offering internal career planning, they are simply misleading their employees and setting up inevitable crises.

Life After Downsizing

In the final analysis, layoff survivor sickness is a good news/bad news proposition. First the bad news. The past 50 years of "enlightened" managerial practice have created codependency between organization and employee. Organizations have been paternalistic; with the best of intentions, they have established systems to hold on to employees by takng care of them. Employees have been seduced and conditioned into letting themselves be captured, often putting their self-esteem and sense of relevance into the company vault. Violations of this dependence lead to anger, betrayal, and depression—the joyless, nonproductive funk of layoff survivor sickness.

Now the good news. The shock of violated dependency is a clear and compelling wake-up call, an alarm that, if heeded, could do more to stimulate a truly empowered and autonomous workforce than all the X, Y, and Z theories; false starts; and rhetoric of the past. The situation we face is frightening, but the means of solving our problems are within our grasp. It only requires leadership from everyone involved and courage.

References

Beattie, M. (1987). *Codependent no more: How to stop controlling others and start caring for yourself*. San Francisco: HarperCollins.

Brockner, J. (1992, Winter). Managing the effects of layoffs on others. *California Management Review, 34*, 9–27.

Brockner, J., Greenberg, J., Brockner, A., Bortz, J., Davy, J., & Carter, C. (1986). Layoffs, equity theory, and work performance: Further evidence of the impact of survivor guilt. *Academy of Management Journal, 29*, 373–384.

Cameron, K. S., Freeman, S. J., & Mishra, A. K. (1991). Best practices in white-collar downsizing: Managing contradictions. *The Executive, 5*(3), 57–72.

Cameron, K. S., Kim, M. U., & Whetten, D. A. (1987). Organizational effects of decline and turbulence. *Administrative Science Quarterly, 32*, 222–240.

Davy, J. A, & Tansik, D. (1986). *Procedural justice and layoff survival: Preliminary evidence for the effects of voice and choice and survivors' attitudes and behavior*. Unpublished manuscript, Arizona State University, Tempe.

Dorfman, J. R. (1991). Heard on the street. *Wall Street Journal*, Dec. 10, pp. C1–C2.

Harvey, J. B. (1981). *Management and marasmus*. Unpublished manuscript, George Washington University.

Harvey, J. B. (1988). *The Abilene paradox and other meditations on management*. Lexington, MA: Lexington Books.

Kuhn, T. S. (1970). *The structure of scientific revolutions* (2nd ed.). Chicago: University of Chicago Press.

Marks, M. L. (1991). Viewpoints. *Los Angeles Times*, Jan. 6, p. D7.

Marshak, R. J., & Katz, J. H. (1992). The symbolic side of OD. *OD Practitioner, 24*, 1–5.

Noer, D. (1993a). *Healing the wounds: Overcoming the trauma of layoffs and revitalizing downsized organizations*. San Francisco: Jossey-Bass.

Noer, D. (1993b). Leadership in an age of layoffs. *Issues and Observations, 13*(3), 1–5.

Right Associates. (1992). *Lessons learned: Dispelling the myths of downsizing* (2nd ed.). Philadelphia: Author.

Schaef, A. W. (1986). *Co-dependence: Misunderstood—mistreated*. San Francisco: Harper-Collins.

Taylor, F. W. (1911). *The principles of scientific management*. New York: Harper & Brothers.

Wyatt Company. (1991). *Restructuring—Cure or cosmetic surgery: Results of corporate change in the '80s with Rxs for the '90s* (published survey report). Washington, DC: Author.

11

Leadership in the New Organization

Robert Rosen

This chapter is the result of observations I have made over a period of many years with top executives and others on how to lead organizations. Ironically, it was the effects of casting darkness that first sparked my interest in leadership. While some leaders inspire others, casting brightness around them, others seem to be operating from what C. G. Jung called "their shadow side," casting darkness. Ineffective leadership casts darkness while inspired leadership can cast brightness. Back in 1980, I was working as a psychologist at the George Washington University School of Medicine, treating the families of executives in business and government. A mother and her 13-year-old son came to see me. The son's performance in school had been deteriorating; he was having trouble concentrating and, in frustration, was growing increasingly unruly.

From my sessions with the boy and his mother, a portrait emerged of a father who was charismatic, smart, and, as the head of a growing and profitable company, extremely successful. Indeed, he was so engrossed in his business that he gave little time to his family.

Later, I came to realize that despite all the time this man put in at the office, he treated his employees exactly as he did his family. He ignored them. Oh, he spent a lot of time supervising them, inspecting their work, and mistrusting their intentions. He rode them extremely hard, demanding late nights and frequent weekend stints. In short, he treated his employees as tools to make a profit, but he refused to recognize their family and community lives. He ignored them as people.

As it turned out, this was one of the major reasons his firm eventually went bankrupt. Turnover and morale problems got out of hand. Bitter infighting divided his top leadership cadre, and not surprisingly, the firm could not develop long-term customer relationships.

Extreme though this story is, I realized that to paint a true portrait of thousands of American managers one would have to use many of the same stark colors. I also saw the profound and critical connection between this man's inner life and his leadership of his family and business. He was casting his shadow side—his insensitivities and self-absorption and excessive ambition—on everyone around him, with disastrous effects. I wanted to understand how this vicious circle worked and to help others reverse it or avoid it altogether. I set about interviewing and studying leaders from all walks of life.

Almost immediately, I encountered leaders who were mature and effective, who were casting brightness rather than darkness on those around them. One of the first such leaders was Max DePree, CEO of Fortune 500 furniture manufacturer Herman Miller and a renowned writer on leadership. In our interview, DePree recounted how an employee came to him and complained that two coworkers had been wrongly fired. Taken aback, DePree investigated and confirmed the complaint. He reinstated the fired employees and gave the offending supervisor the boot.

What sticks most prominently in my mind is not the decisive action DePree took, but how deeply he was affected by the episode. I remember sitting in his office, which was remarkably spare and unassuming for a person of his position, as he told me how thrilled he was that his employees had the confidence to approach him, the top boss, with the expectation of fairness. I had spent several hours with DePree and found him to be pleasant but reserved. Now, for the first time, passion flowed forth: His greatest achievement was not his company's high profit margins, he told me, or even the quality of its products. Instead, it was his creation of a culture where people were treated right, where the open-door policy was not an empty phrase but a reality. "My job," he said, "is to oversee fundamental principles, like fair play and honesty. If I do that, the profits will follow."

As he said this, I felt a twinge of skepticism. Could a person under the kind of pressure Wall Street imposes on CEOs really believe that his duty was to watch "principles" as closely as quarterly earnings? But the more time I spent with leaders, the more I realized that the best of them did exactly that.

Maximizing Companies' Potential: Early Observations

In the early years of my career, I worked mostly with entrepreneurs, and I noticed that those who were able to grow their businesses were the ones who, like DePree, understood human nature and how to tap the best in people. They understood that the bottom line is, ultimately, the result of human endeavor.

I noticed the same dynamic when I was consultant to the Washington Business Group on Health, a national group of Fortune 500 companies. There I saw how some of the most prestigious businesses in America managed, and mismanaged, their human capital. I was dismayed at how many of these corporations undervalued and underinvested in their people.

But something else surprised me: The corporate leaders who did understand the human side of their businesses and who were most effectively motivating and mobilizing their people were operating mostly by instinct. Just like the entrepreneurs, these leaders were acting from the profound intuition that profits follow principles. Why were these leaders, with all the immense resources at their disposal, going with their gut? Because almost no solid data existed to make the cause for investing in people.

Corporate accounting, so sophisticated when it came to finances and hard assets, was downright primitive when it came to measuring human assets. It could not prove how different management techniques affected employee performance, and it certainly could not tell leaders how to maximize their workers' creativity and commitment. It was as if clocks had not yet been invented and people could only guess the time.

By now I was engrossed in these issues. I began to explore a new concept: the "healthy" organization, a high-performance enterprise that nurtures and taps the talents, ideas, and energy of its people. Healthy enterprises start from core human values, such as trust, integrity, and teamwork, and they balance the needs of all their stakeholders: employees, customers, shareholders, and the larger community. They do not do this merely because it is right or fair. They do it because it is better business—because it gives them the profound and enduring competitive advantage of a fast, flexible work culture in which employees act like they own the business, learn on the job, and care deeply about quality and service.

With a growing network of colleagues from business, academia, government, and labor, I pursued key questions: How do we develop robust, successful enterprises? Where and how do people create the most value for business? What investments in people will really make a difference in performance? How can we unleash the full potential of our workers?

The Crisis In American Organizations

In 1990, the John D. and Catherine T. MacArthur Foundation helped me delve even more deeply into these questions by giving a charter grant to the not-for-profit think tank I founded called Healthy Companies Institute. We surveyed the dominant philosophies and practices of American management, and as we did so it became clear that American organizations face two profound crises.

The first is a crisis in commitment. People are not working at their full potential. Competitive advantage comes from the effort workers put in above and beyond "just doing their job." If a line worker in a factory sees a better way to reuse scrap but does not share it with the company, that worker is, technically, still doing his job. He is earning his pay, fulfilling the letter, if not the spirit, of his contract. But in a competitor's factory down the road, or across the ocean, another worker comes up with the same recycling idea and pushes to get it implemented. Suddenly the second factory gets more out of its raw materials than the first, and not because of superior technology or training, but purely because an employee gave more than was strictly required.

We call this *discretionary effort* because no leader can force an employee to give it. Employees provide it at their discretion, and if they choose to give it often enough, the power it gives an enterprise is truly awesome. But across the country and in every sector of the American economy, I saw people withhold their discretionary effort.

Sometimes people were downright passive–aggressive. Other times they were indifferent, as if their spark had been snuffed out. And often they blamed management. The bureaucracy was too cumbersome. The company did not invest in learning opportunities. Top leadership hoarded information, especially financial figures, that would clarify the big picture and enable workers to suggest improvements. The glass ceiling kept women and people of color "in their place." Technology was implemented without any thought about the workers who used it, which caused health problems such as repetitive stress syndrome. A relentless demand for extra hours ate into precious time for family and leisure.

Sometimes these complaints were baseless bellyaching. There are always a few bad apples in any bin. But in many cases, the workers were right. Leaders had created environments that undermined motivation and discouraged discretionary effort. I saw the worst of these companies go out of business, brought to their knees by employee burnout, rampant mistrust, missed market opportunities, and resistance to change—in short, by a colossal waste of human potential.

I saw other companies stumble along by taking partial measures. Management strategies, such as total quality, reengineering, and empowerment programs, helped these enterprises and deepened my own understanding of healthy, high-performing organizations. But unfortunately, they were only fragmentary approaches that did not inspire people to consistently contribute discretionary effort and so did not resolve the commitment crisis.

In fact, employees in these companies were often jaded, quick to deride the new management techniques as "fads." These workers would often tell me that yes, the management "flavor of the month" made sense and even improved things. So what was their gripe? It was that the new technique seemed like a ploy to jack up short-term profits. What these people sensed was something awfully close to hypocrisy. They felt that their leaders were merely tinkering with rhetoric and style and that deep down they were still operating from the same old assumption: that work is something to be extracted from these people, as though employees were a kind of fuel to be burned up and reduced to waste. In short, workers sensed that they were still being managed as costly liabilities and not as valuable assets.

But buried in the complaints of such workers lies an urgent and surprising message that points to the second crisis, which is in leadership. People want to be led. They do not want the old authoritarian leadership style. Nor do they want some clever new management technique. Instead, they want leaders with deeply held human values who respect people's unique talents and contributions. They want leaders who will create an environment that nurtures excellence, risk taking, and creativity. They reject intimidation or manipulation, but they positively yearn for inspiration.

Similarly, in the misguided efforts of leaders is hidden another message: Leaders need followers. Leaders do not want docile, do-only-as-ordered employees. Instead, they want responsible, mature, forward-looking associates. They want partners who are as committed as they are to the success of the enterprise.

The simple fact is that leaders and followers need each other, but they are not working well together. As I travel around the country, I see tensions between them as severe as a chronic ache. These rifts divide not just employers and employees but also politicians and constituents, doctors and patients, teachers and students. Everywhere, our leader–follower relationships are tense, cynical, confused, and mistrustful. This dysfunctional relationship is the primary cause of the crisis in commitment.

But the responsibility for mending the relationship lies with leaders. Leaders must take the first steps, for it is leaders who set the rules, create the culture, and determine the values and principles that guide the organization. Indeed, fostering mature and robust leader–follower partnerships is what leading people is all about. But most leaders are not pulling their weight. To put it another way, followers are not following because leaders are not leading.

A 1995 national survey (Towers Perrin, 1995) found that 98% of executives agreed that improving employee performance would significantly increase company productivity, and 73% claimed that employees were their company's most important asset. But when asked to rank business priorities, these same executives relegated investing in people to fifth place on a six-item list. Such dissonance between rhetoric and reality is almost deafening, but it is only one example. During the last two decades, employees have watched the salaries of top executives rise much faster than those of the average worker, and they have seen failed executives jump with golden parachutes worth tens of millions of dollars. Is it any wonder that workers cock a cynical ear when management asks them to make sacrifices, such as paying part of their health insurance or shouldering more responsibility?

Characteristics of Successful Leaders

Despite these problems, in a small but growing group of enterprises, I found little such cynicism. These were organizations that had leaders committed to ethical values, frank talk, and deep listening. Some use the latest management innovations, others did not. Some of these leaders were well into their 60s, some were surprisingly young. Indeed, they had little in common, except for what really counts: a profound understanding of themselves, of the motivations and aspirations of the people around them, and of the external challenges their enterprises faced.

These leaders knew their business inside and out and were fiercely committed to reality and results, but they defined success broadly. It included making a profit, of course, and it also included making their enterprises valuable to the larger society through quality products and services, healthy and challenged employees, and environmental stewardship.

In their enterprises—which ranged from huge multinational corporations to small family businesses and were scattered across the industry, government, and the nonprofit sectors—I did not find perfection. That does not exist. But I did find excellence, innovation, resilience, and optimism.

I found labor–management relations marked by candor and mutual responsibility. I found workers who wanted to be challenged and stretched by their jobs and to be identified with their organization because they knew it was doing good, meaningful work. I found work cultures in which information was shared rather than hoarded and in which learning and development were valued rather than shortchanged. I found management structures that were flexible and responsive rather than rigid and stifling. I found enterprises steering their way through today's conflicting demands: Innovate but avoid mistakes, think long-term but increase productivity now, downsize but improve teamwork.

And I found profit. But as the leaders of these enterprises were always quick to point out, their profit was the result of creating an environment that liberated people's creativity, nurtured their commitment, and inspired their discretionary effort.

In short, I found healthy, high-performance enterprises, models of the organizations that will succeed in the 21st century. In every case, the key was leadership. Healthy, mature, self-aware leaders were unlocking the best in their employees and therefore the best in the enterprise as a whole. But where leaders were still projecting more of their dark sides, leadership acted as a jailer rather than a liberator, confining creativity and enthusiasm, and keeping the best prospects of the organization shut away.

With growing conviction, I realized that the only way to transform an organization in the deep, long-term ways that inspire people and invigorate their efforts is to transform an organization's leadership. What America needs to thrive in the next century, I realized, is not a new management practice or productivity program. What we need, in all walks of life and all endeavors, is new leadership. This chapter is both a call for and a lesson in this new leadership and is based on research I and my staff conducted at the Healthy Companies Institute.

We live in a time of chaos, marked by breathtaking technological advances, tectonic cultural and political shifts, and vigorous international competition. Our workforce grows more diverse every day, while our attitudes about work are constantly changing. At the same time customers are demanding intensive service and near-perfect quality. Everything has to be better, cheaper, and faster.

That kind of continuous innovation and improvement cannot come from technology alone, which nowadays turns obsolete as quickly as a mayfly. It comes from human creativity and commitment, from employees giving their best at all levels of the organization. In short, success depends on people, and in order to achieve success, people depend on leaders.

It is a simple idea, but one with sweeping consequences. It opens up tremendous opportunities but also gaping pitfalls. To succeed, leaders will have to reinvent their organizations to get the most from their people. But to do that leaders must take a deep look inward and discover the ways they influence their enterprise and their people. More important, they will have to reinvent themselves.

We have not had an honest conversation in this country about leadership, about what we want and expect from our leaders, and about the real-life experience of leading. Instead, leading gets inflated to a John Wayne caricature or deflated to a bloodless "manager." This is not surprising. As a robust, action-oriented society, we usually look outside for answers to competitors, other countries, and new techniques. We mistrust introspection, dismiss our emotions, and generally neglect the "soft" side of business. This cultural bias has given us leaders who are comfortable with operations and marketing but not with inner emotions and human relationships, leaders who are good at manipulating numbers but not at developing people.

That is a real problem, because the only way to succeed in the lightning-quick information age is to nurture independent, motivated people and to build healthy, high-performing organizations. We have known this for a while. The importance of people has become a cliché of annual reports. And more profound is that a whole new social contract is evolving.

This contract requires more from both employees and employers. Workers must pitch in with more than their hands; they must also contribute with their minds and their hearts. They must "own" their work and act as mini-entrepreneurs. The old paternalistic contract rewarded effort and loyalty, long hours, and doing what the boss asked. The new contract rewards results and self-reliance, smart solutions, and taking responsibility without having to be asked.

For their work as whole people, workers need to be treated as whole people. But in survey after study, poll after poll, people tell us they are not getting this from their companies. They want a say in workplace decisions, as voters have in a democracy, but too often they are still treated as children and told what to do. They need the opportunity for camaraderie and teamwork and excellence, but they are often frustrated by rigid hierarchies. They want their labor to have meaning, and they want to learn on the job, but they are often stuck in companies that offer scant opportunity to grow and develop. Leaders must live up to their end of the new contract and offer their people respect, dignity, and fairness.

This results in smart business. The leader's job is to maximize the organization's most valuable asset, people. Their "intellectual capital" is the most appreciable asset in the knowledge economy. Yet a recent national survey of more than 10,000 workers found that current leadership is costing American companies more than half their human potential. To put that another way, improved leadership alone could double worker productivity (Hall, 1994).

To do this, leaders must build organizations that help employees strengthen their competence, creativity, and commitment. Leaders must create healthy environments where people are excited about their work, take pride in their accomplishments, and contribute to their colleagues' doing the same. Their task, in short, is to foment ideas, skills, and energy. This is leading people.

But for the last decade, American business leaders have focused not on appreciating their human assets but on cutting costs. To increase productivity, they have pared their organizations down to the bone. Companies have stripped out management layers, "reengineered" work units, and linked computer networks. And most commonly, they have laid off workers, sometimes in massive one-time reductions, often in protracted downsizing.

The result? Lean enterprises, some of which have emerged healthier and more robust than ever. But where enlightened leadership has been absent, cost cutting has left a demoralized workforce, prone to cynicism, mistrust, and resentment. In these companies, stressed-out employees end up putting in more work in less time, with fewer resources, and then withhold their full potential from executives, who reap excessive bonuses from short-term financial performance. Such organizations—and there are too many of them—are like anorexics; lean, yes, but so thin that they are unable to withstand competitive assault. They are financially solvent, but emotionally bankrupt. And in the long term, they are extremely vulnerable.

The current internal malaise affecting our companies is bound to come to a head. All indications reveal that by the year 2000, the competitive advantage will go to companies that most effectively mobilize their people. Organizations with the best ideas, the most skills, and the most dedicated workforce will succeed. But developing human assets is a whole different ball game from cutting costs. New management practices, such as employee involvement and organizational learning, come closer to what is needed but still fall short. After reengineering, retooling, and restructuring, many companies wonder why they are still lagging behind. Frustrated, they look around for some new technique or management practice. Instead, they should look inward. They should look at the way they are leading their people.

Leaders shed light or impose darkness. This is the most profound power they have. Because people look to leaders for guidance and purpose, their every action and word carries extra impact. In fact, leaders project their attitudes and personality onto the people around them.

The danger is that all personalities have a dark side—secretiveness or insecurity or arrogance. That is part of being human, as is a tendency to cling to old concepts of power, motivation, and diversity.

If leaders lack a deep understanding of themselves, they will cast too much of their shadow side onto their enterprise, with chilling effect. A 1994 study at the Center for Creative Leadership identified the most common reasons why managers derail in their careers. The four most enduring explanations were interpersonal problems, inability to meet business demands, failure to lead, and the inability to adapt to change (Center for Creative Leadership, 1994). The fact is they all had to do with leading people.

This translates directly to the bottom line. The single biggest influence on employee commitment and performance, according to a sweeping national study of more than 25,000 workers, is the leadership skills of their managers (Leimbach, 1994). It is only when leaders learn more about themselves that they will be able to avoid casting their shadow side onto their enterprise.

Does this mean that leaders must shirk painful decisions or be pre-occupied with employees' needs? Of course not. Leadership has always required tough choices, and it always will. The difference lies in how leaders make and carry out these decisions.

Consider two methods, both of which have been used in the real world to lead a company through the same difficult change. In one scenario, top management huddles together, decides that the financial figures call for drastic action, and terminates 10% of the workforce one Friday afternoon, without warning.

In the other scenario, top management shares the dire economic news with the entire company, janitor through CEO, and asks for creative ways to cut costs and boost productivity. As many suggestions as possible are implemented, reaping real improvements. But the situation still looks bad. Top management again communicates this to workers and lets them know that some people will need to be let go, although, thanks to employee suggestions, not as many as management had feared. It offers a combination of options to reduce the workforce by 7%, including early retirement, employee buyouts, and, for those involuntarily laid off, job training.

If you survived the cutbacks, which leaders would you rather work for? Same problem, different leadership. In the first instance, the leaders hoarded information and power; in the second case, they shared it. In the first scenario, the leaders acted on their people; in the second case, they acted with them. In the first case, the leaders cast a pall of secrecy and fear over their enterprise; in the second, they cast a light of candor and common purpose.

This idea, that leadership is the casting of light or darkness, is simple to understand but hard to master. It requires constant introspection, peeling back layers of oneself, and learning about one's self.

But it also requires real-life experience: interacting with colleagues and customers and competitors, coping with hard economic realities, balancing the tensions and trade-offs that leadership decisions inevitably demand. In short, it requires both contemplation and challenge, hard thinking and hard knocks.

In my case, it has taken 15 years to understand leadership, most of my adult career as a psychologist and business consultant, and I am still learning. The leaders I studied come from all three sectors of the American economy: business, government, and nonprofit. Each of these sectors has its special strengths and challenges, and each sector can learn from the others. Business is expert in efficiency, technological innovation, and profitability. Government can teach us about balancing constituencies for the larger public good and about justice and equal treatment. The nonprofit world knows the value of public trust, volunteerism, and the motivational power of a larger purpose. The best leaders adapt traits from the other sectors to their own enterprises.

The Leader's New Work

So what exactly is this new leadership? First, it is not a status. Forget about all the paraphernalia of the high and mighty down the centuries, from scepter and crowns to limousines and corner offices. Just as clothes do not make the man, trappings never made a leader. They just stroked someone's vanity. Such trappings also intimidate people, which is good if you want to be a dictator or run a personality cult but bad if you want to create an open, vibrant, and high-performing team. Leaders inspire rather than intimidate, motivate rather than monitor, and mobilize rather than manage. And these activities do not require the totems of rank and position.

Rather than a status, leadership is an activity. To emphasize this I prefer to use *leading* instead of *leadership*, a verb instead of a noun, a process rather than a position. Leading is like marketing or manufacturing or accounting, it does something. What it does is enable a group of people to pursue a shared vision and create extraordinary results.

Leaderless organizations do not work. Some people have argued that self-managing organizations do not need leaders, that they can operate strictly through an organic, participative, bottom-up process of collaboration and consensus. But my 15 years of working with all manner of organizations, large and small, refute that. At some point, even small, self-managing firms need leaders. People can rotate into the leader's position, or a leader can develop de facto, without a title or job description. But leading is a necessary function, as vital to the life and prosperity of an organization as speaking is to communication.

This function can be learned. Leaders are made, not born. Leading is not some mystical charisma that either you have or you do not. It is more like a language: We all have a capacity for it, some more and some less, but with experience virtually everyone can learn to lead people effectively.

The analogy goes further. For the most part, language is not learned in a classroom. Indeed, we talk before we ever see our first blackboard or scribble our first grammar lesson. We learn it from the people around us. We listen and we imitate what we hear. So too with leading. We emulate those around us: parents, bosses, coaches, teachers. Like kids picking up a language, we learn leadership without even being conscious of it.

Unfortunately, most of our leadership role models reached their positions by climbing up traditional hierarchies. They watched leaders before them hoard control, play politics, and issue edicts, so they do the same. In a truly blighted cycle, that is the style of leadership they are passing on to the next generation. To learn a new and better leadership, we need better role models, people who connect fundamental values to their work.

Leaders are always made, through experience on the job and in their family and community lives. All of the successful leaders I have consulted had key teachable moments in their lives, moments when they were open to new insight and leapt to a new level of understanding.

For many of them, one of those moments was when they realized that leaders are not heroes or villains. That is how our society thinks of leaders.

We love them or hate them, idolize or demonize them, in much the same way as the press portrays our presidents. But this conception of leaders as larger than life, as the organization's all-knowing Big Brain, undermines leaders and followers alike. It puts tremendous stress on the leaders, who know they can never measure up. The results are frustration and workaholism or the arrogance of someone who has begun to believe this fantasy of omnipotence. Both responses are psychologically corrosive.

This impossible ideal makes it all too easy to snipe at a leader's "failures" and "shortcomings." It also infantilizes workers, putting them in the role of children who must depend on the adult leaders. The new leader–associate relationship is not adult–child but adult–adult. Workers have to shoulder more responsibility and independence, and leaders must step down from their pedestals.

But humanizing is a tricky task. We expect both too much and too little of our leaders. On the one hand, we must learn to be more forgiving and gentle, to allow our leaders to be human rather than heroic. We have to recognize that leaders often face dilemmas that pit important interests and parties against one another and that lack a single clear answer. In such cases, decisions can involve painful, even wrenching, trade-offs. But even as we humanize leaders, we must hold them to new, and higher, standards. Leaders must share power and information. They must speak candidly, and they must "walk their talk." They must listen carefully. They must recognize that their personalities get magnified and projected onto the organization, and so they must work to be more aware of their inner lives. They must be willing to admit mistakes, to say that they do not know, to express their feelings, and to ask for help.

But above all, leaders must cultivate healthy adult–adult relationships. Why is this so critical? Because in our fast-paced, complex, and highly technical world, people need to work together and share a common vision to produce high-quality work. Their relationships, therefore, are crucial. Indeed, these relationships are the glue that holds the enterprise together, connecting its strategy, structure, systems, and technology.

This could not be more different from the traditional workplace. The old glue was formal boundaries. Rules, hierarchy, walls, policies, and authority held the old organization together. The new glue is shared values, a common purpose, clear responsibilities, and the relationships between the adults who make up (indeed, who are) the organization.

Effective leaders know this, and so they pay careful attention to these relationships. They manage the "space" between their people, keeping it close enough for collaboration but not for complacency, wide enough for friendly competition but not for conflict.

This is a messy business. Humans are not like technology or numbers. They feel things. They get jealous and angry. They retreat into disappointment. They swell up into overconfidence and arrogance. They play politics. They take drugs. They act thoughtlessly and sometimes meanly. And they are always changing. Just when you think someone is okay, content, and confident, suddenly she or he is not.

Of course, people also act nobly and generously, shoulder responsibility, and show joy and satisfaction. They help each other, and they laugh together. And often their unpredictable changes are for the better. Just when you think you ought to "can" someone, he pulls off a spectacular performance.

Yes, people are any organization's most valuable asset, but like divas and racehorses, people are very high-maintenance. They demand constant attention. Indeed, the everyday work of the leader is human interaction. Building on strong ethical principles, the leader partners with the employees. She or he shares power and lets others shine. He or she challenges people to stretch. In short, she or he recognizes that people have a deep drive for competence and achievement. People yearn for respect and want to feel good about themselves. They want to be full members of a team. They want to know what is going on and to be surrounded by healthy relationships founded on honesty and reciprocal responsibilities. It is the leader's job to create an environment that will liberate the talents and energies lying dormant in people and tap their deep desire for excellence.

Of course, employees are not a leader's only concern. In business there are three fundamental values: a commitment to satisfying customers, a commitment to developing a mature and motivated workforce, and a commitment to earning excellent returns for stockholders or the public. Research shows that companies that focus on all three of these values outperform their competitors. Too narrow a focus on employee satisfaction, for example, can be just as destructive as squeezing out short-term profits to satisfy stockholders.

Keepers of the big picture, leaders have to make sure that all the elements of the business are in synch. Just as a conductor must hear in his mind's ear how all the instruments should harmonize, a leader must visualize how all those with a stake in the organization—employees, customers, stockholders, and the community at large—should interact. It is the leader's job to balance and align people and systems in such a way that all will benefit.

This broad perspective stems from a profound business logic. AT&T, a company profiled in this book, and with which I have worked, put it this way: If an enterprise invests in its human side—in values, respect, pay, learning—then it will reap a healthy, productive workforce. This is *people value added*. That high-performance workforce will then delight the organization's customers with excellent service, high-quality products, and reputation capital. That is *customer value added*. In turn, those satisfied customers will reward the company with profits, *economic value added*. That allows the enterprise to reinvest in its people and keep the cycle going. It also allows the company to benefit the community at large with a stable, vibrant workforce as well as donations and volunteers. That is *society value added*. Figure 1 sums up this idea.

In the healthy, productive enterprise, leaders are always looking for their critical sources of competitive advantage, whether it be their financial capability, their marketing skills, or their state-of-the-art technologies. They know they must build an efficient infrastructure, reengineer their work processes, and continuously manage change.

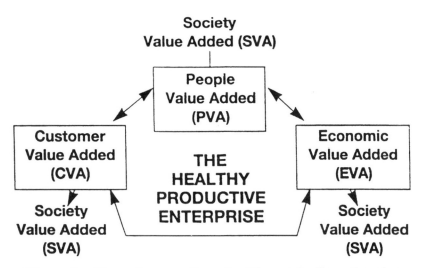

Figure 1.   The cycle supporting a healthy, productive enterprise.

But it is no accident that this cycle begins with an organization's people. A company's people are the prime movers, the first among equals, the leading indicators. Why? It is because people operate the technology and machinery, manufacture the products, provide the services, interact with customers, make the sales, order the supplies, plan for the future, and hold the institutional memory. They are the asset that makes all other assets possible. People are the nerve center of the organizational body.

The best leaders see themselves as the chief people officers of their enterprise, and that is why they spend so much of their day leading people. And the very best leaders know that none of this happens without reinventing themselves and their organizations. Great leaders begin by looking inside themselves. They work to become comfortable with the whole range of human emotions, from happiness and joy to anger and jealousy and insecurity, for they know that they will feel all those emotions themselves and will encounter them in others.

They search for the secret ways by which they sabotage their own efforts. They scrutinize their biases and prejudices. They acknowledge their blind spots: perhaps a narrow definition of success or an excessive competitiveness or a tendency to blame others. They know that the higher they climb the less supervision they receive and the more self-confidence they get, which puts them in danger of the pride that "goeth before a fall." Instead, they pursue humility and maturity.

They seek out reality checks to counter isolation and arrogance, and to allow a constant flow of information. Enlightened pragmatists rather than ideologues, they constantly dart back and forth between the internal and the external, between their own minds and the outside world, challenging their ideas and beliefs. And always they look for ways to learn and grow, for they know that their own development—intellectual, emotional, and spiritual—is their greatest leadership tool. Self-awareness allows them to gauge their effect on people and to calibrate it to diverse individuals with diverse needs. It allows them to tap more effectively the spirit and creativity of their people and to inspire high performance. And self-awareness leads to wisdom.

An all-embracing concept, wisdom includes character as well as intelligence, empathy as well as insight. It implies maturity, the importance of balance, and the necessity of trade-offs. It has depth, of understanding, of caring, and of commitment. With abundant common sense, it recognizes the implacable limitations of the real world, such as money, time, and logistics. But it also knows that the key to transcending those limits, to making possible tomorrow what was impossible yesterday, lies in the unseen world of the human mind and heart. Leading people is wisdom in action.

The Eight Principles of Leading People

In studying and working with these kinds of leaders, I have come to recognize eight principles that run through all their stories, eight strands that when woven together, form wisdom in action.

1. *Vision.* Leaders see the whole picture and articulate that broad perspective with others. By doing so, leaders create a common purpose that mobilizes people and coordinates their efforts into a single, coherent, and agile enterprise.
2. *Trust.* Without trust, vision becomes an empty slogan. Trust binds people together, creating a strong, resilient organization. To build trust, leaders are predictable, and they share information and power. Their goal is a culture of candor.
3. *Participation.* The energy of an organization is the participation and effort of its people. The leader's challenge is to unleash and focus this energy, inspiring people at every level of the enterprise to pitch in with their minds and hearts.
4. *Learning.* Leaders need a deep understanding of themselves. They must know their strengths and shortcomings, which requires a lifelong process of discovery, and they must be able to adapt to new circumstances. The same applies to their organization. It must promote constant innovation, and the leaders must encourage their people to refresh their skills and renew their spirits.
5. *Diversity.* Successful leaders know the power of diversity and the poison of prejudice. They understand their own biases, and they actively cultivate an appreciation of the positive aspects of people's differences. In their organizations, they insist on a culture of mutual respect.
6. *Creativity.* In a world where smart solutions outpace excessive work, creativity is crucial. Leaders pay close attention to people's talents, leaning on their strengths and managing around their weaknesses. They encourage independent, challenging thinking,

and they invest in technologies that facilitate the efforts of their people.

7. *Integrity*. A leader must stand for something. As a public citizen and a private person, he or she knows what is important in life and acts by deep-seated principles. Every wise leader has a moral compass, a sense of right and wrong. Good leaders understand that good ethics is good business.

8. *Community*. Community is mutual commitment, and it inspires the highest performance. It is human nature to go the extra mile for one's neighbors and fellow citizens, and a mature leader stresses the organization's responsibility to the surrounding society. A leader also acts as a steward of the natural environment.

As the chart in Figure 2 makes plain, these eight principles are the components of leading people. They are the DNA of wisdom at work. Of course, none of the leaders I studied are one-dimensional. I tried to focus on an outstanding quality, but any of them could have exemplified several of the principles.

At the same time, no single leader was equally gifted in all the principles. Nobody could be. It is the composite of all these leaders, therefore, that provides a model for leading. No one I know has fully attained it, but the best leaders constantly strive for it, getting ever closer with age and learning and experience.

In the meantime, they compensate by team leadership. Knowing their shortcomings and dark sides, they manage around themselves by assembling a cadre of leaders with diverse talents and backgrounds and outlooks. And in the ultimate act of leadership, they create a culture of leading, nurturing at every level of the organization healthy, ethical, mature employee leaders. In short, the best leaders try not just to become wise themselves but to institutionalize wisdom.

This chapter has been written as a personal guide for leaders. In looking at the eight principles, you might want to sit down with a pad and

Figure 2. The eight leadership principles.

pen and ask yourself some tough questions: How does this resonate with your own situation? What are you doing that is working and not working? And what can you do to change? I have prepared a book entitled *Leading People* (Rosen, 1996), which goes into detail on each of these leadership qualities and presents case studies of individuals who have exemplified that quality.

Do Healthy Enterprises Perform Better?

Yes, they do. An overwhelming amount of research indicates that organizations that incorporate many of the leading principles outlined in this model gain a definite advantage over companies that remain mired in the traditional ways of managing people. Here is a sample of findings:

- An MIT study comparing automotive plants with similar technology found the plants with innovative work practices (including extensive training, work teams, pay for performance, and participative management) manufactured vehicles in an average of 22 hours with 0.5 defects per vehicle. Traditional plants took 30 hours with 0.8 defects per vehicle (MacDuffie & Krafcik, 1992).
- A 1993 survey of 700 publicly held firms from all major industries found that companies using a greater number of innovative human-resource practices had higher annual shareholder returns from 1986 to 1991 and higher gross return on capital. The most "progressive" 25% of firms had an 11% rate of return on capital, more than twice as high as the remaining companies (Huselid, 1993).
- A 1994 report by the U.S. Department of Labor indicates that healthy management practices (open communications, teamwork, employee involvement, extensive training) are associated with increases in productivity and long-term financial performance. The study further found that these effects are most pronounced when they are implemented together (U.S. Department of Labor, 1994).
- A 1994 study examining *Fortune* magazine's annual survey on corporate reputations found that companies that were well respected for their employee practices also had excellent reputations for quality of products and the ability to innovate. These companies also scored highest on long-term corporate performance (U.S. Department of Labor, 1994).
- Firms listed in *The 100 Best Companies to Work for in America* in 1993 had higher total return (the sum of stock price appreciation and dividends paid) over the previous 8 years than did the 3,000 largest companies in America. The difference was substantial: 19.5% for the 100 Best Companies compared with 12% for the others (U.S. Department of Labor, 1994).
- The Domini Social Index—composed of 400 corporations with good records on employee relations, quality, community involvement,

and the environment—has outperformed the Standard & Poor's Index since its inception in 1990, returning 70.11%, whereas the S&P has gained 58.29% (Business for Social Responsibility, 1994).

- A survey of 150 Forbes 500 firms found that the most "progressive" firms (defined by participation, creativity, reward systems, flexibility, culture, and structure) fared considerably better than "nonprogressive" firms in profit growth, sales growth, earnings per share, and dividend growth (Kravetz, 1988).

- Cooperative labor–management relations help company performance. One major study in a manufacturing industry found that innovative workplaces had 75% fewer worker hours lost to waste and scrap, 42% fewer defects per worker, and 17% higher labor productivity (Cutcher-Gershenfeld, 1991).

- A 1994 review of studies in pay and compensation showed a strong connection between productivity and compensation linked to performance. The use of profit sharing was generally associated with 3.5% to 5% higher productivity. The increase for small and midsize firms topped 11% (Kruse, 1995).

- Americans favor socially responsible products and companies. A 1990 Roper poll found that more than two thirds of Americans are concerned about a company's social performance and that 52% would pay up to 10% more for a brand made by a socially responsible company (Business for Social Responsibility, 1994).

- Firms with cultures emphasizing all the key stakeholders (customers, stockholders, and employees) and leadership at all levels outperformed those that did not, by a huge margin. Over an 11-year period, revenue increased 682% for healthy enterprises compared with 166% for unhealthy companies. Net income increased 756% versus 1% (Kotter & Heskett, 1992). These research findings offer compelling evidence in support of a new model of leading and managing. The results of these studies indicate that the eight principles of leading people presented in this chapter offer a significant competitive advantage to companies that work to incorporate them into their organizational culture. As more companies learn the benefits of pursuing this new approach to management, it will become an advantage that few organizations will be able to do without.

References

Business for Social Responsibility. (1994). *Corporate social responsibility and the bottom line: Financial performance*. Internal memo from Business for Social Responsibility. San Francisco, CA

Center for Creative Leadership. (1994). *Why managers derail*. Greensboro, NC: Author.

Cutcher-Gershenfeld, J. (1991). The impact on economic performance of a transformation in workplace relations. *Industrial and Labor Relations Review, 44*, 241–260.

Hall, J. (1994). Americans know how to be productive if managers will let them. *Organizational Dynamics, 23*(3), 33–46.

Huselid, M. (1993, June). *Human resource management practices and firm performance* [Mimeograph]. New Brunswick, NJ: Institute of Management Labor Relations Press, Rutgers University.

Kotter, J., & Heskett, J. (1992). *Corporate culture and performance.* New York: Free Press.

Kravetz, D. (1988). *The human resources revolution.* San Francisco: Jossey-Bass.

Kruse, D. (1995). *Profit-sharing: Does it make a difference?* Kalamazoo, MI: Upjohn Institute.

Leimbach, M. (1994). *Business performance, employee satisfaction and leadership practices.* Eden Prairie, MN: Wilson Learning Corporation.

MacDuffie, J. P., & Krafcik, J. (1992). Integrating technology and human resources for high-performance manufacturing. In T. Kochan & M. Useem (Eds.), *Transforming organizations.* New York: Oxford University Press.

Rosen, R. (1996). *Leading people: Transforming business from the inside out.* New York: Viking Penguin.

Towers Perrin. (1995, January 19). Executives rank people-related issues far below other business priorities [Press release]. New York: Author.

U.S. Department of Labor. (1994). *High performance work practices and firm performance.* Washington, DC: Author.

12

Holistic Stress Management at Corning, Incorporated

Jeff Monroy, Hank Jonas, Joseph Mathey, and Lawrence Murphy

In the last 10 years, downsizing and restructuring in American industry have become the price of doing business in the global economy. The effects have been particularly pronounced among the Fortune 500 companies, which collectively have not created one net new job since 1974 (Block, 1993). This massive redeployment of American workers from large corporations to small business, self-employment, or no employment is a stunning reversal of the migration from small to big business in the early days of the Industrial Revolution.

The negative personal impact of this unprecedented shrinkage on individuals has been well documented ("The downsizing of America," 1996). Other research suggests that such psychological effects may be more pronounced among the "survivors," who must cope with their own guilt as well as increased work loads, than among those who lose their jobs and often use the opportunity to make positive transformations in their lives (Noer, 1993; chapter 10, this volume).

Corporations have responded to this seismic shift by reevaluating the psychological contract with their workers (Noer, 1993, chapter 10, this volume; Sherwood & Glidewell, 1972; Strebel, 1996). They have attempted to develop new models of commitment that emphasize increased empowerment, temporary work contracts, and more challenging work assignments while deemphasizing dependency, lifelong employment, and feelings of entitlement.

This chapter will detail how one American corporation, with help from a federal agency that specializes in the study of workplace stress, is creating a unique approach to reshaping the psychological contract with its workers. The company's particular approach to reengineering, in contrast to those in many other corporations, actually involved minimal downsizing. In fact, in the period described in this study (1993–1995, the same time frame during which reengineering was occurring in virtually every American corporation), the company stayed stable in its overall employment. Instead, we shall describe an intervention that seeks to integrate stress research at the individual level with diagnosis and change efforts at the organizational level. The purpose is to develop a multidimensional response to the short-term needs of survivors of restructuring as well as the long-term need of the corporation to evolve its contract with its future workforce and to revitalize itself.

Creating a Research Partnership

In 1991 a research partnership was formed between Corning, Incorporated, and the National Institute for Occupational Safety and Health (NIOSH). Corning, Incorporated, is an international corporation of approximately 41,000 employees headquartered in Corning, New York. The company manufactures glass, glass/ceramic, and other specialty-material products for the communications, laboratory sciences, environmental sciences, and consumer market segments. The company is well-known for its many alliances and joint ventures as a way of leveraging technology, as well as for its frequent managerial innovations, such as total quality management, high-performance work systems, and diversity initiatives. For example, its Telecommunications Products Division won the Malcolm Baldrige National Quality Award in 1995. NIOSH is the principal federal agency responsible for conducting research that helps to ensure, to the greatest extent possible, safe and healthful working conditions for all workers. Since its establishment as part of the Occupational Safety and Health Act in 1970 (P.L. 91–596, 91st Congress, S. #2193), NIOSH has sponsored and conducted numerous studies of job stress and health in a wide variety of occupations (e.g., nurses, police officers, coal miners, video display terminal operators, and postal workers).

The seed of this research partnership was formed when Corning's corporate medical director visited stress researchers at NIOSH to obtain information on stress and stress management. Six months later, Corning's employee assistance program (EAP) director at the time met with NIOSH researchers to explore further how the latest stress research could be applied to understanding stress in the workplace, how to promote more effective coping skills for employees, and how to successfully link any subsequent interventions to key organizational initiatives.

Defining the Issues

By this time it had become clear that several distinctions would be useful in raising awareness of the issue of stress within the company. First, workplace stress, like other forms of stress, could be separated into value-added stress and non-value-added stress. *Value-added stress* was connected to accomplishing organizational goals and to meeting ever-changing customer demands. *Non-value-added stress* was a product of inefficient internal procedures or dysfunctional organizational politics and relationships. Because it made no sense to talk in terms of totally eliminating stress in the workplace, the focus shifted to identifying sources of non-value-added stress.

Second, as contradictory as it sounds, stress in the workplace could not be confined to stress only on the job. Personal stress at home affects workplace stress, and vice versa. Therefore, any stress management intervention targeted at employees must have the capability to extend to coping skills that have multiple applications to other aspects of employees' lives. Finally, stress management could not be an individual responsibility alone; organizations must extend their contribution beyond simply sponsoring skills training seminars. Because Corning was contemplating a company-wide reengineering effort, it was felt that any truly adequate response to the problems of managing change of this magnitude must contain sufficient tools to address organizational issues as well as promote individual capabilities.

The fruitfulness of these discussions led to the signing of a formal letter of agreement in 1992 describing a multiyear research partnership between Corning and NIOSH. A series of meetings was held to define the scope of the partnership project, and to set forth the goals for the project and the responsibilities of each partner. One of the first decisions was to invite internal consultants in Corning's human resources division to participate in the project. Their involvement was crucial because they were responsible for administering a biannual organizational-climate survey and for feeding back the results to employees and management. The climate survey had been developed several years earlier with the help of a private consulting firm, and it assessed four broad categories: organizational practices, culture, values, and outcomes. These categories were assembled into a functional model of organizational effectiveness that specified that organizational practices, especially managerial policies and behaviors, over time created an organizational culture (consisting of perceptions of the climate and the extent to which the company's values were being actualized), which in turn led to such organizational outcomes as overall satisfaction and commitment. Early on, the climate survey was viewed as a potential key tool for assessing the effectiveness of any subsequent stress management and organizational change initiatives.

Corporate-Wide Reengineering

Although the original impetus for an initiative on managing stress was targeted at the high cost of stress-related health claims within the company, Corning, not unlike many large U.S. companies, soon undertook a company-wide reengineering effort. This created an even more compelling need for a proactive approach to change management. A high-level task force was charged with defining the company position on how it would respond to individual and team needs, such as setting up information hotlines and forums, providing career and personal counseling, and other resources.

The stress management initiative was viewed as just such a natural support resource, although its sponsors were careful not to limit its benefits to the immediate period of the reengineering project; instead, its potential was seen as helping to create a set of positive capabilities that would generalize beyond the workplace, to the home or even to one's work experiences outside of Corning. As it turned out, although there were a number of job transfers, the net workforce reduction was quite small; however, because of its sheer scope and duration, the level of anxiety connected to the reengineering effort was similar to those that have been publicized within other companies.

Exploratory Research Design

The first step in the stress management initiative was to assess the level of stress within the company. Although much anecdotal evidence existed around the implementation of earlier large-scale change interventions, such as total quality management in the early 1980s, and focus groups were often used to measure employee opinion on a variety of topics, no data had been collected on employee perceptions of stress and the effects of change. We decided to pilot a stress-related question in different business units that were conducting their periodic climate surveys. The question stated, "During the last 2 weeks, would you say that you experienced: a lot of stress, a moderate amount of stress, relatively little stress, almost no stress at all?" The advantage of this question was that it was taken from a Special Supplement of the 1985 National Health Interview Survey (NHIS; Silverman, Eichler, & Williams, 1987) and could be compared with the responses of more than 16,000 working adults in the United States. The result was that 38% among Corning's trial sample of several hundred employees answered "a lot of stress," compared with 23% among the national sample.

Although this finding created further support for continuing to develop program objectives related to stress management, the disadvantages of the NHIS question were that it assumed that all stress was dysfunctional, it did not specify the source of stress, and it implied that the individual was simply a passive recipient of stress, without any coping mechanisms. On the basis of these concerns, two additional questions were added to the climate survey that asked how well employees were dealing with stress in their organization (i.e., coping with stress) and the degree to which employees felt they could maintain a healthy balance between their work life and their home life. The latter question reflected the objectives of a company initiative that was being implemented at the time to increase quality of work life.

Data Analysis

These three questions were not intended to characterize completely overall stress in this population. Rather, they were used to provide a first glimpse of the scope of the problem of work-related stress and how well employees were coping with that stress. As mentioned, the complete climate survey contained 120 questions dealing with a wide range of topics, including performance rewards, total quality management, management leadership, strategic planning, training effectiveness, supervisory support, corporate values, openness, diversity, and interunit cooperation. Correlational analyses indicated that the stress, coping, and balance questions were intercorrelated, and they were grouped together to form a composite stress index. Reliability was determined by Cronbach's alpha ($\alpha = .60$), a measure of internal consistency.

Descriptive analyses showed that employees who reported the highest level of stress were three to four times more likely than those who reported moderate or low stress to (a) rate their work group and overall organization as ineffective, (b) not feel valued as employees, (c) rate the job-related training they received as ineffective, (d) be dissatisfied with their jobs, and (e) leave the company within the next 5 years. Hierarchical multiple regression analyses revealed that higher employee ratings of management practices (i.e., management leadership, recognition and rewards, strategic planning) and organizational climate and culture (i.e., inclusion, capacity to act, empowerment) were generally associated with less perceived stress. Finally, we discovered that the relationships between organizational practices and organizational effectiveness outcomes (i.e., job satisfaction, satisfaction with the company) were weaker among high-stress employees. Overall, the results suggested that by reducing organizational sources of stress and improving worker coping abilities, Corning could improve organizational effectiveness as well as employee health and well-being.

Meanwhile, discussions were taking place with senior managers to position the emerging program as a key resource for managers and employees who would be affected by restructuring and reengineering efforts that were being contemplated at the time. The human resources consulting group took the lead role in the analysis of the climate survey data to identify organizational practices associated with employee stress. For example, patterns could be seen among various work units and business groups in terms of stress and overall satisfaction. In addition, the medical department began to collect aggregate health and personal adjustment data and feed this information back to the collaborating groups and corporate managers. An example was the annualized health care costs connected to stress-related ailments. Each of these analyses formed the basis for later discussions of specific stress interventions.

A Dual-Phase Intervention Model

Stress interventions can be classified as primary, secondary, or tertiary prevention (Quick, Murphy, & Hurrell, 1992). *Primary prevention* focuses on increasing the employee's ability to cope with stress by eliminating or reducing the sources of non-value-added stress (e.g., revise supervisory practices, expand promotion and career ladders, install flexible work

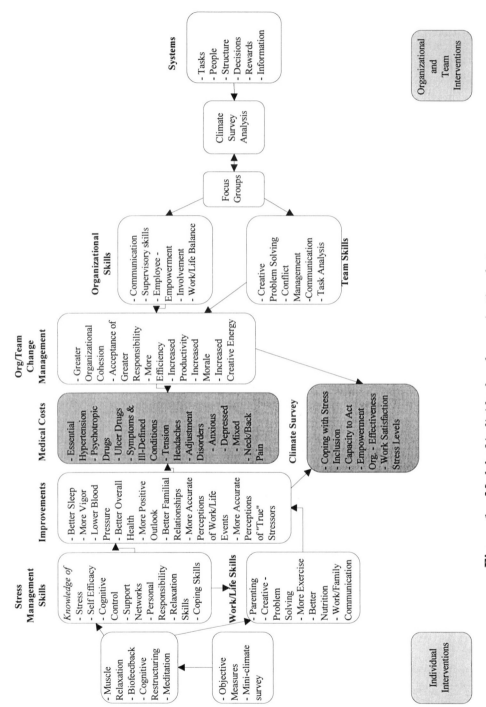

Figure 1. Model of individual and organizational stress.

schedules, increase worker autonomy). *Secondary prevention* strategies seek to reduce the symptoms of stress (acute reactions) and usually are implemented before employees demonstrate clinical signs of illness (e.g., progressive muscle relaxation, stress inoculation, improved coping skills). Finally, *tertiary prevention* deals with treatment or therapy for individuals experiencing chronic disease (e.g., substance abuse counseling, psychotherapy, hospitalization).

A review of the relevant research literature, together with benchmarking of corporate practices, indicated that the dominant model of program intervention tended to emphasize secondary and tertiary prevention. Although corporations frequently implemented the kinds of primary prevention strategies just listed, such initiatives were often disconnected from a systematic diagnosis of associated stress patterns. Few examples were found of primary prevention aimed at identifying and ameliorating the organizational sources of stress. Because Corning already had an excellent tertiary prevention program in place, a stress intervention model was formulated that emphasized the two strategies of primary and secondary prevention. Essentially, these consisted of organizational and individual assessment and skills development, respectively (see Figure 1).

Individual interventions focused on helping workers understand the nature of stress and its health effects and on improving their stress coping skills. Many organizations currently offer some type of stress management training to employees, and training packages and support materials are readily available commercially. The left side of the model shown in Figure 1 indicates that stress management training leads to enhanced stress management skills, which in turn lead to (a) improvements in health and behavior and (b) improved work and life skills. Both of these effects in turn lead to reduced medical costs and to improved organizational climate, as measured by Corning's annual climate survey.

Organization and team interventions, shown on the right side of Figure 1, were designed to target stressful aspects of the work environment for change. As of this writing, examples of these interventions had been deployed through the diagnostic phase (described later), and plans are in place to design several unique interventions. The design process used focus groups of employees, the purpose of which was to react to, and clarify results of, a "mini" climate survey administered to all employees prior to the initiation of group or team interventions. The model specifies that organizational interventions will ultimately affect the identical set of outcomes as do individual interventions, namely, medical costs and organizational climate.

Building Individual Capability

Individual interventions sought to provide workers with introductory information about the nature and sources of stress, the mental and physical signs of stress, and the long-term health consequences of unresolved stress. This information was delivered through multiple channels, from simple in-house media communications to formal symposia featuring well-known researchers and personalities such as Ken Pelletier, Diane Fassel, and Art Ulene. The centerpiece of this part of the intervention was a series of skill acquisition sessions that taught workers specific, well-established stress management skills, including muscle relaxation, biofeedback, meditation, and cognitive restructuring (Murphy, Hurrell, Sauter, & Keita, 1995). The common thread of each of these methods was the desire to build individual capability to view work experiences and events in a proactive manner that favored taking action versus avoidance or blaming others.

These classes were conducted by local professionals who were not only experienced in stress management training, but most important, they could translate their knowledge to varied types of workers in corporate and manufacturing settings. Weekly training sessions lasting from 60 to 90 minutes were conducted during lunchtime, before or after normal working hours. The entire training period consisted of 12 weeks. On the assumption that practice makes perfect, the initial design called for employees to receive an overview of multiple techniques during Weeks 1 through 8 and then to choose a single technique for an in-depth focus for Weeks 9 through 12. However, because actual attendance was more irregular due to immediate work demands and shifting schedules, the in-depth option in the later weeks of training was often changed to allow more practice with each of the techniques. More important, stress management in a corporate setting needed to provide the flexibility to discuss the work implications of the material presented and do less training for training's sake. These and other departures from standard experimental protocol were made regularly in order to support the more important overall objectives of individual and organizational change.

Individual evaluations, using a standard symptoms checklist, were conducted at Weeks 1, 8, and 12. The questionnaire (see Exhibit 1) contained 25 items grouped into three categories: (a) *symptoms of stress* (17 items), such as headache, trouble concentrating, and depressed feeling; (b) *stress management skills* (3 items), for example, the ability to recognize stress and the ability to relax; and (c) *other life areas* (5 items), such as talking with one's spouse and engaging in physical exercise. All items were answered on a 5-point frequency-of-occurrence response scale (1 = *almost never*, 5 = *nearly daily*). Participants did not put their names on the questionnaires; rather, they entered a group code, class code, and a personal identification number of their choosing. The identification information was used to link or match the participants' Weeks 1, 8, and 12 questionnaires together for statistical analysis.

Results of Individual Skills Training

Table 1 summarizes the changes in stress symptoms, coping abilities, and other life areas before training began (Week 1) and after the 8th and 12th weeks of training, as reported in the symptom checklist. Mean scores on each measure are shown for Weeks 1, 8, and 12, the percentage gain at

Exhibit 1. Coping With Stress and Change

Behavior Checklist

1. Please indicate how often each of the following behaviors or feelings occurred *during the past month* by darkening the appropriate circle.

	Almost never	Less than once/ month	Less than once/ week	Several times/ week	Nearly daily
a. was easily distracted	O	O	O	O	O
b. felt full of energy	O	O	O	O	O
c. had trouble "unwinding" after work	O	O	O	O	O
d. had a positive outlook on life	O	O	O	O	O
e. was able to recognize stress	O	O	O	O	O
f. had difficulty completing tasks	O	O	O	O	O
g. felt insecure in your job	O	O	O	O	O
h. was able to relax	O	O	O	O	O
i. had a "hot" or explosive temper	O	O	O	O	O
j. talked with spouse/friends about stress	O	O	O	O	O
k. ate well-balanced meals	O	O	O	O	O
l. had arguments at work	O	O	O	O	O
m. engaged in physical exercise	O	O	O	O	O

2. Below is a list of health symptoms. Darken the circle which best indicates how often you experienced each symptom *during the past month*.

	Almost never	Less than once/ month	Less than once/ week	Several times/ week	Nearly daily
a. headaches	O	O	O	O	O
b. trouble sleeping	O	O	O	O	O
c. nervousness	O	O	O	O	O
d. upset stomach	O	O	O	O	O
e. aches and pains (not backache)	O	O	O	O	O
f. backache	O	O	O	O	O
g. restlessness	O	O	O	O	O
h. poor appetite	O	O	O	O	O
i. arguments at work	O	O	O	O	O
j. depressed feeling	O	O	O	O	O
k. overeating	O	O	O	O	O
l. excessive worry	O	O	O	O	O

Note. Almost never = 1; Nearly daily = 5.

Table 1. Results of Individual Skills Training (*N* = 41)

Skills and Symptoms	Means Week 1	Means Week 8	Means Week 12	Week 1 vs. Week 8*	Week 1 vs. Week 12*	% gain Weeks 1–18	% gain Weeks 1–12
Managerial skills							
Able to relax	3.67	4.29	4.24	−3.35	−3.08	17	16
Recognize stress	3.54	4.20	4.08	−3.37	−3.48	19	15
Positive outlook	4.08	4.32	4.34	−1.60	−2.00	6	6
Symptoms of stress							
Depressed feeling	2.54	1.95	1.78	3.58	4.90	23	30
Excessive worry	2.95	2.27	2.17	3.49	4.11	23	26
Restlessness	3.15	2.29	2.33	4.91	4.32	27	26
Easily distracted	3.76	3.20	2.83	3.29	5.64	15	25
Trouble unwinding	3.07	2.56	2.35	2.49	3.51	17	23
Aches/pains	2.68	2.44	2.07	1.14	2.90	9	23
Nervousness	2.98	2.34	2.34	3.46	3.46	21	21
Hot temper	2.07	1.76	1.65	1.94	2.71	15	20
Not complete tasks	2.78	2.34	2.24	2.26	2.84	16	19
Insecure	2.46	1.95	2.03	2.62	2.05	21	17
Headache	2.61	2.23	2.17	1.90	2.20	15	17
Backache	2.15	1.77	1.80	2.17	1.89	18	16
Trouble sleeping	2.93	2.37	2.46	2.60	2.29	19	16
Full of energy	3.44	3.88	3.93	−2.51	−2.88	13	14
Upset stomach	1.95	1.70	1.68	1.52	1.69	13	14
Arguments at work	1.46	1.34	1.37	1.09	0.86	8	6
Other life areas							
Overeating	2.98	2.46	2.12	2.67	4.41	17	29
Talked with spouse	3.22	3.76	3.80	−3.37	−3.52	17	18
Poor appetite	1.71	1.56	1.46	0.94	1.56	9	15
Physical exercise	3.37	3.61	3.71	−1.45	−2.00	7	10
Well-balanced meals	4.00	4.31	4.27	−2.21	−1.80	8	7

Note. Data gathered for more than 400 additional cases that were missing a checklist from either of Weeks 1, 8, or 12 showed highly similar results.
*t test, two-tailed.

the 8th and 12th week compared with that of Week 1, as well as tests of statistical significance for the changes (*t* tests, two-tailed). The data reveal significant changes on measures of stress symptoms, stress management skills, and other life areas after the 8th week of training. The largest changes occurred in selected stress symptoms (e.g., restlessness, depressed feeling, trouble sleeping, excessive worry), followed by stress management skills (e.g., ability to relax). The smallest changes occurred in other life areas (e.g., physical exercise, nutrition habits, and talking with spouse). After 12 weeks of training, additional reductions were found in the frequency of some stress symptoms (depressed feeling, excessive worry, restlessness, easily distracted) and in problems in other life areas (overeating, talking with spouse). No additional improvements in stress management skills were seen after 12 weeks of training.

The data shown in Table 1 represent the responses of approximately 40 employees who scrupulously filled out the proper identity codes on all three surveys. Partial data were also gathered on 464 employees who completed surveys for at least two of the three time periods, and the patterns of improvement are very similar for this larger, incomplete sample. The similarity of results for the large and small samples reinforces the effectiveness of the individual training.

Discussion

Although all are in the expected direction, many of the findings shown in Table 1 may not seem that dramatic. Some improvements, however, such as the symptom of depressed feeling, have clinical significance. If an employee goes from reporting feeling depressed slightly less than once a week to almost never, it has significant implications for improved personal and work effectiveness.

Perhaps more significant than the impact of concentrated skill practice on specific stress symptoms is the larger generalization of these types of results. Individual participants could extend the benefits of skill development to the workplace by talking about specific stressors in the company of sympathetic trainers and colleagues. Because the focus of the Phase 1 stress management training was clearly on individual proactivity, as opposed to organizational change, participants were encouraged to break out of their standard behavioral patterns. In addition, benefits could be extended to home life as participants feel safe to raise more personal concerns. Course materials included information on assessing further specialized help for families and family members.

Building Organizational Capability

Unlike the individual interventions, team and organizational interventions could not be taken off the shelf, but needed to be customized to the stressors and work experiences in each business unit. The organizational performance model developed by Hanna (1988) was used as a guide for preliminary organizational assessment and design. This high-performance work-systems framework contains six basic organizational design elements: tasks, rewards, structure, people, information, and decisions.

Tasks refer to the extent to which duties are organized into flexible roles that help to create a partnership between workers and management. *Rewards* deal with the type of performance reward system in place (e.g., pay and promotion are based on a worker's contribution to the organization). *Structure* refers to the extent to which workers are organized into teams, instead of segmented roles, and each organizational unit is characterized by a whole task. The *people* element involves the kinds of knowledge, skills and capabilities selected for the high-performance environment. *Information* involves the amount and timeliness of information provided to workers at all levels in the organization. Finally, *decisions* refer to the level of decision-making authority granted to all members of the organization. These design elements are influenced by the business situation (stakeholder and environmental needs that must be satisfied and pressures that must be managed); business results (what the organization delivers now in terms of profits, quality, etc.); business strategy (the organization's plan for responding to stakeholder pressures); and organizational culture (how the organization really operates, such as the embedded work habits, norms, and values).

The six design elements were measured using an abbreviated version of Corning's organizational climate survey. This mini climate survey (see Exhibit 2) contained 14 questions selected from the larger survey. The questions collectively provided measures of each of the six design elements: tasks (two items), rewards (two items), structure (two items), people (three items), information (one item), and decisions (one item), plus three items for each of the elements of the stress index (amount of stress, coping ability, and work–life balance). The survey was administered by telephone. Employees in selected locations could participate in the survey by dialing a toll-free number and recording their answers on a touch-tone telephone. Answers to the mini climate survey were instantly recorded in an *Excel*™ spreadsheet, and organizational charts were produced to depict (a) a profile of the entire organization and (b) a profile of those workers who reported low stress, good coping, and good work–family balance.

Examples of the graphical depiction of the data are shown in Figures 2 and 3. These graphical representations were chosen to illustrate to managers in a somewhat idealized fashion how their organization would look if all employees reported the same level of positive scores on the stress index as the smaller sample of those reporting good coping skills, manageable levels of stress, and a positive work–life balance. For example, Figure 2 shows considerable differences on the two dimensions of Information and Decisions. The entire organization had a mean score of 16% favorable on Information, whereas the positive coping group had a mean score of 38% favorable. The corresponding scores for the Decisions dimension were 28% and 53% favorable, respectively. The purpose of these illustrations was to demonstrate how perceived stress and one's ability to cope effectively color multiple perceptions of organizational life. As mentioned earlier, although stress cannot be eliminated, raising employees' coping skills in essence raises their morale and their outlook on the organization.

Figure 3 also shows a less extreme pattern, with opportunities for intervention in multiple areas. For purposes of this diagnostic step, the ideal case is shown in Figure 2, where clear gaps in a limited number of areas allow organizational managers to target specific improvement ideas. This was found to be necessary as a simple entry strategy that helped connect the general issues of employee outlooks on the organization, perceived stress, and possible remedial steps. Naturally, as Hanna's (1988) framework implies, all organizational systems are interconnected, and any successful intervention ultimately must acknowledge and build on this

Exhibit 2.   Phone Survey: Coping With Stress and Change

Thank you for calling the Corning Survey Line. This survey of Corning associates is designed to better understand your experiences of change in the workplace.

We will ask you several questions which will take approximately five minutes to answer. You will respond by pressing keys on your telephone's touch-tone pad. At any time during the survey if you do not respond within 5 seconds, or if you press an invalid key, the question will be repeated. The system will not allow you to skip a question.

For each of the following questions, please use a scale of 1 to 5 for your responses. If you *strongly disagree* with the statement, *press 1*. If you *disagree*, *press 2*. If you neither *disagree or agree*, *press 3*. If you *agree*, *press 4*. If you *strongly agree*, *press 5*. Let's begin.

My job makes good use of my skills and abilities. Please enter your response now.

I receive constructive feedback about my job performance. Please enter your response now.

I am given a real opportunity to improve my skills in this organization. Please enter your response now.

I receive help in planning my future. Please enter your response now.

In this organization people are recognized for outstanding work. Please enter your response now.

The people in this organization recognize me in ways I personally value. Please enter your response now.

In my work group we have the resources and tools we need to do a quality job. Please enter your response now.

Sufficient effort is made to get the opinions and thinking of people who work here. Please enter your response now.

I have the authority to make decisions that help meet customer needs. Please enter your response now.

When changes are announced, my supervisor or team leader takes time to explain how the changes will affect me. Please enter your response now.

I have enough information to do my job well. Please enter your response now.

I am effectively dealing with the stress in this organization. Please enter your response now.

I am able to maintain a healthy balance between my work life and my home life. Please enter your response now.

During the last two weeks, would you say that you experienced: a lot of stress? *Press 1*; a moderate amount of stress? *Press 2*; relatively little stress? *Press 3*; almost no stress? *Press 4*. Please enter your response now.

Thank you for calling the Corning Survey line. The results of this survey will be used to better understand how your organization can address areas of nonproductive stress. Thanks again for calling. Goodbye.

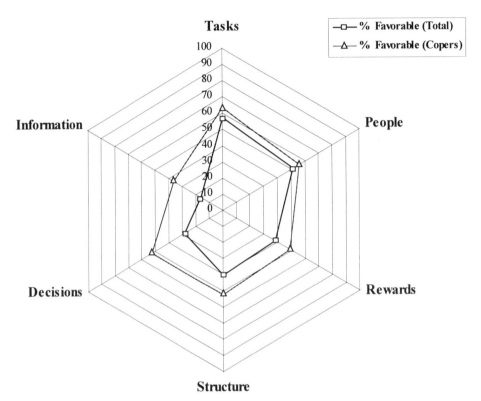

Figure 2.   Organizational Profile "A."

interconnection. A companion resource guide (Corning, 1995) was provided to line managers and human resource managers that provided a menu of intervention options based on the areas showing the largest gaps between well-functioning employees and those under high stress. Managers were encouraged to select internal or external consultants to facilitate this phase of the organizational exploration.

A careful examination of Figures 2 and 3 may lead to the question why the majority of workers who could be considered positive "copers" would still be reporting unfavorable scores on some of the organizational dimensions. Although the immediate aim of this study was to bring the scores of "copers" and "noncopers" on targeted organizational dimensions more in line with each other, obviously there will be areas of employee perception that may be negative across the board, regardless of one's coping ability. In such cases, a longer term approach to organizational development may be required. However, this was not the objective of the present study.

As of this writing, negotiations were continuing to move beyond the diagnostic phase in several different organizations (service vs. manufacturing, large vs. small). The key variable affecting timely progress toward a truly holistic approach to managing stress and change during periods of organizational upheaval appears to be explained by Hanna's variable of

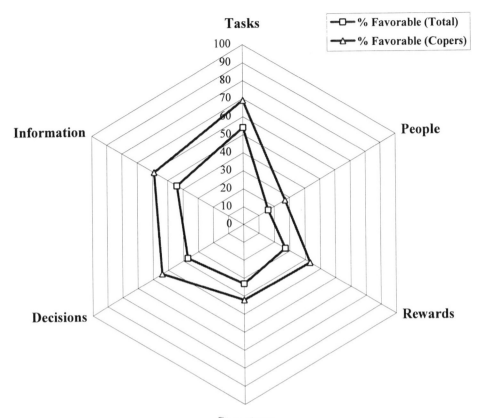

Figure 3.   Organizational Profile "B."

culture. Deep-seated assumptions about the proper relationship between the individual and the organization and the ability to see connections clearly among all aspects of the employee's life can be either enablers or barriers to a more complete understanding of stress in the workplace. For example, some managers had a difficult time appreciating the distinction between value-added and non-value-added stress, preferring to view all stress as either inevitable or as an inappropriate topic for discussion.

Conclusions

On the basis of participant reaction sheets and the pre–post symptom checklists, the individual skills training interventions were judged to be extremely effective by the participants, and they produced significant reductions in reported symptoms of stress and improved coping skills at the conclusion of the training. The visibility of various stress management techniques, many of which were practiced at the work site, helped to create an environment where stress could be discussed and dealt with. Results of the organizational diagnostic surveys reinforced the connection between employee attitudes toward organizational issues and stress levels. Several business units successfully created an environment where stress issues could be openly discussed and, as of this writing, were beginning to consider potential interventions based on results of their mini-climate surveys.

In addition, although we do not have empirical data to support our impressions, we observed that the two most important contextual variables in program success appeared to be the attitude of the leadership, including front-line supervision of each facility, and the skills of the trainer. It is our impression that the more the leader has experienced stress and change in his or her own life (even if vicariously through a son or daughter who brings a new perspective on life's priorities), the more supportive he or she is toward (a) sponsoring the individual training and (b) examining the organization itself and its impact on employees. This is consistent with Schein's (1992) view of the impact of leadership in helping to shape organizational culture. Another observation is that the more open and human the trainer was, the higher the likelihood that employees would respond positively to the training. The ability of the trainer to challenge participants empathically to consider new behaviors, to make the training relevant to the job situation, and to connect work and home life was far more influential than whether the content was systematic relaxation or biofeedback.

Future Directions

The changing demographics of the workforce and the continued trend toward reorganization and downsizing suggest that we are likely to see increases in employee stress levels. In fact, newer generations of employees are signaling that quality-of-life concerns will be more important than those expressed by older generations of workers (Jamrog, 1996). At the same time, downsizing, restructuring, and reengineering are likely to be common organizational responses to the rapid pace of change. Increasingly, companies will need to equip themselves to understand and manage work stress and its health and performance consequences, so as to reduce health care costs, improve productivity, and remain competitive in a world economy. Yet, many corporate human resource programs have taken a reactive, as opposed to a proactive, approach. They emphasize reacting to individual needs through beefed-up employee assistance programs and treating problems after they arise rather than preventing their occurrence, although the costs of preventing stress reactions may ultimately be far less than the costs of a strict treatment approach. One mechanism for meeting this challenge is close collaboration among various in-house corporate professionals, bringing expertise from different disciplines to bear on the problem of stress. The collaboration between human resource management and medical groups described in this article was presented as a cost-effective mechanism for addressing the problem of job stress and one step toward creating healthier work organizations (Murphy, 1995).

Future work in the research partnership between Corning, Incorporated, and NIOSH will continue to use team and organizational interventions to reduce workplace stressors and to collect objective measures of medical costs and company performance data across multiple years to evaluate the success of both individual and organizational interventions. Long-term results of this study will be used not only to reevaluate the psychological contract among Corning employees and their employer but as a catalyst to examine the issue of workplace stress on a national and global level. In this way, more innovative tools and approaches might be made available to other companies that wish to revitalize themselves as a response to unprecedented levels of tumultuous change.

References

Block, P. (1993). *Stewardship: Choosing service over self-interest.* San Francisco: Berrett-Koehler.

Corning, Inc. (1995). *Managing stress and change: A handbook for organizations* [Internal document]. Corning, NY: Author.

The downsizing of America [Special series]. (1996, March 3–December 29, 1996). *The New York Times.*

Hanna, D. P. (1988). *Designing organizations for high performance.* Reading, MA: Addison-Wesley.

Jamrog, J. (1996). *The link between business trends and employee opinions.* Invited address presented by the Human Resource Institute at the Mayflower Group Spring Meeting, St. Petersburg, FL.

Murphy, L. R. (1995). Managing job stress: An employee assistance/human resource management partnership. *Personnel Review, 24,* 41–50.

Murphy, L. R., Hurrell, J. J., Sauter, S. S., & Keita, G. (Eds.). (1995). *Job stress interventions.* Washington, DC: American Psychological Association.

Noer, D. M. (1993). *Healing the wounds: Overcoming the trauma of layoffs and revitalizing downsized organizations.* San Francisco: Jossey-Bass.

Quick, J. C., Murphy, L. R., & Hurrell, J. J. (1992). *Stress and well-being at work: Assessments and interventions for occupational mental health.* Washington, DC: American Psychological Association.

Schein, E. H. (1992). *Organizational culture and leadership* (2nd ed.). San Francisco: Jossey-Bass.

Sherwood, J., & Glidewell, J. (1972). Planned renegotiation: A norm-setting OD intervention. In W. Burke (Ed.), *Contemporary organization development: Approaches and interventions* (pp. 142–149). Washington, DC: NTL Learning Resources Corporation.

Silverman, M. M., Eichler, A., & Williams, G. D. (1987). Self-reported stress: Findings from the 1985 National Health Interview Survey. *Public Health Reports, 102,* 47–53.

Strebel, P. (1996). Why do employees resist change? *Harvard Business Review, 74,* 86–92.

Part IV ————————————————

Conclusion

13

A Conceptual Framework for Coping With the New Organizational Reality

Marilyn K. Gowing, John D. Kraft, and James Campbell Quick

In this concluding chapter, we provide a conceptual framework to guide strategies for coping with the new organizational reality and for revitalizing the workforce and organizations (see Figure 1). We have formulated these strategies based upon the discussions of the internal and external consultants who prepared chapters for our book.

The Environment

The strategies within this framework or model must continually be reevaluated depending upon the environmental context. The environmental context represents the kinds of data we presented in our opening discussion of the evolution from the agrarian economy, to the industrial age, to the information age. The systemic changes which we presented and which were summarized by Martin and Freeman are not limited to the United States. In fact, as Levi, Burke, and Nelson point out in their contributions, the new organizational reality is sweeping western and eastern Europe as well as North America. This new reality is not monolithic downsizing; rather, it is an array of organizational responses to environmental change, including the privatization of some previously public workloads, restructuring of intra- and interorganizational resources, mergers and acquisitions, and divestitures and outsourcing.

In the United States, such major organizational transformations are likely to continue as they are credited with transforming the United States economy into one with low unemployment (below 5%), low inflation (Consumer Price Index at 1.5 in April of 1997), a reduced federal deficit (projected to be as low as $37 billion in 1997), and record levels of corporate profit and stock market performance. Median household income is rising and poverty rates are falling. Simultaneously, Congress and the President have agreed to a plan to balance the budget by the year 2002. Pearlstein

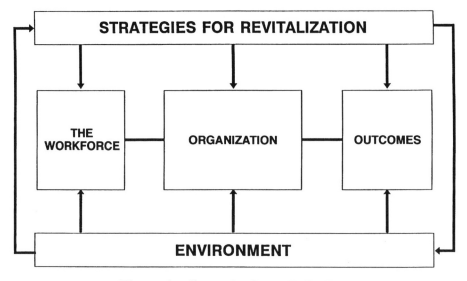

Figure 1. Strategies for revitalization.

(1997) characterized the current economic condition as "the 'virtuous circle'—the opposite of the better-known vicious circle—in which one positive development generates another in a tight, reinforcing pattern, feeding on its own momentum. Strong economic growth, for example, generates extra revenues for the government that makes it easier to balance the budget, which leads to lower interest rates, which in turn leads to more economic growth" (p. H2). Government policies such as ending the Cold War, deregulating many industries, embracing free trade, and adopting anti-inflationary monetary policies have also contributed to the 7-year economic recovery in the United States.

Although corporate America and the consumers express tremendous optimism regarding this new economic environment, some challenging issues remain. One issue is the inequality of income levels among the rich and the poor. The new welfare-to-work initiatives sponsored by the Clinton administration, with support of the state governments, may make some progress in this area.

Another issue is occupational underemployment. While the unemployment rate is remarkably low, the question remains as to whether individuals laid off from downsized organizations accepted positions that provided significantly less income than their former positions. Certainly there is some evidence that this has been happening to displaced managers and executives. We need more empirical data on the current employed workforce to determine the extent to which underemployment is still an issue and the extent to which members of the workforce are feeling "occupationally locked-in." Underemployment is a concern to employers because, as Burke and Nelson reported, underemployment has been consistently found to be related to poorer general mental health, lower overall life satisfaction, and lower job satisfaction.

Strategies for revitalization must consider current domestic and global environmental conditions. These strategies must focus on the *workforce* (our human capital), the organizational practices and procedures for coping with the new organizational reality, the *organization*, the measures employed for assessing organizational effectiveness and, the *outcomes* (including value added to stockholders, employees, and customers).

The Workforce

Strategy 1: Maintain the Health of the Workforce To Increase Productivity

Adam Smith (1776/1909) tells us that the wealth of a nation rests on the productivity of its people and that the economic wealth of a nation is one key to the nation's overall well-being. We believe that the productivity of a people is determined by their health; that is, good health is a necessary condition for productivity. A study by the Massachusetts Institute of Technology in 1993 reported that employers lose $23.8 billion annually just in absenteeism and lost productivity from employees suffering from depression (*Wall Street Journal*, February 26, 1996). Clearly, there is an economic need to focus on strategies to reduce employees' stress and increase their sense of well-being. A wealthy nation requires a healthy workforce. Yet as organizations reduce the size of their workforces in order to become more efficient and to meet stronger and more challenging worldwide competition, workforce health is increasingly difficult to sustain. As Noer notes, survivors of downsizing feel angry, fearful, and depressed. Such a workforce can hardly be expected to turn the organization around to meet and exceed the standards produced by global competition. Such workers become risk aversive and less productive.

Larry Murphy and the professionals from Corning, Inc. present a comprehensive model for enhancing the health and well-being of a workforce in the face of environmental change and organizational transformation. Like many organizations around the world, Corning has a dual focus on its financial success in a challenging business environment and on the health and well-being of its workforce, which is the engine for that success. Corning was able to demonstrate a direct link between stress management training for their workers and reductions in stress symptoms and improvements in stress coping ability. The leadership of Corning understands that economic wealth and workforce health do, in fact, work together for the success of the organization.

Strategy 2: Invest in the Workforce for Competitive Advantage

Many of the authors in this book suggest that workers should be viewed as long-term assets for the organization, not short-term costs (e.g., Noer

and Cascio). Graddick and Cairo noted that even in the midst of potentially dramatic downsizing, AT&T established incentives to retain individuals who were considered essential to the core business of the new organization. They also suggested that AT&T would be challenged in the future
to find ways to retain intellectual capital. Graddick and Cairo noted that
as the number of knowledge workers increases, retaining intellectual capital will clearly be a source of competitive advantage.

With the dramatic reduction in the unemployment rate, employers
will need to begin finding ways of building or rebuilding employee commitment to the organization. We have discussed the new employer/em-
ployee contract in a number of chapters (e.g., chapter 4, chapter 9). Certainly the expectation now is that employers will invest in their workers
and provide them with the necessary skills to ensure their career mobility
in the event of a downturn at their current organization. While we have
been speaking in terms of one new employee/employer contract, the reality
may be that there are several new contracts in place. As Martin and Freeman point out, those employees who have organization-specific and job-
specific knowledge will have greater job security as long as their particular
skills are required. As long as there is a tight labor market, these core
organizational employees may well be in a position to negotiate new employee contracts guaranteeing security, investment in skills, salary increases, and even promotion potential. Other employees who are not so
highly valued or viewed as competitive assets may have to settle for the
employer/employee contract guaranteeing only the organization's investment in skills training.

Gordon points out that investments in training and development coupled with empowerment create an environment that is conducive to continuous improvement and, thus, a significant competitive advantage.
Burke and Nelson suggest that training and development for those who
are fortunate to stay in the organization are essential as those people often
face a more demanding work setting. They believe that the training and
development result in a "career-resilient" workforce which is committed
to (a) learning continuously, (b) reinventing themselves to keep pace with
change, (c) taking responsibility for their own career management, and (d)
dedicating themselves to their company's success. The American Management Association published a report in February 1996 stating that an increasing percentage of firms that eliminate positions are also investing in
retraining. Those firms that did increase retraining enjoyed higher profits
and greater productivity compared with those who did not.

The Organization

Strategy 3: Restructure Responsibly

Organizational transformation and change are inevitable in this era of
global competition and technological advancements. Martin and Freeman

note that the optimal structure of any given firm is constantly changing. Ideally, the firm's organizational structure should evolve continuously as market conditions evolve. Firms always will have to balance the need for structure with the need for flexibility. Structure is necessary to accomplish the tasks at hand, and flexibility is necessary to accomplish the future set of tasks and demands placed on the workforce. Although evolutionary change will always be shaping the organizations of the future, we join Cascio in calling for responsible restructuring that treats our workers as human capital or long-term assets to be developed and nurtured.

The evidence is mixed as to the financial impact of significant corporate downsizing. Cascio shows that the level of downsizing did not systematically affect a company's postdownsizing financial or stock performance. Burke and Nelson report that 6 months to a year after downsizing, key indicators, including expense ratios, profits, return on investments to shareholders, and stock prices did not improve. Noer suggests that in some cases stock performance dropped, while Burke and Nelson cite evidence from a Canadian study that showed positive results from restructuring (85% cut costs, 63% improved earnings, 58% improved productivity, 36% improved customer service). Burke and Nelson also report that between 50% and 80% of all mergers are financial disappointments. A dramatic and often unanticipated side effect of mergers is the loss of human capital. Typically, in acquired firms 50% of the executives seek other jobs within 1 year, and another 25% plan to leave within 3 years. In a study conducted by the Society for Human Resource Management, more than half of the 1,468 firms surveyed reported that productivity stayed the same or deteriorated after downsizing. While the outcome evidence involving downsizing and restructuring is mixed, evidence does show that the aftermath of corporate layoffs includes reductions in job satisfaction, job involvement, organizational commitment, and the intention to remain with the organization (Burke & Nelson, chapter 2, this volume; Noer, chapter 10, this volume).

Faced with the need to respond to evolutionary changes in the workplace and the world, how does an organization meet the challenge of restructuring while avoiding the negative consequences of downsizing with massive layoffs? There are many recommendations presented in this book along with a number of innovative approaches to restructuring. Gordon reports that Chaparral's leadership asked its managers to cut $5 million from the organization saying that if they were unable to identify cuts, then the $5 million would be taken out of the managerial salaries. Not surprisingly, the managers found ways to save $8 million by eliminating some consultants and handling the work internally. So one strategy is to ask the workforce and managerial personnel how to cut costs and to save money to avoid layoffs.

AT&T seems to have come up with a viable alternative to heavy layoffs in the future. They have formed a collaborative partnership with other organizations to share talent and to create a national job bank. As one of the organizations finds it necessary to downsize, the others in the partnership will do their best to find displaced employees alternative work assignments in their companies. This strategy of collaborative labor force management is a creative solution and one which we expect to see used more in the future.

It is important to remember that in any downsizing and restructuring effort, the employer must pay attention to the feelings of the people who are going through the change, including the survivors who will remain with the organization. The employer should strive to support the people's needs during the time of change (Jaffe & Scott, chapter 9, this volume). Certainly one of the greatest needs in a time of change is the need for communication. We were impressed by the results of offering a realistic merger preview to affected personnel (Schweiger & DeNisi, 1991). The organization using this realistic preview had higher employee commitment and greater perceptions of the company's trustworthiness than the control organization which did not receive the realistic preview. This is an important result because the new organizational reality will succeed only to the extent to which trust and collaboration remain intact and will fail to the extent to which trust is lost in the transition from old to new. For workers to be truly empowered and to maximize the use of their new development and training, they must trust the organization's leaders. For workers to take the risks associated with maintaining a competitive advantage, they must have this trust. Any practice, such as realistic communication previews, that will help to build and support the retention of worker trust during organizational restructuring, will hasten the restoration of that company to world class leadership. Employers must successfully manage the restructuring process or be left with surviving employees who lack trust and are narrow-minded, self-absorbed, and risk aversive (Burke & Nelson, chapter 2, this volume).

The case studies presented in this book are also full of practices that could be characterized as responsible restructuring. Joyce Adkins' chapter on the closure of Williams Air Force Base in Arizona is one case example of the shrinking military presence in the United States. Psychologists may, given the nature of their professional training and development, run the risk of overpersonalizing problems and challenges. Adkins takes a very counterintuitive perspective for many psychologists by using a systemic perspective on the transition through which Williams and the U.S. military is moving. This perspective involves avoiding blame attributions and embracing a balanced perspective on being neither detached nor engaged with the people at Williams. Adkins moves us in the direction of flexibility and competence in working through the transition.

The AT&T chapter by Mirian Graddick and Peter Cairo is another example of embracing a balanced perspective. Early in the downsizing process the AT&T team looked to models in the organizational literature to help them guide their strategic planning for downsizing and restructuring. This chapter provides a wealth of specific organizational strategies and processes for helping employees become adjusted to the new corporate assignments as well as lessons learned that will greatly benefit organizations currently confronting major organizational transformation. The important thing to remember about AT&T is that the actual number of people who were laid off was nowhere near the projected 40,000; in fact, it was less than 10,000.

John Gordon's case study chapter is about Chaparral Steel, one of the best examples of a learning organization. Created in the U.S. steel industry during its period of decline, Chaparral Steel had no right to expect to achieve the kind of success which it has experienced throughout its history. However, Chaparral Steel has attempted to lead a new American revolution in the industrial sector of the economy through the design of a unique organizational culture that emphasizes human resources and human capital, learning, growth, and human development (Forward, Beach, Gray & Quick, 1991).

Clarence Hardy and Eduardo Rodela's chapter is a case example of an organization in the midst of transition. The Office of Human Resources and Organizational Services in the U.S. Environmental Protection Agency is a leading edge unit in planning and preparing for change. The Future Search conference is a planning method for developing, deciding and deploying strategies for restructuring and reinventing the human resources office. Early results seem to indicate that customer involvement and employee empowerment have helped to shape a successful change process.

Grant and Kraft provide an excellent example of outcome measurement during three iterations of downsizing at the U.S. Office of Personnel Management. Their "Results-Based Career Transition Program" provided management with tangible evidence of the effectiveness of the organizational practices used to place employees in new jobs during the reductions in force within the agency. The successful placements argue for serious consideration of the components of the OPM program, including peer counseling, in strategic restructuring efforts.

David Noer helps us to learn how to heal the wounds of the layoff survivors. He provides a four-level model for intervening in organizational systems to revitalize the employees. Organizations wishing to regain and even surpass their previous productivity levels would be wise to adopt the strategy recommended by Noer.

Dennis Jaffe and Cynthia Scott teach us about transformational change in the organization and how to introduce empowerment after the social contract has changed. Drawing upon their extensive consulting practice in organizational psychology, the authors provide vivid insights into the organizational policies and practices that support and strengthen the new culture.

Robert Rosen recognizes that the leadership is the key to organizational health and renewal. He argues convincingly that employees want to be led by enlightened leaders. His eight principles present an excellent road map for leaders guiding their organizations through downsizing and restructuring. Others share Rosen's vision of leaders in the next millennium who create a culture based on principles (Hesselbein, Goldsmith, & Beckhard, 1996).

Outcomes

Strategy 4: Manage the Health and Development of the Workforce and the Health of the Organization During Transition: Successful Outcomes Will Follow

Organizational effectiveness is often defined in terms of a type of "balanced scorecard," with outcomes representing economic-value-added (e.g., increased earnings and return on investment for stockholders), people-value-added (e.g., employee satisfaction and motivation through organizational culture) and customer-value-added (e.g., improvements in customer service, see Kaplan & Norton, 1996). Mergers, acquisitions, downsizings, and restructurings often have negative results on some of these important outcome measures. Our thesis states that if employers manage the health and development of their workforce and the health of their organization during the time of transformation, then the employer will be assured of positive outcome measures. This thesis is supported by the guidance from the authors presented in this book.

Employers should adopt ways of measuring the health of their workforce. This includes the stress levels of their workforce even prior to the anticipation of any major organizational change. They should understand the factors contributing to those levels of stress and, if necessary, develop programs designed to reduce stress as in the case of Corning. Corning's program is noteworthy because it included in its stress measurement some items that had been used in some nationwide studies. This enabled the company to benchmark the national results. Reduction of stress levels will result in less absenteeism, and greater employee health and productivity.

If employers are going to invest in the training and development of their workers, then they need to know about the competencies required to perform the work of the organization both now and in the future. Once the competencies have been identified, employers should assess their employees on those competencies. While many organizations are using 360-degree assessments (i.e., assessments by supervisors, peers, subordinates, and sometimes customers) which do provide some useful information, it would be best to obtain objective assessments of the competencies through the use of psychometric test instruments.

Employers should have an automated skills bank of employee competencies including training and development activities. Such a skills bank will be invaluable to their human resource planning process as they are charting their organization's future. They will be able to determine which individuals have the core competencies for the new organization, as well as those who are easily retrainable. Finally, the tight labor market will make buying talent difficult. More and more companies will be choosing to build talent from within.

Just as it is possible to measure through objective measures employee health and competency attainment, it is also possible to measure the health of an organization through cultural assessment tools. AT&T measured their organizational culture on a biweekly basis during their downsizing initiative to determine what issues should be addressed by the policy and program personnel. Kraut (1996) presents a comprehensive review of many such instruments. Organizations have been collaborating in consortia and agreeing to administer the same cultural items in their organizations for benchmarking purposes. The Mayflower Group includes private sector members (Johnson, 1996) while Performance America is the public sector counterpart with all members using the Organizational Assessment Survey (Gowing & Lancaster, 1996). These survey instruments include items that gauge your progress in communication (considered so vital for a transformation by Noer and Jaffe, Scott, and others), leadership (considered essential by Rosen), teamwork, strategic planning, and other dimensions that have been found to be characteristic of high performing organizations.

Rosen provides one of the most comprehensive reviews of the literature linking healthy organizational and leadership practices to a variety of organizational outcomes such as increases in bottom line statistics, customer satisfaction, and overall productivity. Contrary to Rosen, others have argued convincingly with outcome data (sustained stock performance) that the emphasis should not be so much on visionary leaders when attempting to build organizations that last, but rather should be on "visionary companies" with visionary cultures (Collins & Porras, 1994).

In summary, if organizations value and invest in their human capital through training and retraining, if they establish a visionary organization with enlightened, principled leadership, if they attend to their employees in times of organizational change and transformation by addressing their feelings as well as their organizational needs, then we shall see impressive results in terms of financial and nonfinancial measures. The revitalization of our organizations depends upon the adoption of strategies relating to our people and our organizational practices and procedures. Only through a comprehensive, systematic integration of these strategies will we truly be able to achieve the organizational effectiveness necessary to master our new organizational reality.

References

American Management Association. (1996, February). *AMA survey on downsizing, job elimination, and job creation*. New York: Author.

Collins, J. C., & Porras, J. I. (1994). *Built to last: Successful habits of visionary companies*. New York, Harper Business.

Forward, G. E., Beach, D. E., Gray, D. A., & Quick, J. C. (1991). Mentofacturing: A vision for American industrial excellence. *Academy of Management Executives, 5*, 32–44.

Gowing, M. K., & Lancaster, A. R. (1996). Federal government surveys: Recent practices and future directions. In A. I. Kraut (Ed.), *Organizational Surveys: Tools for Assessment and Change* (pp. 360–380). San Francisco: Jossey-Bass.

Hesselbein, F., Goldsmith, M., & Beckhard, R. (Eds.) (1996). *The Leader of the Future*. San Francisco: Jossey-Bass.

Johnson, R. H. (1996). Life in the consortium: The Mayflower group. In A. I. Kraut (Ed.), *Organizational Surveys: Tools for Assessment and Change*. San Francisco: Jossey-Bass.

Kaplan, R. S., & Norton, D. P. (1996). *The balanced scorecard*. Boston: Harvard Business School Press.

Kraut, A. I. (Ed.) (1996). *Organizational Surveys: Tools for Assessment and Change*. San Francisco: Jossey-Bass.

Pearlstein, S. (1997, May 3). The thriving economy that keeps on surprising: In past decade, U.S. transformed itself. *The Washington Post*, pp. H1–H2.

Shweiger, D. M., & DeNisi, A. A. (1991). Communication with employees following a merger: A longitudinal field experiment. *Academy of Management Journal, 34*, 110–135.

Smith, A. (1909). *An inquiry into the nature and causes of the wealth of nations*. In C. J. Bullock (Ed.), *The Harvard classics* (Vol. 10). New York: Collier. (Original work published 1776)

Index

About the Editors

Marilyn K. Gowing, PhD, is Director of the Personnel Resources and Development Center of the U.S. Office of Personnel Management (OPM), the human resource management agency of the Federal Government based in Washington, DC. Dr. Gowing is a member of the Senior Executive Service and has served as a national officer in the Society of Industrial and Organizational Psychology as well as President of the Personnel Testing Council/Metropolitan Washington. Dr. Gowing has written journal articles, technical reports, book chapters, and was coauthor for a book on occupational analysis. Dr. Gowing has held positions in research and consulting firms and served as Director of Assessment Services and Professional Development for the International Personnel Management Association. Dr. Gowing has been recognized as a Distinguished Alumna by George Washington University and received awards from the Internal Revenue Service, the U.S. Department of Housing and Urban Development, the U.S. Office of Personnel Management, and the American Society of Association Executives.

John D. Kraft, MS, retired as the Director of Assessment Services Division, Personnel Resources and Development Center, U.S. Office of Personnel Management. In his federal career he directed the examination development program in the federal government and conducted and directed institutional and organizational research. Prior to working at OPM, he was Deputy Director of Institutional Research at the U.S. Military Academy. He helped plan the organizational response to downsizing in the federal government to insure that employees who were terminated through no fault of their own effectively transitioned into new employment or other activities of their choosing. He currently is consulting with three federal agencies on selection and organizational intervention issues and serves as an examiner for the President's Quality Award. He earned a master's degree from Butler University, Indianapolis, Indiana. He also has taken many additional graduate courses related to his work.

James Campbell Quick, PhD, is Professor of Organizational Behavior at The University of Texas at Arlington and Editor of *Journal of Occupational Health Psychology*. He was APA's stress expert to the National Academy of Sciences on National Health Objectives for the Year 2000. Recognized by the American Heart Association with the Texas Volunteer Recognition Award and listed in the 7th Edition of *Who's Who in the World*, he received the Maroon Citation from the Colgate University Alumni Corporation in 1993. Colonel Quick is in the U.S. Air Force Reserve and serves as Senior Individual Mobilization Augmentee to the Director of Financial Management, San Antonio Air Logistics Center (AFMC), Kelly AFB, Texas. His military awards and decorations include the Meritorious Service Medal and National Defense Service Medal with Bronze Star. He is married to the former Sheri Grimes Schember.